WHOLE 30 COOKBOOK 2019

~ 600 ~

Simple, Easy and Delicious Recipes to Help You Succeed: Fast and Healthy Meals with 30 Day Meal Plan For Whole Family: The Big Whole30 Cookbook for Beginners

By
LISA BENNETT

TABLE OF CONTENTS

DESCRIPTION

Are you contemplating living a healthy diet and eliminating any harmful substances in your diet? Well, the whole30 diet program is the best chose you got! The point of this diet is to slowly eradicate some foods and observe the impact it has on your body for a period of 30-day, after this period, you can reinstate them back gradually and eliminate that which causes inflammation.

This diet recommends elimination of the following grains and legumes, and anything containing MSG, carrageenan, sulfites and soy. This guide has the best collection of 600 whole30 recipes and a meal plan for easy planning in 30-days.

Here are some of the meals covered in this guide:

- Breakfast
- Mains
- Sides
- Seafood

- Poultry
- Meat
- Vegetables
- Soups

- Snacks
- Desserts

There is no better way of living a healthy lifestyle and cleaning up your gut than choosing a whole30 diet. Let's get cooking!!!

INTRODUCTION

After the monthly detox program, the second chapter of your Whole Food 30-day challenge begins – you have to reinstate those products that were eliminated from the diet slowly. Each group of products must be entered separately from the other. You can start with any, but the best is to choose dairy and milk products. So, on the first day after your one-month diet has finished, you start eating dairy products. You eat them throughout the day, and then for four days, you again go back to the whole food diet. It is a time to observe your condition carefully.

You have to note any unpleasant symptoms that have not been seen all month, and now they have appeared again after the first day of reintroduction. It can be anything: bloating and diarrhea, itchy skin and queasiness, headache and increased blood pressure. Anything that makes you feel bad.

If you did not notice any unpleasant symptoms within four days after the first "milk day," go on to reinstate into the diet the second group of excluded foods, for example, legumes.

Theoretically, you can return all the excluded products. However, if you seriously approach to tracking your health after introducing a product group into the diet, you will find that not all of them are consumed by your body normally.

In addition, there are groups of products that you should never consume; like harmful vegetable oils, trans fats, sugar.

01. Egg Salad

Preparation time: 10 minutes
Cooking time: 0 minutes
Servings: 4

Ingredients:

- 8 eggs, hard boiled, peeled and cut into wedges
- ¼ cup onion, chopped
- 3 cups cherry tomatoes, cut in half
- 2 avocados, peeled, pitted and chopped
- Juice of 2 lemons
- ½ cup fresh parsley, chopped
- A pinch of salt and black pepper

Directions:

1. In a salad bowl, mix the avocados with the eggs, onion, tomatoes, salt, pepper, parsley, and lemon juice, toss well, and serve for breakfast

Nutrition Value: Calories - 250, Fat - 5, Fiber - 3, Carbs - 8, Protein - 12

02. Banana Pudding

Preparation time: 30 minutes
Cooking time: 0 minutes
Servings: 6

Ingredients:

- 1 cup coconut milk
- ½ teaspoon ground cinnamon
- 2 bananas, peeled
- 2 tablespoons chia seeds
- 1 cup water

Directions:

1. Put the chia seeds in a bowl, add the water, cover, and set aside for 30 minutes. In a food processor, mix the banana with the coconut milk and cinnamon. Pulse well, transfer to a bowl, add the chia mix, toss and serve for breakfast.

Nutrition Value: Calories - 140, Fat - 3, Fiber - 3, Carbs - 7, Protein - 6

03. Brussels Sprout, Potato and Sausage Mix

Preparation time: 10 minutes
Cooking time: 30 minutes
Servings: 6

Ingredients:

- 1 pound Italian sausage, chopped
- 1 tablespoon olive oil
- 2 garlic cloves, peeled and min
- 2 cups sweet potatoes, cubed
- 2 cups Brussels sprouts, cut into wedges
- 1 onion, peeled and chopped
- 1 red bell pepper, seeded and chopped

Directions:

2. Heat a pan over medium-high heat; add the sausage, stir, brown for 10 minutes, and transfer to a plate. Heat the same pan with the oil over medium heat, add the Brussels sprouts, the sweet potatoes, garlic, bell pepper, and onion, stir, cook for 15 minutes, return the sausage to the pan, stir again, divide between plates, and serve for breakfast.

Nutrition Value: Calories - 245, Fat - 6, Fiber - 3, Carbs - 16, Protein - 15

04. Yam Hash

Preparation time: 10 minutes
Cooking time: 25 minutes
Servings: 4

Ingredients:

- 7 bacon slices, cooked and crumbled
- 2 yams, peeled and cubed
- 1 teaspoons sweet paprika
- 2 tablespoons coconut oil, melted
- 4 garlic cloves, peeled and minced
- 1 onion, peeled and chopped
- 2 tablespoons fresh parsley, chopped
- A pinch of salt and black pepper

Directions:

1. Put some water in a pot, bring to a boil over medium heat, add the yams and some salt, cook for 15 minutes, drain and put them into a bowl. Heat a pan with the oil over medium heat, add the onions, stir, and cook for 5 minutes. Add the yams, garlic, bacon, paprika, and parsley, salt and ground black pepper, stir, cook for 5 minutes, divide between plates, and serve for breakfast.

Nutrition Value: Calories - 200, Fat - 3, Fiber - 3, Carbs - 6, Protein - 12

05. Pork and Chard Bowls

Preparation time: 10 minutes
Cooking time: 20 minutes
Servings: 4

Ingredients:

- 2 tablespoons olive oil
- 1 bunch chard, torn
- 1 pound ground pork
- ½ cup raisins
- 2 cups sweet potato, chopped
- 3 garlic cloves, peeled and minced
- 1 teaspoon turmeric, ground
- ½ teaspoon ground cinnamon
- 1 teaspoon apple cider vinegar

Directions:

1. Heat a pan over medium-high heat, add the pork, brown for 4 minutes and transfer to a bowl. Heat the same pan with the oil over medium heat, add the sweet potatoes, stir, and cook for 5 minutes. Add the chard, cinnamon, garlic, and turmeric, stir, and cook 5 minutes. Add the raisins, vinegar, and return the meat to the pan as well, stir, cook for 5 more minutes, divide between plates and serve for breakfast.

Nutrition Value: Calories - 300, Fat - 4, Fiber - 4, Carbs - 12, Protein - 17

Turkey Breakfast Pan

Preparation time: 10 minutes
Cooking time: 22 minutes
Servings: 4

Ingredients:

- 3 teaspoons olive oil
- 3 tablespoons water
- 3 cups kale, torn
- 1 butternut squash, peeled and cubed
- 12 ounces ground turkey meat
- 1 yellow onion, chopped
- 1 apple, cored, peeled, and chopped
- ¼ teaspoon dried thyme
- ½ teaspoon dried sage
- A pinch of ground nutmeg
- ¼-teaspoon garlic powder

Directions:

1. In a bowl, mix the turkey with the nutmeg, thyme, and sage and garlic powder and stir well. Heat a pan with half of the oil over medium heat, add the squash and onion, stir, and cook for 10 minutes. Add the apple, water, turkey mixture and the rest of the oil, stir, and cook for 10 minutes. Add the kale, stir, cook for 2 minutes, divide between plates, and serve for breakfast.

Nutrition Value: Calories - 300, Fat - 12, Fiber - 4, Carbs - 20, Protein - 23

07. Chicken, Squash and Apple Mix

Preparation time: 10 minutes
Cooking time: 40 minutes
Servings: 3

Ingredients:

- 1 summer squash, peeled and cubed
- 1 bunch kale, torn
- 2 tablespoons olive oil
- 1 apple, cored and cubed
- 2 chicken breasts, skinless and boneless
- 1 tablespoon fresh thyme, chopped
- A pinch of salt and black pepper

Directions:

1. In a bowl, mix the apple with salt, pepper, thyme, squash and half of the oil and toss. Heat a pan with the rest of the oil over medium heat, add the chicken, season with salt and black pepper, and cook for 5 minutes on each side. Add the squash mixture, stir, bake in the oven at 425°F for

20 minutes, add the kale, bake for 10 minutes, shred the meat, divide everything between plates and serve for breakfast.

Nutrition Value: Calories - 200, Fat - 4, Fiber - 3, Carbs - 10, Protein - 15

08. Chicken Bowls

Preparation time: 10 minutes
Cooking time: 35 minutes
Servings: 4

Ingredients:

- 2 chicken breasts, skinless and boneless
- 2 cups butternut squash, cubed
- 2 tablespoons olive oil
- 6 cups mixed greens
- 1 tablespoon lemon juice
- ¼ cup tahini paste
- 1 avocado, peeled, pitted, and cubed
- 3 tablespoons water
- 1 tablespoon apple cider vinegar
- A pinch of salt and black pepper

Directions:

1. Arrange the squash pieces on a lined baking sheet, season with salt and pepper, drizzle half of the oil and roast in the oven at 425°F for 25 minutes. Heat a pan with the rest of the oil over medium-high heat, add the chicken, season with salt and black pepper, and cook for 5 minutes on each side and shred with a fork. In a bowl, mix the lemon juice with the tahini, vinegar, salt, pepper and water, and whisk well. Put the mixed greens in a bowl, add roasted squash, shredded chicken and avocado, drizzle the lemon and tahini dressing you've made, toss and serve for breakfast.

Nutrition Value: Calories - 245, Fat - 4, Fiber - 3, Carbs - 6, Protein - 12

09. Sprout Salad and Vinaigrette

Preparation time: 10 minutes
Cooking time: 0 minutes
Servings: 10

Ingredients:

- 24 ounces Brussels sprouts, shredded
- 1 cup onion, chopped
- 6 bacon slices, cooked and chopped
- ⅔ cup almonds, toasted and sliced
- ⅔ cup cherries, pitted and sliced
- For the vinaigrette:
- 1 teaspoon orange zest, grated
- 1 teaspoon mustard
- Juice of 1 orange
- Juice of 1 lemon
- 2 tablespoons shallots, chopped
- ¾ cup olive oil
- 2 teaspoons fresh cilantro, chopped
- A pinch of salt and black pepper

Directions:

1. In a salad bowl, mix the Brussels sprouts with the onion, almonds, cherries, and bacon and toss. In another bowl, mix the orange zest with the mustard, lemon juice, orange juice, shallots, oil, salt, pepper and cilantro and whisk well.
2. Add 1 cup of this mix over the salad, toss, divide between plates and serve for breakfast.

Nutrition Value: Calories - 150, Fat - 4, Fiber - 4, Carbs - 7, Protein - 8

10. Sweet Potato and Tomato Sauce Mix

Preparation time: 10 minutes
Cooking time: 45 minutes
Servings: 3

Ingredients:

- 2 tablespoons olive oil
- 3 tablespoons tomato sauce, no-salt added
- 3 tablespoons green onions, chopped
- 1 pound pork sausage, chopped
- 2 sweet potatoes, cubed
- 4 cups kale, chopped
- A pinch of salt and black pepper

Directions:

1. In a bowl, mix the sweet potatoes with the salt, pepper, and oil, toss, arrange on a lined baking sheet and bake in the oven at 400°F for 30 minutes. Heat a pan over medium heat, add the sausage, tomato sauce, green onions and kale, toss and cook

for 15 minutes. Divide this mix into bowls, add toasted potatoes, toss and serve for breakfast.

Nutrition Value: Calories - 220, Fat - 4, Fiber - 2, Carbs - 6, Protein - 7

11. Turkey and Apple Breakfast Cakes

Preparation time: 10 minutes
Cooking time: 10 minutes
Servings: 12

Ingredients:

- ½ teaspoon garlic powder
- ¼ teaspoon fennel seeds, crushed
- 1 pound ground turkey meat
- ½ cup apples, peeled, cored and minced
- ½ teaspoon sweet paprika
- A pinch of salt and black pepper
- 2 tablespoons olive oil

Directions:

1. In a bowl, mix the turkey meat with garlic powder, fennel, apple, and paprika, salt and pepper, stir and shape 12 cakes out of this mix. Heat a pan with the oil over medium heat, add the turkey cakes to the pan, cook for 5 minutes on each side, divide between plates and serve.

Nutrition Value: Calories - 104, Fat - 4, Fiber - 0, Carbs - 3, Protein - 12

12. Pork Cakes with Blackberries

Preparation time: 10 minutes
Cooking time: 10 minutes
Servings: 8

Ingredients:

- 1 pound ground pork meat
- ½ cup blackberries, chopped
- ½ teaspoon garlic powder
- A pinch of salt and black pepper
- ½ teaspoon dried thyme
- ½ teaspoon dried sage
- 2 tablespoons olive oil

Directions:

1. In a bowl, combine the pork meat with the blackberries, garlic powder, salt, pepper,

thyme and sage, stir well and shape 8 cakes out of this mix. Heat a pan with the oil over medium-high heat, add the cakes into the pan, and cook for 5 minutes on each side, divide between plates and serve for breakfast.

Nutrition Value: Calories - 233, Fat - 5, Fiber - 2, Carbs - 8, Protein - 12

13. Blueberry Smoothie

Preparation time: 10 minutes
Cooking time: 10 minutes
Servings: 2

Ingredients:

- 12 ounces blueberries
- 2 teaspoons cinnamon powder
- 5 cups water

Directions:

1. Heat a pot with 4 cups water over medium-high heat, add the cinnamon, boil for 10 minutes and strain into a blender. Add the rest of the water and the blueberries, pulse well, strain this again into 2 bowls and serve.

Nutrition Value: Calories - 68, Fat - 0, Fiber - 1, Carbs - 0, Protein - 2

14. Pineapple and Cucumber Bowls

Preparation time: 5 minutes
Cooking time: 0 minutes
Servings: 1

Ingredients:

- 1 cup pineapple, cubed
- ½ cup cucumber, sliced
- 1 small banana, peeled and chopped
- 1 teaspoon lime zest
- 2 tablespoons lime juice
- ½ cup kale leaves

Directions:

1. In a salad bowl, mix the pineapple with the cucumber, banana, lime zest, lime juice and kale, toss and serve for breakfast.

Nutrition Value: Calories - 78, Fat - 1, Fiber - 1, Carbs - 2, Protein - 2

15. Minty Cucumber Smoothie

Preparation time: 5 minutes
Cooking time: 0 minutes
Servings: 2

Ingredients:

- 1 cup cucumber, peeled, and chopped
- ¼ cup water
- 6 ice cubes
- ⅓ cup natural apple juice
- ¼ cup mint leaves, chopped

Directions:

1. In a blender, mix the cucumber with the water, apple juice, mint and ice, pulse well, divide into 2 glasses and serve.

Nutrition Value: Calories - 76, Fat - 1, Fiber - 0, Carbs - 0, Protein - 3

16. Cucumber and Berry Smoothie

Preparation time: 5 minutes
Cooking time: 0 minutes
Servings: 3

Ingredients:

- 2 big cucumbers, peeled and chopped
- 1 cup blackberries
- 1 tablespoon lemon juice
- 1 cup almond milk

Directions:

1. In a blender, mix the cucumbers with the blackberries, milk and lemon juice, pulse well, pour into 3 glasses and serve.

Nutrition Value: Calories - 80, Fat - 0, Fiber - 1, Carbs - 2, Protein - 3

17. Apple and Spinach Smoothie

Preparation time: 6 minutes
Cooking time: 0 minutes
Servings: 2

Ingredients:

- 1 cucumber, peeled and chopped
- 1 cup baby spinach
- 1 cup water
- ½ green apple, peeled and chopped

Directions:

1. In a blender, mix the cucumber with the apple, water and spinach, pulse well, divide into 2 glasses and serve.

Nutrition Value: Calories - 60, Fat - 1, Fiber - 1, Carbs - 2, Protein - 4

18. Cucumber and Ginger Smoothie

Preparation time: 5 minutes
Cooking time: 0 minutes
Servings: 3

Ingredients:

- 2 cucumbers, sliced
- 1 tablespoon ginger, grated
- 1 cup water
- ½ cup kale, torn
- 1 apple, peeled and chopped
- Juice of 1 lime

Directions:

1. In a blender, mix the cucumbers with the ginger, water, apple, kale and lime juice, pulse well, divide into 3 glasses and serve.

Nutrition Value: Calories - 78, Fat - 1, Fiber - 1, Carbs - 2, Protein - 2

19. Strawberry Smoothie

Preparation time: 5 minutes
Cooking time: 0 minutes
Servings: 2

Ingredients:

- 2 cups strawberries
- 1 cup coconut milk
- ½ cucumber, seedless and chopped
- 1 tablespoon lemon juice

Directions:

1. In a blender, mix the strawberries with the coconut milk, lemon juice and cucumber, pulse well, divide into bowls and serve for breakfast.

Nutrition Value: Calories - 100, Fat - 0, Fiber - 1, Carbs - 1, Protein - 2

20. Squash Boats

Preparation time: 10 minutes
Cooking time: 45 minutes
Servings: 4

Ingredients:

- 1 onion, peeled and chopped
- 1 pound Italian sausage, casings removed and chopped
- 2 acorn squash, cut in half and deseeded
- 3 tablespoons olive oil
- 2 cups spinach, chopped
- 2 garlic cloves, peeled and minced
- 1 apple, cored and chopped
- 1 tablespoon fresh rosemary, chopped
- A pinch of salt and black pepper

Directions:

1. Arrange the acorn squash halves on a lined baking sheet, place in the oven at 400°F, and roast for 20 minutes. Heat a pan with the oil over medium heat, add the onion, stir, reduce heat to low, cook them for 15 minutes, add the garlic, apples, salt, pepper, spinach, rosemary and sausage, stir, cook for 7 minutes more and take off heat. Stuff the roasted acorn halves with this mix, broil for 10 minutes over medium heat, divide between plates, and serve.

Nutrition Value: Calories - 300, Fat - 4, Fiber - 4, Carbs - 7, Protein - 12

21. Almond Milk and Berries Smoothie Bowls

Preparation time: 10 minutes
Cooking time: 3 minutes
Servings: 3

Ingredients:

- ½ cup coconut flakes
- 2 and ½ cups almond milk
- 1 tablespoon ground cinnamon
- 1 teaspoon allspice
- 2 teaspoons ground ginger
- 1 teaspoon cardamom powder
- 2 tablespoons pumpkin seeds
- 1½ cups berries
- 1 tablespoon chia seeds

Directions:

1. In a blender, mix the almond milk with the coconut flakes, cinnamon, allspice, ginger, cardamom and berries, pulse well, divide into 3 bowls, top with pumpkin seeds and chia seeds and serve.

Nutrition Value: Calories - 150, Fat - 4, Fiber - 2, Carbs - 6, Protein - 3

22. Grapes Smoothie

Preparation time: 10 minutes
Cooking time: 0 minutes
Servings: 3

Ingredients:

- 1 cup apple juice
- 1 small avocado, pitted and peeled
- ¼ cup mint leaves
- 3 cups grapes
- 2 cups baby spinach
- 1 teaspoon green tea powder
- ½ tablespoon chia seeds

Directions:

1. In a blender, mix the apple juice with the avocado, mint, grapes, spinach, tea powder and pulse well. Add the chia seeds, stir, divide into glasses and serve.

Nutrition Value: Calories - 90, Fat - 1, Fiber - 2, Carbs - 5, Protein - 2

23. Blueberry Pudding

Preparation time: 3 hours and 10 minutes
Cooking time: 0 minutes
Servings: 2

Ingredients:

- 2 cups almond milk
- 1 cup matcha green tea powder
- 4 tablespoons chia seeds
- 2 cups blueberries
- 1 banana, peeled and sliced

Directions:

1. In a bowl, mix the almond milk with the tea powder and chia seeds, stir and leave aside for 10 minutes. Add the blueberries and the banana, toss and serve.

Nutrition Value: Calories - 130, Fat - 1, Fiber - 1, Carbs - 4, Protein - 2

24. Spinach Omelette

Preparation time: 10 minutes
Cooking time: 6 minutes
Servings: 3

Ingredients:

- 3 tablespoons coconut milk
- 2 eggs
- 1 teaspoon olive oil
- 2 green onions, chopped
- 1 red bell pepper, seeded and chopped
- 1 cup spinach, torn

Directions:

1. In a bowl, mix the eggs with the milk, green onions, bell pepper and spinach, and whisk. Heat a pan with the oil over medium-high heat, add the eggs mix, stir, cook for about 3 minutes on each side, slice, divide between plates, and serve.

Nutrition Value: Calories - 160, Fat - 3, Fiber - 3, Carbs - 7, Protein - 3

25. Stuffed Mushroom Caps

Preparation time: 10 minutes
Cooking time: 32 minutes
Servings: 12

Ingredients:

- 1 pound chorizo, chopped
- 1 small onion, peeled and chopped
- 1 tablespoon olive oil
- 2 pounds button mushroom caps, half of the stems reserved and chopped
- 3 garlic cloves, peeled and minced
- 2 cups spinach, chopped
- ¼ cup fresh parsley, chopped

Directions:

1. Heat a pan with the oil over medium heat, add the mushroom stems, stir, and cook for 3 minutes. Add the onion and the garlic, stir, and cook for 5 minutes. Add the spinach and parsley, stir, take off the heat, mix with the chorizo, stuff the mushroom caps with mix, arrange them on a lined

baking sheet, bake in the oven at 350°F for 25 minutes, divide between plates and serve.

Nutrition Value: Calories - 124, Fat - 4, Fiber - 1, Carbs - 3, Protein - 9

26. Chicken, Apple and Grape Salad

Preparation time: 10 minutes
Cooking time: 0 minutes
Servings: 4

Ingredients:

- 2 tablespoons lemon juice
- 1 avocado, peeled, pitted and cubed
- 3 tablespoons fresh basil, chopped
- 1 tablespoon olive oil
- A pinch of salt and black pepper
- 2 cups chicken, cooked and shredded
- 1 onion, peeled and chopped
- ⅓ cup celery, chopped
- ½ cup apple, cored and chopped
- ½ cup grapes, cut in half
- ¼ cup walnuts, chopped

Directions:

1. In a salad bowl, mix the onion with the chicken, apples, celery, walnuts, and grapes and toss. In a food processor, mix the avocado with the oil, basil, lemon juice, salt and pepper, pulse well, and add over the salad, toss and serve.

Nutrition Value: Calories - 243, Fat - 12, Fiber - 4, Carbs - 10, Protein - 22

27. Pear and Berry Sandwich

Preparation time: 10 minutes
Cooking time: 0 minutes
Servings: 6

Ingredients:

- 1 pear, cored and sliced
- 2 tablespoons almonds, chopped
- 6 tablespoons almond butter
- 6 tablespoons blueberries

Directions:

1. Spread the almond butter on the pear

slices, arrange them on a platter, sprinkle the almonds all over, divide the blueberries and serve.

Nutrition Value: Calories - 154, Fat - 12, Fiber - 2, Carbs - 9, Protein - 4

28. Avocado Boats

Preparation time: 10 minutes
Cooking time: 0 minutes
Servings: 4

- Ingredients:
- ½ cup red cabbage, shredded
- 2 cups chicken breasts, skinless, boneless, cooked, and chopped
- ½ cup mango, peeled and cubed
- 3 tablespoons fresh cilantro, chopped
- 3 green onions, chopped
- 2 tablespoons olive oil
- 2 tablespoon red vinegar
- A pinch of salt and black pepper
- 2 avocados, pitted and halved
- 2 tablespoons lemon juice

Directions:

1. In a bowl, mix the cabbage with the chopped chicken, mango, cilantro, onions, lemon juice, salt, pepper, vinegar and oil and toss well. Stuff the avocado boats with the mix and serve.

Nutrition Value: Calories - 265, Fat - 12, Fiber - 5, Carbs - 12, Protein - 27

29. Whole30 Morning Bowl

Preparation time: 5 minutes
Servings: 1

Ingredients:

- 1 cup coconut milk
- 1 teaspoon raw honey
- 1 teaspoon walnuts; chopped.
- 1 teaspoon pistachios; chopped.
- 1 teaspoon almonds; chopped.
- 1 teaspoon pine nuts; raw
- 1 teaspoon pepitas; raw
- 2 teaspoons raspberries
- 1 teaspoon pecans; chopped.

- 1 teaspoon sunflower seeds; raw

Directions:

1. In a bowl, mix milk with honey and stir.
2. Add pecans, walnuts, almonds, pistachios, sunflower seeds, pine nuts and pepitas
3. Stir, top with raspberries and serve

Nutrition Values: Calories: 100; Fat : 2; Fiber : 4; Carbs : 5; Protein : 6

30. Quick Whole30 Burrito

Preparation time: 26 minutes
Servings: 1

Ingredients:

- 1/4 pound beef meat; ground
- 1 teaspoon sweet paprika
- 1 teaspoon cumin; ground
- 1 teaspoon onion powder
- 1 small red onion; julienned
- 3 eggs
- 1 teaspoon coconut oil
- 1 teaspoon garlic powder
- 1 teaspoon cilantro; chopped.
- Salt and black pepper to the taste.

Directions:

1. Heat up a pan over medium heat; add beef and brown for a few minutes
2. Add salt, pepper, cumin, garlic and onion powder and paprika; stir, cook for 4 minutes more and take off heat.
3. In a bowl, mix eggs with salt and pepper and whisk well.
4. Heat up a pan with the oil over medium heat; add egg, spread evenly and cook for 6 minutes
5. Transfer your egg burrito to a plate, divide beef mix, add onion and cilantro, roll and serve

Nutrition Values: Calories: 280; Fat : 12; Fiber : 4; Carbs : 7; Protein : 14

31. Whole30 Bacon And Lemon Muffins

Preparation time: 30 minutes
Servings: 12

Ingredients:

- 1 cup bacon; finely chopped.
- 1 teaspoon baking soda
- 4 eggs
- 1/2 cup ghee; melted
- 3 cups almond flour
- 2 teaspoons lemon thyme
- Salt and black pepper to the taste.

Directions:

1. In a bowl, mix flour with baking soda and eggs and stir well.
2. Add ghee, lemon thyme, bacon, salt and pepper and whisk well.
3. Divide this into a lined muffin pan, introduce in the oven at 350 degrees F and bake for 20 minutes
4. Leave muffins to cool down a bit, divide between plates and serve them.

Nutrition Values: Calories: 213; Fat : 7; Fiber : 2; Carbs : 9; Protein : 8

32. Awesome Avocado Muffins

Preparation time: 30 minutes
Servings: 12

Ingredients:

- 6 bacon slices; chopped.
- 1 yellow onion; chopped.
- 1/2 teaspoon baking soda
- 1/2 cup coconut flour
- 1 cup coconut milk
- 2 cups avocado; pitted, peeled and chopped.
- 4 eggs
- Salt and black pepper to the taste.

Directions:

1. Heat up a pan over medium heat; add onion and bacon; stir and brown for a few minutes
2. In a bowl, mash avocado pieces with a fork and whisk well with the eggs
3. Add milk, salt, pepper, baking soda and coconut flour and stir everything.
4. Add bacon mix and stir again.
5. Grease a muffin tray with the coconut oil, divide eggs and avocado mix into the tray, introduce in the oven at 350 degrees F and

bake for 20 minutes

6. Divide muffins between plates and serve them for breakfast.

Nutrition Values: Calories: 200; Fat : 7; Fiber : 4; Carbs : 7; Protein : 5

33. Breakfast Hash

Preparation time: 26 minutes
Servings: 2

Ingredients:

- 2 cups corned beef; chopped.
- 1 pound radishes; cut in quarters
- 1 yellow onion; chopped.
- 1/2 cup beef stock
- 1 tablespoon coconut oil
- 2 garlic cloves; minced
- Salt and black pepper to the taste.

Directions:

1. Heat up a pan with the oil over medium high heat; add onion; stir and cook for 4 minutes
2. Add radishes; stir and cook for 5 minutes
3. Add garlic; stir and cook for 1 minute more
4. Add stock, beef, salt and pepper; stir, cook for 5 minutes, take off heat and serve

Nutrition Values: Calories: 240; Fat : 7; Fiber : 3; Carbs : 12; Protein : 8

34. Whole30 Breakfast Dish

Preparation time: 50 minutes
Servings: 6

Ingredients:

- 1 pound sausage; chopped.
- 6 asparagus stalks; chopped.
- 8 eggs; whisked
- 1 tablespoon coconut oil; melted
- 1 tablespoon dill; chopped.
- 1 leek; chopped.
- 1/4 cup coconut milk
- 1/4 teaspoon garlic powder
- Salt and black pepper to the taste.

Directions:

1. Heat up a pan over medium heat; add sausage pieces and brown them for a few

minutes

2. Add asparagus and leek; stir and cook for a few minutes
3. Meanwhile; in a bowl, mix eggs with salt, pepper, dill, garlic powder and coconut milk and whisk well.
4. Pour this into a baking dish which you've greased with the coconut oil.
5. Add sausage and veggies on top and whisk everything.
6. Introduce in the oven at 325 degrees F and bake for 40 minutes Serve warm.

Nutrition Values: Calories: 340; Fat : 12; Fiber : 3; Carbs : 8; Protein : 23

35. Herbed Biscuits

Preparation time: 25 minutes
Servings: 6

Ingredients:

- 6 tablespoons coconut oil
- 6 tablespoons coconut flour
- 2 garlic cloves; minced
- 1/4 cup yellow onion; minced
- 1/2 teaspoon apple cider vinegar
- 1/4 teaspoon baking soda
- 1 tablespoons parsley; chopped.
- 2 tablespoons coconut milk
- 2 eggs
- Salt and black pepper to the taste.

Directions:

1. In a bowl, mix coconut flour with eggs, oil, garlic, onion, coconut milk, parsley, salt and pepper and stir well.
2. In a bowl, mix vinegar with baking soda; stir well and add to the batter.
3. Drop spoonful of this batter on lined baking sheets and shape circles
4. Introduce in the oven at 350 degrees F and bake for 15 minutes
5. Serve these biscuits for breakfast.

Nutrition Values: Calories: 140; Fat : 6; Fiber : 2; Carbs : 10; Protein : 12

36. Whole30 Poached Eggs

Preparation time: 45 minutes
Servings: 4

Ingredients:

- 3 tomatoes; chopped.
- 3 garlic cloves; minced
- 1 tablespoon ghee
- 1/4 teaspoon chili powder
- 1 tablespoon cilantro; chopped.
- 6 eggs
- 1 white onion; chopped.
- 1 red bell pepper; chopped.
- 1 teaspoon paprika
- 1 teaspoon cumin
- 1 Serrano pepper; chopped.
- Salt and black pepper to the taste.

Directions:

1. Heat up a pan with the ghee over medium heat; add onion; stir and cook for 10 minutes
2. Add Serrano pepper and garlic; stir and cook for 1 minute
3. Add red bell pepper; stir and cook for 10 minutes
4. Add tomatoes, salt, pepper, chili powder, cumin and paprika; stir and cook for 10 minutes
5. Crack eggs into the pan, season them with salt and pepper, cover pan and cook for 6 minutes more
6. Sprinkle cilantro at the end and serve

Nutrition Values: Calories: 300; Fat : 12; Fiber : 3. 4; Carbs : 22; Protein : 14

37. Tasty Whole30 Pancakes

Preparation time: 15 minutes
Servings: 4

Ingredients:

- 2 ounces cream cheese
- 1 teaspoon stevia
- 1/2 teaspoon cinnamon; ground
- 2 eggs
- Cooking spray

Directions:

1. In your blender, mix eggs with cream cheese, stevia and cinnamon and blend well.
2. Heat up a pan with some cooking spray

over medium high heat; pour 1/4 of the batter, spread well, cook for 2 minutes, flip and cook for 1 minute more

3. Transfer to a plate and repeat the action with the rest of the batter.
4. Serve them right away.

Nutrition Values: Calories: 344; Fat : 23; Fiber : 12; Carbs : 3; Protein : 16

38. Pumpkin Pancakes

Preparation time: 25 minutes
Servings: 6

Ingredients:

- 2 ounces hazelnut flour
- 2 ounces flax seeds; ground
- 1 ounce egg white protein
- 1 teaspoon coconut oil
- 1 tablespoon chai masala
- 1 teaspoon vanilla extract
- 1 teaspoon baking powder
- 1 cup coconut cream
- 1 tablespoon swerve
- 1/2 cup pumpkin puree
- 3 eggs
- 5 drops stevia

Directions:

1. In a bowl, mix flax seeds with hazelnut flour, egg white protein, baking powder and chai masala and stir.
2. In another bowl, mix coconut cream with vanilla extract, pumpkin puree, eggs, stevia and swerve and stir well.
3. Combine the 2 mixtures and stir well.
4. Heat up a pan with the oil over medium high heat; pour 1/6 of the batter, spread into a circle, cover, reduce heat to low, cook for 3 minutes on each side and transfer to a plate
5. Repeat with the rest of the batter and serve your pumpkin pancakes right away.

Nutrition Values: Calories: 400; Fat : 23; Fiber : 4; Carbs : 5; Protein : 21

39. Breakfast Stir Fry

Preparation time: 40 minutes
Servings: 2

Ingredients:

- 1/2 pounds beef meat; minced
- 1 tablespoon tamari sauce
- 2 bell peppers; chopped.
- 2 teaspoons red chili flakes
- 1 teaspoon chili powder
- 1 tablespoon coconut oil
- Salt and black pepper to the taste.
- For the bok choy:
- 6 bunches bok choy; trimmed and chopped.
- 1 teaspoon ginger; grated
- 1-tablespoon coconut oil
- Salt to the taste.
- For the eggs:
- 2 eggs
- 1 tablespoon coconut oil

Directions:

1. Heat up a pan with 1 tablespoon coconut oil over medium high heat; add beef and bell peppers; stir and cook for 10 minutes
2. Add salt, pepper, tamari sauce, chili flakes and chili powder; stir, cook for 4 minutes more and take off heat.
3. Heat up another pan with 1 tablespoon oil over medium heat; add bok choy; stir and cook for 3 minutes
4. Add salt and ginger; stir, cook for 2 minutes more and take off heat.
5. Heat up the third pan with 1 tablespoon oil over medium heat; crack eggs and fry them.
6. Divide beef and bell peppers mix into 2 bowls
7. Divide bok choy and top with eggs

Nutrition Values: Calories: 248; Fat : 14; Fiber : 4; Carbs : 10; Protein : 14

40. Cheese And Oregano Muffins

Preparation time: 35 minutes
Servings: 6

Ingredients:

- 1 cup cheddar cheese; grated
- 1 cup almond flour
- 1/2 teaspoon oregano; dried

- 1/2 cup coconut milk
- 1/4 teaspoon baking soda
- 2 tablespoons olive oil
- 1 egg
- 2 tablespoons parmesan cheese
- Salt and black pepper to the taste.

Directions:

1. In a bowl, mix flour with oregano, salt, pepper, parmesan and baking soda and stir.
2. In another bowl, mix coconut milk with egg and olive oil and stir well.
3. Combine the 2 mixtures and whisk well.
4. Add cheddar cheese; stir, pour this a lined muffin tray, introduce in the oven at 350 degrees F for 25 minutes
5. Leave your muffins to cool down for a few minutes, divide them between plates and serve

Nutrition Values: Calories: 160; Fat : 3; Fiber : 2; Carbs : 6; Protein : 10

41. Whole30 Egg Porridge

Preparation time: 14 minutes
Servings: 2

Ingredients:

- 2 eggs
- 2 tablespoons ghee; melted
- 1/3 cup heavy cream
- 1 tablespoon stevia
- A pinch of cinnamon; ground

Directions:

1. In a bowl, mix eggs with stevia and heavy cream and whisk well.
2. Heat up a pan with the ghee over medium high heat; add egg mix and cook until they are done
3. Transfer to 2 bowls, sprinkle cinnamon on top and serve

Nutrition Values: Calories: 340; Fat : 12; Fiber : 10; Carbs : 3; Protein : 14

42. Whole30 Waffles

Preparation time: 30 minutes
Servings: 5

Ingredients:

- 5 eggs; separated
- 4 ounces ghee; melted
- 3 tablespoons almond milk
- 1 teaspoon baking powder
- 4 tablespoons coconut flour
- 2 teaspoon vanilla
- 3 tablespoons stevia

Directions:

1. In a bowl, whisk egg white using your mixer.
2. In another bowl mix flour with stevia, baking powder and egg yolks and whisk well.
3. Add vanilla, ghee and milk and stir well again.
4. Add egg white and stir gently everything.
5. Pour some of the mix into your waffle maker and cook until it's golden.
6. Repeat with the rest of the batter and serve your waffles right away.

Nutrition Values: Calories: 240; Fat : 23; Fiber : 2; Carbs : 4; Protein : 7

43. Whole30 Bread

Preparation time: 13 minutes
Servings: 4

Ingredients:

- 1/3 cup almond flour
- 1 egg; whisked
- 1/2 teaspoon baking powder
- 2 ½ tablespoons coconut oil
- A pinch of salt

Directions:

1. Grease a mug with some of the oil.
2. In a bowl, mix the egg with flour, salt, oil and baking powder and stir.
3. Pour this into the mug and cook in your microwave for 3 minutes at a High temperature
4. Leave the bread to cool down a bit, take out of the mug, slice and serve with a glass of almond milk for breakfast.

Nutrition Values: Calories: 132; Fat : 12; Fiber : 1; Carbs : 3; Protein : 4

44. Whole30 Cereal Nibs

Preparation Time: 55 minutes
Servings: 4

Ingredients:

- 4 tablespoons hemp hearts
- 1/2 cup chia seeds
- 2 tablespoons coconut oil
- 1 tablespoon swerve
- 2 tablespoons cocoa nibs
- 1 tablespoon vanilla extract
- 1 tablespoon psyllium powder
- 1 cup water

Directions:

1. In a bowl, mix chia seeds with water; stir and leave aside for 5 minutes
2. Add hemp hearts, vanilla extract, psyllium powder, oil and swerve and stir well with your mixer.
3. Add cocoa nibs, and stir until you obtain a dough.
4. Divide dough into 2 pieces, shape into cylinder form, place on a lined baking sheet, flatten well, cover with a parchment paper, introduce in the oven at 285 degrees F and bake for 20 minutes
5. Remove the parchment paper and bake for 25 minutes more
6. Take cylinders out of the oven, leave aside to cool down and cut into small pieces
7. Serve in the morning with some almond milk.

Nutrition Values: Calories: 245; Fat : 12; Fiber : 12; Carbs : 2; Protein : 9

45. Steak And Eggs

Preparation time: 20 minutes
Servings: 1

Ingredients:

- 1 small avocado; pitted, peeled and sliced
- 3 eggs
- 4 ounces sirloin
- 1 tablespoon ghee
- Salt and black pepper to the taste.

Directions:

1. Heat up a pan with the ghee over medium high heat; crack eggs into the pan and cook them as you wish.
2. Season with salt and pepper, take off heat and transfer to a plate
3. Heat up another pan over medium high heat; add sirloin, cook for 4 minutes, take off heat; leave aside to cool down and cut into thin strips
4. Season with salt and pepper to the taste and place next to the eggs
5. Add avocado slices on the side and serve

Nutrition Values: Calories: 500; Fat : 34; Fiber : 10; Carbs : 3; Protein : 40

46. Mouthwatering Breakfast Pie

Preparation time: 55 minutes
Servings: 8

Ingredients:

- 3/4 pound beef; ground
- 1/2 onion; chopped.
- 1 pie crust
- 3 tablespoons taco seasoning
- 1 teaspoon baking soda
- Mango salsa for serving
- 1/2 red bell pepper; chopped.
- A handful cilantro; chopped.
- 8 eggs
- 1 teaspoon coconut oil
- Salt and black pepper to the taste.

Directions:

1. Heat up a pan with the oil over medium heat; add beef, cook until it browns and mixes with salt, pepper and taco seasoning.
2. Stir again, transfer to a bowl and leave aside for now.
3. Heat up the pan again over medium heat with cooking juices from the meat, add onion and bell pepper; stir and cook for 4 minutes
4. Add eggs, baking soda and some salt and stir well.
5. Add cilantro; stir again and take off heat.
6. Spread beef mix in pie crust, add veggies mix and spread over meat, introduce in the oven at 350 degrees F and bake for 45 minutes
7. Leave the pie to cool down a bit, slice,

divide between plates and serve with mango salsa on top.

Nutrition Values: Calories: 198; Fat : 11; Fiber : 1; Carbs : 12; Protein : 12

47. Whole30 Cauliflower And Chorizo

Preparation time: 55 minutes
Servings: 4

Ingredients:

- 1 cauliflower head; florets separated
- 4 eggs; whisked
- 1/2 teaspoon garlic powder
- 2 tablespoons green onions; chopped.
- 1 pound chorizo; chopped.
- 12 ounces canned green chilies; chopped.
- 1 yellow onion; chopped.
- Salt and black pepper to the taste.

Directions:

1. Heat up a pan over medium heat; add chorizo and onion; stir and brown for a few minutes
2. Add green chilies; stir, cook for a few minutes and take off heat.
3. In your food processor mix cauliflower with some salt and pepper and blend.
4. Transfer this to a bowl, add eggs, salt, pepper and garlic powder and whisk everything.
5. Add chorizo mix as well, whisk again and transfer everything to a greased baking dish.
6. Bake in the oven at 375 degrees F and bake for 40 minutes
7. Leave casserole to cool down for a few minutes, sprinkle green onions on top, slice and serve

Nutrition Values: Calories: 350; Fat : 12; Fiber : 4; Carbs : 6; Protein : 20

48. Special Almond Cereal

Preparation time: 5 minutes
Servings: 1

Ingredients:

- 2 tablespoons almonds; chopped.

- 1/3 cup coconut milk
- 1 tablespoon chia seeds
- 2 tablespoon pepitas; roasted
- A handful blueberries
- 1 small banana; chopped.
- 1/3 cup water

Directions:

1. In a bowl, mix chia seeds with coconut milk and leave aside for 5 minutes
2. In your food processor, mix half of the pepitas with almonds and pulse them well.
3. Add this to chia seeds mix.
4. Also add the water and stir.
5. Top with the rest of the pepitas, banana pieces and blueberries and serve

Nutrition Values: Calories: 200; Fat : 3; Fiber : 2; Carbs : 5; Protein : 4

49. Whole30 Salad In A Jar

Preparation time: 10 minutes
Servings: 1

Ingredients:

- 1 ounce favorite greens
- 1 ounce red bell pepper; chopped.
- 4 ounces rotisserie chicken; roughly chopped.
- 4 tablespoons extra virgin olive oil
- 1/2 scallion; chopped.
- 1 ounce cucumber; chopped.
- 1 ounce cherry tomatoes; halved
- Salt and black pepper to the taste.

Directions:

1. In a bowl, mix greens with bell pepper, tomatoes, scallion, cucumber, salt, pepper and olive oil and toss to coat well.
2. Transfer this to a jar, top with chicken pieces and serve for breakfast.

Nutrition Values: Calories: 180; Fat : 12; Fiber : 4; Carbs : 5; Protein : 17

50. Whole30 Brussels Sprouts

Preparation time: 22 minutes
Servings: 3

Ingredients:

- 12 ounces Brussels sprouts; thinly sliced
- 2 ounces bacon; chopped.
- 2 shallots; minced
- 2 garlic cloves; minced
- 1½ tablespoons apple cider vinegar
- 3 eggs
- 1 tablespoon ghee; melted
- Salt and black pepper to the taste.

Directions:

1. Heat up a pan over medium heat; add bacon; stir, cook until it's crispy, transfer to a plate and leave aside for now.
2. Heat up the pan again over medium heat; add shallots and garlic; stir and cook for 30 seconds
3. Add Brussels sprouts, salt, pepper and apple cider vinegar; stir and cook for 5 minutes
4. Return bacon to pan; stir and cook for 5 minutes more
5. Add ghee; stir and make a hole in the center.
6. Crack eggs into the pan, cook until they are done and serve right away.

Nutrition Values: Calories: 240; Fat : 7; Fiber : 4; Carbs : 7; Protein : 12

51. Scrambled Eggs

Preparation time: 5 minutes
Cooking time: 5 minutes
Servings: 2

Ingredients:

- 1 tomato, chopped
- 1 tablespoon vegetable oil
- 1 cup baby spinach
- ½ cup feta cheese, cubed
- Salt and black pepper to taste
- 3 eggs

Directions:

1. Heat a pan with the oil over medium heat, add spinach and tomatoes, stir and cook for a few minutes. Add eggs, mix to scramble and cook for 30 seconds.
2. Add cheese, salt and pepper, stir, cook for 20 seconds more, divide between plates and serve.

Nutrition Value: calories 150, fat 2, fiber 0, carbs 2, protein 10

52. Egg Salad

Preparation time: 10 minutes
Cooking time: 0 minutes
Servings: 4

Ingredients:

- ½ cup sun-dried tomatoes, chopped
- 8 eggs, hard-boiled, peeled and chopped
- ¼ cup olives, pitted and chopped
- 1 small cucumber, chopped
- 1 small red onion, finely chopped
- ½ cup Greek yogurt
- ¼ teaspoon cumin
- A splash of lemon juice
- Salt and black pepper to taste
- 1 and ½ teaspoon oregano

Directions:

1. In a bowl, mix eggs with onion, olives, cucumber and tomatoes.
2. Add salt, pepper, lemon juice, Greek yogurt, cumin and oregano, stir well and keep in the fridge until you serve it.

Nutrition Value: calories 230, fat 1, fiber 2, carbs 1.4, protein 7

53. Breakfast Bowl

Preparation time: 10 minutes
Cooking time: 20 minutes
Servings: 6

Ingredients:

- 1 teaspoon onion powder
- ¼ cup Greek yogurt
- 12 eggs
- 1 teaspoon garlic powder
- Salt and black pepper to taste
- 1 teaspoon extra virgin olive oil
- 1 pint cherry tomatoes cut in halves
- 2 cups quinoa, already cooked
- 5 ounces baby spinach leaves
- 1 cup feta cheese, crumbled

Directions:

1. In a bowl, mix eggs with salt, pepper,

onion powder, garlic powder and yogurt, whisk well and leave aside for now.

2. Heat a pan with the oil over medium high heat, add spinach, stir and cook for 3 minutes.
3. Add tomatoes, stir and cook 3 more minutes.
4. Add eggs mix, cook for 9 minutes and stir to scramble. Add quinoa and cheese, stir, cook for 2 minutes more, transfer to bowls and serve hot.

Nutrition Value: calories 357, fat 20, fiber 2, carbs 20, protein 23

54. **Walnut Breakfast Oats**

Preparation time: 5 minutes
Cooking time: 0 minutes
Servings: 1

Ingredients:

- 2 tablespoons walnuts, chopped
- ½ cup oats
- ¾ cup almond milk
- 1 date, chopped
- 1 tablespoon chia seeds
- 1 tablespoon vanilla powder
- ½ teaspoon cinnamon

Directions:

1. In a bowl, mix milk with walnuts, oats, date, chia seeds, vanilla powder and cinnamon.
2. Stir well, keep in the fridge overnight and serve the next day cold.

Nutrition Value: calories 345, fat 18, fiber 3, carbs 38, protein 16

55. **Figs and Yogurt**

Preparation time: 10 minutes
Cooking time: 5 minutes
Servings: 4

Ingredients:

- 8 ounces figs cut in halves
- 2 cups Greek yogurt
- 1 tablespoon honey
- A pinch of cinnamon
- ¼ cup pistachios, chopped

Directions:

1. Heat a pan over medium heat, add honey and warm through.
2. Add figs, stir and caramelize for 5 minutes.
3. Divide yogurt into bowls, add caramelized figs on top, sprinkle cinnamon and pistachios and serve.

Nutrition Value: calories 200, fat 5, fiber 2, carbs 24, protein 5

56. **Olive and Feta Frittata**

Preparation time: 10 minutes
Cooking time: 20 minutes
Servings: 6

Ingredients:

- ¼ cup kalamata olives, pitted and chopped
- 6 eggs
- ½ cup milk
- ½ cup tomatoes, chopped
- ¼ cup black olives, pitted and chopped
- ¼ cup feta cheese, crumbled
- 1 cup spinach
- Salt and black pepper to taste
- 1 teaspoon oregano, dried
- A drizzle of olive oil

Directions:

1. Grease a baking dish with a drizzle of oil. In a bowl, mix eggs with milk, salt, pepper, tomatoes, black olives, kalamata olives, spinach, cheese, oregano and whisk well.
2. Pour into the pan, spread, place in the oven at 400 degrees F and bake for 20 minutes. Serve hot.

Nutrition Value: calories 176, fat 3, fiber 7, carbs 21, protein 16

57. **Spanish Baked Eggs**

Preparation time: 10 minutes
Cooking time: 20 minutes
Servings: 6

Ingredients:

- 2 green bell peppers, chopped
- 2 garlic cloves, minced
- 3 tablespoons olive oil
- 1 yellow onion, chopped

- 1 teaspoon sweet paprika
- 1 teaspoon coriander, ground
- Salt and black pepper to taste
- A pinch of red pepper flakes
- ½ cup tomato sauce
- 6 tomatoes, chopped
- 6 eggs
- ¼ cup parsley, chopped
- ¼ cup mint, chopped

Directions:

1. Heat a pan with the oil over medium heat, add bell peppers, onion, garlic, salt, pepper, paprika, coriander, pepper flakes and cumin, stir and cook for 10 minutes.
2. Add tomatoes and tomato sauce, stir and simmer for 10 minutes.
3. Add more salt and pepper to taste and make 6 holes in the mix.
4. Crack an egg into each, cover pan, reduce heat and cook until eggs are done.
5. Sprinkle parsley and mint over to serve.

Nutrition Value: calories 300, fat 18, fiber 4, carbs 23, protein 15

58. Breakfast Casserole

Preparation time: 10 minutes
Cooking time: 1 hour
Servings: 4

Ingredients:

- 2 garlic cloves, minced
- 3 tablespoons butter
- 1 cup mushrooms, sliced
- 2 shallots, chopped
- 6 cups white bread, cubed
- 1 teaspoon marjoram, dried
- ½ cup artichoke hearts, chopped
- ¼ cup kalamata olives, pitted and cut in quarters
- 4 ounces mozzarella cheese balls, cut in halves
- 1/5 cup sun-dried tomatoes, marinated and chopped
- ¼ cup parmesan, grated
- 6 eggs
- 1 and ½ cups half and half

- Salt to taste
- ¼ cup basil, chopped

Directions:

1. Heat a small pan over medium heat, add 1 tablespoon butter, melt and use to brush 4 baking cups.
2. Heat the same pan with remaining butter over medium heat, add shallot, garlic, stir and cook for 2 minutes.
3. Add mushrooms and marjoram, stir, cook for 4 minutes and transfer to a bowl.
4. Add artichoke pieces, bread cubes, olives, tomatoes, salt, mozzarella, parmesan and toss everything well.
5. Divide mix into greased baking cups. In a bowl, mix eggs with half and a half and whisk well.
6. Divide this over mushroom mix and place in the oven at 325 degrees F and bake for 50 minutes.
7. Leave cups aside to cool down for 5 minutes.
8. Scatter with fresh basil to serve.

Nutrition Value: calories 300, fat 6, fiber 8, carbs 20, protein 15

59. Breakfast Pancakes

Preparation time: 10 minutes
Cooking time: 5 minutes
Servings: 2

Ingredients:

- 6 ounces Greek yogurt
- ½ cup flour
- 1 egg
- 1 teaspoon baking soda

Directions:

1. Put yogurt in a bowl and whisk it well.
2. Add the egg and stir again. In another bowl, mix baking soda with flour and stir.
3. Combine the 2 mixtures and stir well.
4. Heat a pan over medium high heat, spoon some of the batter into the pan, spread, cook until it turns golden, flip and cook on the other side then transfer pancake to a plate.
5. Repeat with the rest of the batter and serve your pancakes with some maple syrup.

Nutrition Value: calories 111, fat 1.4, fiber 2, carbs 15, protein 10

60. Whole30 Galettes

Preparation time: 10 minutes
Cooking time: 50 minutes
Servings: 4

Ingredients:

- 2 yellow onions, cut into medium wedges
- 2 red bell peppers, cut into thin strips
- 1 teaspoon coriander
- 1 teaspoon cumin
- Salt and black pepper to taste
- Some thyme leaves
- 6 tablespoons olive oil
- A handful cilantro, chopped
- A handful parsley, chopped
- 1 puff pastry sheet
- 1 egg, whisked
- 6 eggs
- 12 teaspoons sour cream

Directions:

1. In a bowl, mix onions with bell pepper, thyme, salt, pepper, oil, cumin and coriander and toss to coat.
2. Spread into a baking dish, place in the oven at 400 degrees F and bake for 30 minutes.
3. Take veggies out of the oven, add half of the cilantro and parsley, toss to coat and leave aside.
4. Roll out puff pastry, cut into 6 squares, place them on a lined baking sheet, prick them with a fork and keep in the fridge for 30 minutes.
5. Take pastry squares out of the fridge, brush with whisked egg, spread 3 teaspoons sour cream on each, divide veggie mix and also spread, lift square edges a bit, place in the oven at 425 degrees F and bake for 10 minutes.
6. Take galettes out of the oven, crack an egg in each, place in the oven again and bake for 10 minutes.
7. Take galettes out of the oven, sprinkle salt, pepper to the taste, the rest of the cilantro and parsley, drizzle a little oil and serve.

Nutrition Value: calories 340, fat 20, fiber 3, carbs

20, protein 11

61. Arugula and Roasted Pepper Frittata

Preparation time: 10 minutes
Cooking time: 45 minutes
Servings: 12

Ingredients:

- 3 garlic cloves, minced
- 1 tablespoon olive oil
- 1 cup white onion, chopped
- 8 eggs, whisked
- 12 ounces canned roasted bell peppers, chopped
- 2 handfuls arugula, chopped
- Salt and black pepper to taste
- ¼ cup basil pesto
- 1 cup mozzarella cheese, shredded
- Cooking spray

Directions:

1. Heat a pan with the olive oil over medium high heat, add onion, stir and cook for 5 minutes.
2. Add garlic, stir and cook 2 minutes then take off heat. In a bowl, whisk eggs with arugula, red peppers, salt, pepper, cheese and pesto.
3. Add onions mix and stir well again.
4. Pour into a lightly greased baking dish, place in the oven at 350 degrees F and bake for 45 minutes.
5. Take frittata out of the oven, slice and serve hot.

Nutrition Value: calories 200, fat 12, fiber 1, carbs 0, protein 10

62. Banana Toast

Preparation time: 10 minutes
Cooking time: 20 minutes
Servings: 6

Ingredients:

- 2 eggs
- ½ cup milk
- 6 bread slices
- 1 teaspoon vanilla extract

- ½ teaspoon cinnamon, ground
- A pinch of salt
- 2 tablespoons sugar
- 2 tablespoons butter
- For the banana syrup:
- 3 tablespoons whipping cream
- ¼ cup butter
- 2 tablespoons sugar
- 1 teaspoon vanilla extract
- ¼ teaspoon cinnamon, ground
- 2 bananas, chopped
- 4 tablespoons rum

Directions:

1. In a bowl, mix milk with eggs, salt, vanilla, ½ teaspoon cinnamon and 2 tablespoons sugar and stir well.
2. Heat a pan with 2 tablespoons butter over medium high heat, dip bread slices in egg mix, place them in the pan, fry for 2 minutes on each side and transfer to a plate.
3. Heat a pan with ¼ cup butter over medium high heat and melt it.
4. Add 2 more tablespoons of sugar, stir until it dissolves, cook for 2 minutes and take off heat.
5. Add whipping cream, 1 teaspoon vanilla and ¼ teaspoon cinnamon and stir well.
6. Spoon sauce over toasted slices, top with sliced banana and serve.

Nutrition Value: calories 180, fat 7, fiber 4, carbs 32, protein 5

63. Artichokes and Fennel Omelet

Preparation time: 10 minutes
Cooking time: 10 minutes
Servings: 4

Ingredients:

- 6 eggs
- 2 cups fennel, chopped
- 1 tablespoon olive oil
- ¼ cup green olives, pitted and chopped
- 1 plum tomato, chopped
- 2 tablespoons parsley, chopped
- ¼ cup artichoke hearts, chopped

- Salt and black pepper to the taste
- ½ cup goat cheese, crumbled

Directions:

1. Heat up a pan with the oil over medium heat, add the artichokes and fennel, stir and cook for about 5 minutes.
2. Add tomato and olives, stir and cook for 3 more minutes.
3. In a bowl, mix eggs with salt and pepper, whisk well, add to the pan, stir gently and cook for 2 minutes.
4. Sprinkle cheese all over, bake the omelet at 325 degrees F for 5 minutes, divide it between plates, sprinkle the parsley on top and serve.

Nutrition Value: calories 210, fat 12, fiber 1, carbs 6, protein 5

64. Pepper and Spinach Frittata

Preparation time: 10 minutes
Cooking time: 45 minutes
Servings: 6

Ingredients:

- 1 cup red bell pepper, chopped
- 2 tablespoons butter
- 1 yellow onion, chopped
- 1 and ½ cups spinach
- ½ cup milk
- Salt and black pepper to taste
- 8 eggs
- 1 teaspoon olive oil
- 2 ounces feta cheese, crumbled
- 1 cup tomato, chopped
- 1 tablespoon basil, chopped

Directions:

1. Heat a pan with butter over medium high heat, add onion and bell pepper, stir and cook for 6 minutes.
2. Add spinach, stir and cook for 2 minutes.
3. Meanwhile, in a bowl, mix eggs with salt, pepper, cheese and stir well.
4. Add cooked onions and stir well again.
5. Heat another pan with olive oil over medium heat, add eggs and spread evenly.
6. Place pan in the oven at 350 degrees F and bake for 35 minutes.

7. Take out of oven, spread tomatoes and
    basil all over, leave aside to cool down for
    5 minutes, cut and serve.

**Nutrition Value: calories 250, fat 13, fiber 0, carbs
12, protein 17**

65. Cauliflower Rice Soup

Preparation time: 10 minutes
Cooking time: 4 hours
Servings: 6

Ingredients:

- 5 cups cauliflower rice
- 1 cup yellow onion, chopped
- 1 tablespoon olive oil
- 2 carrots, chopped
- 1 jalapeno pepper, chopped
- 3 garlic cloves, minced
- 1 teaspoon cumin, ground
- 1 teaspoon chili powder
- 1 teaspoon oregano, dried
- A pinch of salt and black pepper
- 2 tablespoons tomato paste
- 4 cups veggie stock
- 1 tablespoon cilantro, chopped

Directions:

1. Drizzle the olive oil on the bottom of your slow cooker, add cauliflower rice, onion, carrots, jalapenos, garlic, cumin, chili powder, oregano, salt, pepper, tomato paste, stock and cilantro, toss, cover and cook on High for 4 hours.
2. Ladle into bowls and serve.
3. Enjoy!

Nutrition Value: calories 394, fat 5, fiber 8, carbs 18, protein 4

66. Easy Butternut Squash Soup

Preparation time: 10 minutes
Cooking time: 8 hours
Servings: 6

Ingredients:

- 3 pounds butternut squash, peeled and cubed
- 1 yellow onion, chopped
- 4 cups veggie stock
- 14 ounces coconut milk

- Salt and black pepper to the taste
- 3 tablespoons red curry paste
- 1 tablespoon cilantro, chopped

Directions:

1. In your slow cooker, mix squash with onion, stock, milk, curry paste, salt and pepper, stir, cover, cook on Low for 8 hours; blend using an immersion blender, ladle into bowls, sprinkle cilantro on top and serve.
2. Enjoy!

Nutrition Value: calories 271, fat 5, fiber 6, carbs 22, protein 6

67. Green Beans and Thyme Soup

Preparation time: 10 minutes
Cooking time: 4 hours
Servings: 4

Ingredients:

- 1 pound green beans
- 1 yellow onion, chopped
- 4 carrots, chopped
- 4 garlic cloves, minced
- A pinch of salt and black pepper
- 1 tablespoon thyme, chopped
- 7 cups veggie stock

Directions:

1. In your slow cooker, mix green beans with onion, carrots, garlic, stock, salt and pepper, stir, cover, cook on High for 4 hours, add thyme, stir, ladle soup into bowls and serve.
2. Enjoy!

Nutrition Value: calories 201, fat 4, fiber 6, carbs 13, protein 5

68. Potato and Chard Soup

Preparation time: 10 minutes
Cooking time: 8 hours
Servings: 6

Ingredients:

- 1 yellow onion, chopped
- 1 tablespoon olive oil
- 1 carrot, chopped
- 1 celery stalk, chopped
- 1 bunch Swiss chard, leaves torn
- 2 garlic cloves, minced
- 4 sweet potatoes, cubed
- 6 cups veggie stock
- A pinch of salt and black pepper
- 1 tablespoon coconut aminos

Directions:

1. In your slow cooker, mix oil with onion, carrot, celery, chard, garlic, potatoes, stock, salt, pepper and aminos, stir, cover, cook on Low for 8 hours, ladle soup into bowls and serve right away.
2. Enjoy!

Nutrition Value: calories 212, fat 5, fiber 7, carbs 10, protein 5

69. Chinese Veggies Soup

Preparation time: 10 minutes
Cooking time: 8 hours
Servings: 6

Ingredients:

- 2 celery stalks, chopped
- 1 yellow onion, chopped
- 1 cup carrot, chopped
- 8 ounces water chestnuts
- 8 ounces canned bamboo shoots, drained
- 2 teaspoons garlic, minced
- 2 teaspoons ginger paste
- ½ teaspoon red pepper flakes
- 3 tablespoons coconut aminos
- 1-quart veggie stock
- 2 bunches bok choy, chopped
- 5 ounces white mushrooms, sliced
- 6 scallions, chopped

Directions:

1. In your slow cooker, mix onion with carrot, celery, chestnuts, bamboo shoots, garlic paste, ginger paste, pepper flakes, coconut aminos, stock, bok choy, mushrooms and scallions, stir, cover, cook

on Low for 8 [‘/hours, ladle into bowls and serve.

2. En.,mkyteretiii[]joy!

Nutrition Value: calories 281, fat 4, fiber 6, carbs 13, protein 4

70. Veggie Stew

Preparation time: 10 minutes
Cooking time: 4 hours
Servings: 6

Ingredients:

- 1 tablespoon ginger, grated
- 3 garlic cloves, minced
- 1 date, pitted and chopped
- 1 and ½ teaspoon coriander, ground
- ½ teaspoon mustard powder
- 1 and ¼ teaspoon cumin, ground
- A pinch of salt and black pepper
- ½ teaspoon turmeric powder
- 1 tablespoon white wine vinegar
- ¼ teaspoon cardamom powder
- 2 carrots, chopped
- 1 yellow onion, chopped
- 4 cups cauliflower florets
- 2 zucchinis, chopped
- 6 ounces tomato paste
- 1 green bell pepper, ch#
- opped

Directions:

1. In your slow cooker, mix ginger with garlic, date, coriander, dry mustard, cumin, salt, pepper, turmeric, vinegar, cardamom, carrots, onion, cauliflower, zucchinis, tomato paste and bell pepper, stir, cover, cook on High for 4 hours, divide into bowls and serve.
2. Enjoy!

Nutrition Value: calories 205, fat 2, fiber 10, carbs 12, protein 9

71. Spinach and Cauliflower Curry

Preparation time: 10 minutes
Cooking time: 6 hours
Servings: 8

Ingredients:

- 10 ounces spinach
- 1 tablespoon garlic, minced
- 15 ounces canned tomatoes, chopped
- 3 cups cauliflower florets
- 1 teaspoon ginger, grated
- 1 yellow onion, chopped
- 4 cups veggie stock
- 2 tablespoons curry paste
- ½ teaspoon cumin, ground
- ½ teaspoon coriander powder
- A pinch of salt and black pepper
- ¼ cup cilantro, chopped

Directions:

1. In your slow cooker, mix spinach with garlic, tomatoes, cauliflower, ginger, onion, stock, curry paste, cumin, coriander, salt and pepper, stir, cover, cook on Low for 6 hours, add cilantro, stir, divide into bowls and serve.
2. Enjoy!

Nutrition Value: calories 325, fat 1, fiber 7, carbs 22, protein 7

72. Red Cabbage Soup

Preparation time: 10 minutes
Cooking time: 7 hours
Servings: 4

Ingredients:

- 1 small yellow onion, chopped
- 1 tablespoon olive oil
- 2 garlic cloves, minced
- 1 and ½ cups mushrooms, sliced
- 3 teaspoons ginger, grated
- A pinch of salt and black pepper
- 4 cups red cabbage, chopped
- 4 cups water
- 2 teaspoons tomato paste
- 1 teaspoon coconut aminos

Directions:

1. In your slow cooker, mix the olive oil with the onion, garlic, mushrooms, ginger, salt, pepper, cabbage, water and tomato paste, stir, cover and cook on Low for 7 hours.

2. Add aminos, stir, and leave soup aside for a few minutes, ladle into bowls and serve.
3. Enjoy!

Nutrition Value: calories 238, fat 4, fiber 4, carbs 14, protein 4

73. Tomatoes and Okra Soup

Preparation time: 10 minutes
Cooking time: 5 hours
Servings: 6

Ingredients:

- 1 green bell pepper, chopped
- 1 small yellow onion, chopped
- 3 cups veggie stock
- 3 garlic cloves, minced
- 16 ounces okra, sliced
- A pinch of salt and black pepper
- 29 ounces canned tomatoes, crushed
- 1 and ½ teaspoon smoked paprika
- 1 teaspoon marjoram, dried
- 1 teaspoon thyme, dried
- 1 teaspoon oregano, dried

Directions:

1. In your slow cooker, mix bell pepper with onion, stock, garlic, okra, tomatoes, smoked paprika, marjoram, thyme, oregano, salt and pepper, stir, cover, cook on High for 5 hours, ladle into bowls and serve.
2. Enjoy!

Nutrition Value: calories 271, fat 4, fiber 6, carbs 14, protein 7

74. Coconut Carrot Soup

Preparation time: 10 minutes
Cooking time: 6 hours
Servings: 6

Ingredients:

- 3 pounds carrots, cubed
- 1 yellow onion, chopped
- 1-quart veggie stock
- Salt and black pepper to the taste
- 1 teaspoon thyme, dried
- 3 tablespoons coconut milk

- 2 teaspoons curry powder
- A handful cilantro, chopped

Directions:

1. In your slow cooker, mix onion with carrots, stock, salt, pepper, thyme and curry powder, stir, cover, cook on Low for 6 hours.
2. Add coconut milk, stir, blend soup using an immersion blender, ladle soup into bowls, sprinkle cilantro on top and serve.
3. Enjoy!

Nutrition Value: calories 281, fat 4, fiber 7, carbs 13, protein 5

75. Baby Carrots and Ginger Cream

Preparation time: 10 minutes
Cooking time: 7 hours
Servings: 6

Ingredients:

- 2 pounds baby carrots, peeled
- 2 teaspoons ginger paste
- 1 yellow onion, chopped
- 4 cups veggie stock
- 2 teaspoons curry powder
- Salt and black pepper to the taste
- 14 ounces coconut milk

Directions:

1. In your slow cooker, mix baby carrots with ginger paste, onion, stock, curry powder, salt and pepper, stir, cover and cook on High for 7 hours.
2. Add coconut milk, blend soup using an immersion blender, divide soup into bowls and serve.
3. Enjoy!

Nutrition Value: calories 281, fat 2, fiber 4, carbs 15, protein 7

76. Seafood Soup

Preparation time: 10 minutes
Cooking time: 8 hours and 30 minutes
Servings: 4

Ingredients:

- 2 cups water

- ½ fennel bulb, chopped
- 2 sweet potatoes, cubed
- 1 yellow onion, chopped
- 2 bay leaves
- 1 tablespoon thyme, dried
- 1 celery rib, chopped
- A pinch of salt and black pepper
- A pinch of cayenne pepper
- 2 tablespoons tapioca powder
- 2 cups coconut milk
- 1 pounds salmon fillets, peeled and cubed
- 24 shrimp, peeled and deveined
- ¼ cup parsley, chopped

Directions:

1. In your slow cooker, mix water with fennel, potatoes, onion, bay leaves, thyme, celery, cayenne, salt, black pepper and tapioca, stir, cover and cook on Low for 8 hours.
2. Add salmon, coconut milk, shrimp and parsley, cover, cook on Low for 30 minutes more, ladle into bowls and serve.
3. Enjoy!

Nutrition Value: calories 288, fat 10, fiber 2, carbs 16, protein 8

77. Salmon with Cauliflower and Broccoli

Preparation time: 10 minutes
Cooking time: 3 hours
Servings: 2

Ingredients:

- 2 medium salmon fillets
- A pinch of salt and black pepper
- 2 tablespoons coconut aminos
- 8 ounces broccoli florets
- 8 ounces cauliflower florets
- 2 tablespoons lemon juice
- 1 teaspoon sesame seeds

Directions:

1. Put the cauliflower and broccoli florets in your slow cooker and top with salmon fillets.
2. In a bowl, mix aminos and lemon juice, whisk well, pour into the slow cooker,

sprinkle sesame seeds, season with salt and pepper, cover, cook on Low for 3 hours, divide everything between plates and serve.

3. Enjoy!

Nutrition Value: calories 230, fat 4, fiber 2, carbs 14, protein 6

78. Tuna Loin and Veggies

Preparation time: 10 minutes
Cooking time: 4 hours and 10 minutes
Servings: 2

Ingredients:

- ½ pound tuna loin, cubed
- 1 garlic clove, minced
- 4 jalapeno peppers, chopped
- 1 cup olive oil
- 3 red chili peppers, chopped
- 2 teaspoons black peppercorns, ground
- A pinch of salt and black pepper

Directions:

1. Put the oil in your slow cooker, add chili peppers, jalapenos, peppercorns, salt, pepper and garlic, cover and cook on Low for 4 hours.
2. Add tuna cubes, stir, cook on High for 10 minutes more, divide between plates and serve.
3. Enjoy!

Nutrition Value: calories 251, fat 4, fiber 3, carbs 10, protein 7

79. Asian Squid

Preparation time: 10 minutes
Cooking time: 7 hours
Servings: 4

Ingredients:

- 1 pound squid, cleaned and cut into rings
- 1-inch ginger piece, grated
- 1 garlic head, peeled and crushed
- 3 tablespoons coconut aminos
- 1/4 cup veggie stock
- 2 leeks stalks, chopped
- 2 bay leaves
- A pinch of salt and black pepper

Directions:

1. Put the squid in your slow cooker, add ginger, garlic, aminos, leeks, stock, black pepper and bay leaves, stir, cover, cook on Low for 8 hours, divide into bowls and serve.
2. Enjoy!

Nutrition Value: calories 280, fat 2, fiber 4, carbs 16, protein 7

80. Salmon with Cilantro Sauce

Preparation time: 10 minutes
Cooking time: 2 hours and 30 minutes
Servings: 4

Ingredients:

- 2 garlic cloves, minced
- 4 salmon fillets, boneless and skin-on
- ¾ cup cilantro, chopped
- 3 tablespoons lime juice
- 1 tablespoon olive oil
- A pinch of salt and black pepper

Directions:

1. Grease your slow cooker with the oil, place salmon fillets inside skin side down, add garlic, cilantro, limejuice, salt and pepper, cover and cook on Low for 2 hours and 30 minutes.
2. Divide salmon fillets on plates, drizzle the cilantro sauce all over and serve.
3. Enjoy!

Nutrition Value: calories 271, fat 3, fiber 2, carbs 16, protein 7

81. Spiced Salmon

Preparation time: 10 minutes
Cooking time: 2 hours
Servings: 2

Ingredients:

- 1 medium salmon fillets, boneless and skin-on
- ½ teaspoon nutmeg, ground
- ½ teaspoon cloves, ground
- ½ teaspoon ginger powder
- 2 tablespoons olive oil
- A pinch of salt and black pepper

- 1 teaspoon onion powder
- ¼ teaspoon chipotle chili powder
- ½ teaspoon cinnamon powder

Directions:

1. In a bowl, mix salmon with nutmeg, cloves, ginger, salt, pepper, onion powder, chili powder, cayenne and cinnamon, rub well, transfer to your slow cooker, drizzle the oil all over, cover and cook on Low for 2 hours.
2. Divide between plates and serve.
3. Enjoy!

Nutrition Value: calories 220, fat 4, fiber 2, carbs 17, protein 4

82. Cod and Asparagus

Preparation time: 10 minutes
Cooking time: 2 hours
Servings: 4

Ingredients:

- 4 tilapia fillets, boneless and skinless
- 1 bundle asparagus
- 12 tablespoons lemon juice
- A pinch of lemon pepper
- 2 tablespoons olive oil

Directions:

1. Divide the cod on tin foil pieces, top each fillet with asparagus spears, lemon juice, lemon pepper and oil, wrap them, place them in your slow cooker, cover and cook on High for 2 hours.
2. Unwrap the fish, divide it and asparagus between plates and serve.
3. Enjoy!

Nutrition Value: calories 276, fat 3, fiber 6, carbs 15, protein 3

83. Beef and Cauliflower Rice Mix

Preparation time: 10 minutes
Cooking time: 6 hours
Servings: 4

Ingredients:

- 4 cups cauliflower rice
- 2 pound beef chuck roast
- 1 poblano pepper, chopped

- 6 ounces tomato paste
- 1 white onion, chopped
- 1 cup veggie stock
- 2 tablespoons cumin, ground
- 2 tablespoons olive oil
- 1 tablespoon garlic, minced
- 1 tablespoon oregano, chopped
- 1 tablespoon smoked paprika
- ½ cup cilantro, chopped

Directions:

1. In your slow cooker, mix the oil with beef, poblano pepper, tomato paste, onion, stock, cumin, garlic, oregano, cauliflower rice and smoked paprika, toss well, cover and cook on Low for 6 hours.
2. Slice meat, divide it between plates and serve with cilantro sprinkled on top.
3. Enjoy!

Nutrition Value: calories 285, fat 7, fiber 8, carbs 18, protein 17

84. Asian Beef Chuck Roast

Preparation time: 10 minutes
Cooking time: 8 hours
Servings: 4

Ingredients:

- 5 pounds beef chuck roast
- 1 tablespoon coconut aminos
- 10 pepperoncinis
- 1 cup veggie stock
- 2 tablespoons ghee, melted

Directions:

1. In your slow cooker, mix the roast with the aminos, pepperoncinis, stock and ghee, toss well, cover and cook on Low for 8 hours.
2. Transfer roast to a cutting board, shred using 2 forks, return to pot, toss, divide between plates and serve.
3. Enjoy!

Nutrition Value: calories 381, fat 4, fiber 8, carbs 17, protein 17

85. Lamb Stew

Preparation time: 10 minutes

Cooking time: 8 hours

Servings: 6

Ingredients:

- 1 and ½ pound lamb steak, cubed
- 1 yellow onion, chopped
- 1 tablespoon olive oil
- 1 carrot, sliced
- A pinch of salt and black pepper
- 1 teaspoon lemon zest, grated
- 1 teaspoon cinnamon powder
- 1 and ½ teaspoon cumin powder
- ½ teaspoon allspice, ground
- 2 tablespoons lemon juice
- 1 teaspoon onion powder
- 2 garlic cloves, minced
- 7 apricots, dried and sliced
- 1 tablespoon tomato paste
- 1 and ½ cups water
- 1 tablespoon parsley, chopped

Directions:

1. In your slow cooker, mix lamb with onion, oil, carrot, salt, pepper, lemon zest, cinnamon, cumin, allspice, lemon juice, onion powder, garlic, apricots, tomato paste and water, toss, cover, cook on Low for 8 hours, add parsley, stir, divide into bowls and serve.
2. Enjoy!

Nutrition Value: calories 361, fat 4, fiber 8, carbs 22, protein 15

86. Savoy Cabbage and Veggies Soup

Preparation time: 10 minutes

Cooking time: 7 hours

Servings: 6

Ingredients:

- 10 cups water
- 2 tablespoons apple cider vinegar
- 1 Serrano pepper, chopped
- 2 tablespoons avocado oil
- 2 leeks, chopped
- 1 yellow onion, chopped
- 4 garlic cloves, minced

- 1 sweet potato, cubed
- 2 celery stalks, chopped
- 2 carrots, chopped
- 2 turnips, chopped
- ½ Savoy cabbage head, cut into medium strips
- 1 tablespoon thyme, chopped
- 1 handful parsley, chopped
- A pinch of salt and black pepper

Directions:

1. In your slow cooker, mix the water with the vinegar, Serrano pepper, oil, leeks, onion, garlic, sweet potato, celery, carrots, turnips, cabbage, thyme, parsley, salt and pepper, stir, cover and cook on High for 5 hours.
2. Ladle into bowls and serve.
3. Enjoy!

Nutrition Value: calories 371, fat 8, fiber 12, carbs 28, protein 12

87. Beef and Cauliflower Soup

Preparation time: 10 minutes

Cooking time: 6 hours

Servings: 4

Ingredients:

- 1 pound beef, ground
- 2 cups cauliflower, chopped
- 1 cup yellow onion, chopped
- 2 red bell peppers, chopped
- 15 ounces tomato sauce
- 15 ounces tomatoes, chopped
- 3 cups beef stock
- ½ teaspoon basil, dried
- ½ teaspoon oregano, dried
- 3 garlic cloves, minced
- A pinch of salt and black pepper

Directions:

1. In your slow cooker, mix beef with cauliflower, onion, bell peppers, tomato sauce, tomatoes, stock, basil, oregano, garlic, salt and pepper, stir, cover, cook on Low for 6 hours, ladle into bowls and serve.
2. Enjoy!

Nutrition Value: calories 316, fat 6, fiber 6, carbs 18, protein 7

88. Easy Beef Short Ribs

Preparation time: 10 minutes
Cooking time: 6 hours
Servings: 6

Ingredients:

- 4 pounds beef short ribs
- ½ cup beef stock
- ½ cup coconut aminos
- 2 tablespoons apple cider vinegar
- 1 tablespoon ginger, grated
- 4 garlic cloves, minced
- 1 tablespoon green onions, chopped

Directions:

1. In your slow cooker, mix ribs with stock, aminos, vinegar, ginger, garlic and green onions, stir, cover and cook on Low for 6 hours.
2. Divide between plates and serve with cooking juices drizzled all over.
3. Enjoy!

Nutrition Value: calories 349, fat 8, fiber 12, carbs 29, protein 4

89. Beef Brisket and Orange Mix

Preparation time: 10 minutes
Cooking time: 5 hours
Servings: 6

Ingredients:

- 4 pounds beef brisket
- 2 oranges, peeled and cut into segments
- 2 garlic cloves, minced
- 2 yellow onions, thinly sliced
- 11 ounces celery, thinly sliced
- 1 tablespoon dill, dried
- 1 teaspoon cinnamon powder
- A pinch of salt and black pepper
- 17 ounces veggie stock

Directions:

1. In your slow cooker, mix beef with orange, garlic, onion, celery, dill, bay leaves, cinnamon, salt, pepper and stock, stir,

cover, cook on High for 5 hours, slice the meat, divide it and orange mix between plates and serve.
2. Enjoy!

Nutrition Value: calories 300, fat 5, fiber 7, carbs 28, protein 8

90. Coconut Beef and Mushrooms Mix

Preparation time: 10 minutes
Cooking time: 5 hours
Servings: 4

Ingredients:

- 10 pounds beef, cubed
- 1 yellow onion, chopped
- 2 and ½ tablespoons olive oil
- 2 garlic cloves, minced
- 4 ounces mushrooms, sliced
- 1 and ½ tablespoon tomato paste
- A pinch of salt and black pepper
- 13 ounces beef stock
- 8 ounces coconut cream

Directions:

1. In your slow cooker, mix beef with onion, oil, garlic, mushrooms, tomato paste, salt, pepper, beef stock and cream, stir, cover, cook on High for 5 hours, divide between plates and serve.
2. Enjoy!

Nutrition Value: calories 383, fat 7, fiber 6, carbs 22, protein 11

91. Whole30 Lamb Shanks

Preparation time: 10 minutes
Cooking time: 7 hours
Servings: 4

Ingredients:

- 4 lamb shanks
- 2 tablespoons olive oil
- 1 yellow onion, chopped
- 3 carrots, roughly chopped
- 2 garlic cloves, minced
- 2 tablespoons tomato paste
- 1 tablespoon oregano, chopped

- A pinch of salt and black pepper
- 1 tomato, roughly chopped
- 4 ounces chicken stock

Directions:

1. In your slow cooker, mix lamb with oil, onion, garlic, carrots, tomato paste, tomato, oregano, stock, salt and pepper, stir, cover, cook on Low for 7 hours, divide into bowls and serve.
2. Enjoy!

Nutrition Value: calories 381, fat 13, fiber 4, carbs 27, protein 16

92. Baked Mushrooms

Preparation time: 10 mins
Cooking time: quarter-hour
Servings: 4

Ingredients:

- 1 and ½ pounds white mushrooms, sliced
- ¼ cup fresh fresh lemon juice
- 3 tablespoons extra virgin olive oil
- Zest of a single lemon, grated
- 3 garlic cloves, minced
- 2 teaspoons thyme, dried
- ¼ cup low-fat parmesan, grated
- A pinch of salt and black pepper

Directions:

1. 1.In a bowl, combine the mushrooms with all the freshly squeezed freshly squeezed lemon juice, oil, lemon zest, garlic, thyme, parmesan, salt and pepper, toss, spread for the lined baking sheet, introduce within the oven at 375 degrees F for quarter-hour, divide between plates and serve as a side dish.
2. Enjoy!

Nutrition Value: calories 164, fat 12, fiber 3, carbs 10, protein 7

93. Garlic Potatoes

Preparation time: ten mins
Cooking time: 30 minutes
Servings: 6

Ingredients:

- 3 pounds red potatoes, halved
- 4 garlic cloves, minced
- 2 tablespoons organic extra virgin olive oil
- 1 teaspoon thyme, dried
- ½ teaspoon basil, dried
- 1/3 cup low-fat parmesan, grated
- 2 tablespoons low-fat butter, melted
- 2 tablespoons parsley, chopped
- Black pepper on the taste

Directions:

1. 1.In a roasting pan, combine the red potatoes with garlic, oil, thyme, basil, parmesan, butter and black pepper, toss, introduce in the oven and cook at 400 degrees F for 30 minutes.
2. 2.Add parsley, toss, divide between plates and serve as being a side dish.
3. Enjoy!

Nutrition Value: calories 251, fat 12, fiber 4, carbs 13, protein 6

94. Corn Pudding

Preparation time: 10 mins
Cooking time: quarter-hour
Servings: 4

Ingredients:

- 8 ears corn, grated
- 3 bacon slices, chopped
- 1 yellow onion, chopped
- ½ cup coconut milk
- ½ cup basil, torn
- A pinch of black pepper
- ½ teaspoon red pepper flakes

Directions:

1. 1.Heat up a pan over medium-high heat, add bacon, stir and cook for two minutes.
2. 2.Add corn, onion, black pepper and pepper flakes, stir and cook for 8 minutes.
3. 3.Add milk and basil, stir and cook for 5 minutes more, divide between plates and serve like a side dish.
4. Enjoy!

Nutrition Value: calories 201, fat 3, fiber 5, carbs 14, protein 7

95. Corn Sauté

Preparation time: 10 minutes
Cooking time: 12 minutes
Servings: 4

Ingredients:

- 4 cups corn
- 4 bacon slices, cut into strips
- A pinch of red pepper flakes
- 3 scallions, chopped
- A pinch of black pepper

Directions:

1. 1.Heat up a pan over medium-high heat, add bacon, toss and cook for 5 minutes.
2. 2.Add corn, pepper flakes, black pepper and scallions, toss, cook for 7 minutes more, divide between plates and serve being a side dish.
3. Enjoy!

Nutrition Value: calories 199, fat 3, fiber 6, carbs 13, protein 8

96. Pineapple Potato Salad

Preparation time: ten minutes
Cooking time: 40 minutes
Servings: 4

Ingredients:

- 2 cups pineapple, peeled and cubed
- 4 sweet potatoes, cubed
- 1 tablespoon essential olive oil
- ¼ cup coconut, unsweetened and shredded
- 1/3 cup almonds, chopped
- 1 cup coconut cream

Directions:

1. 1.Arrange sweet potatoes on the lined baking sheet, add the essential olive oil, introduce within the oven at 350 degrees F, roast for 40 minutes, place them within a salad bowl, add coconut, pineapple, almonds and cream, toss, divide between plates and serve as being a side dish.
2. Enjoy!

Nutrition Value: calories 200, fat 4, fiber 3, carbs 7, protein 8

97. Coconut Sweet Potatoes

Preparation time: ten minutes

Cooking time: one hour
Servings: 4

Ingredients:

- 4 sweet potatoes, sliced
- A drizzle of organic olive oil
- A pinch of salt and black pepper
- 1 small thyme bunch, chopped
- 1/3 cup coconut cream
- ½ teaspoon parsley, chopped
- 1 tablespoon Dijon mustard
- ½ teaspoon garlic

Directions:

1. 1.Arrange sweet potato slices using a lined baking sheet, sprinkle thyme, drizzle oil, season with a pinch of salt and black pepper, toss well, introduce within the oven at 400 degrees F and bake for about an hour.
2. 2.Meanwhile, in a very very bowl, mix coconut cream with parsley, garlic and mustard and whisk well.
3. 3.Arrange baked potatoes on plates, drizzle the mustard sauce around and serve as a side dish.
4. Enjoy!

Nutrition Value: calories 237, fat 5, fiber 4, carbs 12, protein 9

98. Cashew and Coconut Sweet Potatoes

Preparation time: ten mins
Cooking time: an hour
Servings: 4

Ingredients:

- 2 sweet potatoes, peeled and sliced
- ½ cup cashews, soaked to get a couple of hours and drained
- 1 cup coconut milk
- ¼ teaspoon cinnamon powder

Directions:

1. 1.In your meal processor, mix cashews, milk and cinnamon and pulse.
2. 2.Spread some inside potato slices in a very greased baking pan and drizzle some within the cashews cream.

3. 3.Repeat while using the rest inside the potatoes and cream, bake in the oven for 60 minutes at 350 degrees F, divide between plates and serve like a side dish.
4. Enjoy!

Nutrition Value: calories 200, fat 5, fiber 3, carbs 9, protein 8

99. Sage Celery Mix

Preparation time: ten minutes
Cooking time: ten mins
Servings: 6

Ingredients:

- 2 tablespoons extra virgin essential olive oil
- 5 celery ribs, chopped
- 1 yellow onion, chopped
- 1 teaspoon sage, dried
- 8 ounces walnuts, chopped
- A pinch of black pepper
- 3 tablespoons sage, chopped

Directions:

1. 1.Heat up a pan while using oil over medium heat, add celery and onion, stir and cook for 5 minutes.
2. 2.Add dried sage, pepper, fresh sage and walnuts, stir, cook for 5 minutes more, divide between plates and serve as a side dish.
3. Enjoy!

Nutrition Value: calories 250, fat 7, fiber 5, carbs 9, protein 4

100. Garlic Zucchini Fries

Preparation time: ten minutes
Cooking time: twenty approximately minutes
Servings: 4

Ingredients:

- 4 zucchinis, cut into medium fries
- A pinch of black pepper
- ½ teaspoon chili powder
- 1 tablespoon organic organic olive oil
- ¼ teaspoon garlic powder

Directions:

1. 1.Spread the zucchini fries on the lined

baking sheet, add black pepper, chili powder, garlic powder and oil, toss, introduce inside oven, bake at 400 degrees F for twenty roughly minutes, divide between plates and serve as like a side dish.
2. Enjoy!

Nutrition Value: calories 185, fat 3, fiber 2, carbs 6, protein 8

101. Tahini Green Beans

Preparation time: ten mins
Cooking time: ten mins
Servings: 4

Ingredients:

- 1 and ½ tablespoons tahini paste
- Juice of 1 lemon
- Zest of a single lemon, grated
- 2 tablespoons essential olive oil
- 1 garlic oil, minced
- 1 red onion, sliced
- 1 yellow bell pepper, sliced
- 10 ounces green beans, halved
- A pinch of black pepper

Directions:

1. 1.In a bowl, mix lemon zest, fresh freshly squeezed lemon juice, tahini and black pepper and whisk well.
2. 2.Heat up a pan while using the oil over medium-high heat, add onion, stir and cook for 5 minutes.
3. 3.Add the bell pepper, garlic and green beans, toss and cook for ten mins.
4. 4.Add tahini dressing, toss, cook for just two main minutes more, divide between plates and serve as being a side dish.
5. Enjoy!

Nutrition Value: calories 180, fat 10, fiber 6, carbs 13, protein 8

102. Mustard Tarragon Beets

Preparation time: 10 minutes
Cooking time: 0 minutes
Servings: 5

Ingredients:

- 1 tablespoon Dijon mustard

- 1 and ½ tablespoon essential olive oil
- 8 ounces beets, cooked and sliced
- 2 tablespoons tarragon, chopped
- A pinch of black pepper

Directions:

1. 1.In a bowl, mix mustard with oil and black pepper and whisk.
2. 2.In a bowl, combine the beets with all the tarragon at the same time as the mustard mix, toss, divide between plates and serve as a side dish.
3. Enjoy!

Nutrition Value: calories 170, fat 5, fiber 7, carbs 8, proteins 10

103. Almond Green Beans

Preparation time: ten mins
Cooking time: 20 mins
Servings: 6

Ingredients:

- 5 tablespoons extra virgin olive oil
- 3 pounds green beans, halved
- 8 tablespoons almonds, toasted and sliced
- A pinch of black pepper
- 2 yellow onions, chopped
- 2 and ½ tablespoons parsley, chopped

Directions:

1. 1.Heat up a pan over medium-high heat, add green beans, cook them for 5 minutes and transfer to some bowl.
2. 2.Heat inside the same pan with all the extra virgin organic olive oil over medium heat, add onions along using a pinch of black pepper, stir and cook for 10 mins.
3. 3.Add beans, almonds and parsley, toss, cook for 5 minutes, divide between plates and serve as being a side dish.
4. Enjoy!

Nutrition Value: calories 130, fat 1, fiber 2, carbs 7, protein 6

104. Tomatoes Side Salad

Preparation time: 10 mins
Cooking time: 0 minutes
Servings: 4

Ingredients:

- ½ bunch mint, chopped
- 8 plum tomatoes, sliced
- 1 teaspoon mustard
- 1 tablespoon rosemary vinegar
- A pinch of black pepper

Directions:

1. 1.In a bowl, mix vinegar with mustard and pepper and whisk.
2. 2.In another bowl, combine the tomatoes with all the mint as well as the vinaigrette, toss, divide between plates and serve just like a side dish.
3. Enjoy!

Nutrition Value: calories 70, fat 2, fiber 2, carbs 6, protein 4

105. Squash Salsa

Preparation time: 10 mins
Cooking time: 13 minutes
Servings: 6

Ingredients:

- 3 tablespoons olive oil
- 5 medium squash, peeled and sliced
- 1 cup pipits, toasted
- 7 tomatillos
- A pinch of black pepper
- 1 small onion, chopped
- 2 tablespoons fresh lime juice
- 2 tablespoons cilantro, chopped

Directions:

1. 1.Heat up a pan over medium heat, add tomatillos, onion and black pepper, stir, cook for 3 minutes, transfer to your food processor and pulse.
2. 2.Add lime juice and cilantro, pulse again and transfer for some bowl.
3. 3.Heat the kitchen grill over high heat, drizzle the oil over squash slices, grill them for 10 mins, divide them between plates, add pepitas and tomatillos mix on the top and serve like a side dish.
4. Enjoy!

Nutrition Value: calories 120, fat 2, fiber 1, carbs 7, protein 1

106. Apples and Fennel Mix

Preparation time: 10 minutes
Cooking time: 0 minutes
Servings: 3

Ingredients:

- 3 big apples, cored and sliced
- 1 and ½ cup fennel, shredded
- 1/3 cup coconut cream
- 3 tablespoons apple vinegar
- ½ teaspoon caraway seeds
- Black pepper for the taste

Directions:

1. 1.In a bowl, mix fennel with apples and toss.
2. 2.In another bowl, mix coconut cream with vinegar, black pepper and caraway seeds, whisk well, add inside the fennel mix, toss, divide between plates and serve as as being a side dish.
3. Enjoy!

Nutrition Value: calories 130, fat 3, fiber 6, carbs 10, protein 3

107. Simple Roasted Celery Mix

Preparation time: ten mins
Cooking time: 25 minutes
Servings: 3

Ingredients:

- 3 celery roots, cubed
- 2 tablespoons extra virgin organic olive oil
- A pinch of black pepper
- 2 cups natural and unsweetened apple juice
- ¼ cup parsley, chopped
- ¼ cup walnuts, chopped

Directions:

1. 1.In a baking dish, combine the celery with all the oil, pepper, parsley, walnuts and apple juice, toss to coat, introduce in the oven at 450 degrees F, bake for 25 minutes, divide between plates and serve as as being a side dish.
2. Enjoy!

Nutrition Value: calories 140, fat 2, fiber 2, carbs 7, protein 7

108. Thyme Spring Onions

Preparation time: ten mins
Cooking time: 40 minutes
Servings: 8

Ingredients:

15 spring onions
A pinch of black pepper
1 teaspoon thyme, chopped
1 tablespoon essential extra virgin olive oil

Directions:

1. Put onions inside the baking dish, add thyme, black pepper and oil, toss, bake in the oven at 350 degrees F for 40 minutes, divide between plates and serve as as being a side dish.
2. Enjoy!

Nutrition Value: calories 120, fat 2, fiber 2, carbs 7, protein 2

109. Carrot Slaw

Preparation time: 10 minutes
Cooking time: 10 mins
Servings: 4

Ingredients:

- ¼ yellow onion, chopped
- 5 carrots, cut into thin matchsticks
- 1 tablespoon essential organic olive oil
- 1 garlic herb, minced
- 1 tablespoon Dijon mustard
- 1 tablespoon red vinegar
- A pinch of black pepper
- 1 tablespoon freshly squeezed lemon juice

Directions:

1. 1.In a bowl, mix vinegar with black pepper, mustard and fresh lemon juice and whisk.
2. 2.Heat up a pan while using the oil over medium heat, add onion, stir and cook for 5 minutes.
3. 3.Add garlic and carrots, stir, cook for 5 minutes more, transfer for a salad bowl, cool-down, add the vinaigrette, toss, divide between plates and serve as a side dish.
4. Enjoy!

Nutrition Value: calories 120, fat 3, fiber 3, carbs 7, protein 5

110. Watermelon Tomato Salsa

Preparation time: 10 mins
Cooking time: 0 minutes
Servings: 16

Ingredients:

- 4 yellow tomatoes, seedless and chopped
- A pinch of black pepper
- 1 cup watermelon, seedless and chopped
- 1/3 cup red onion, chopped
- 2 jalapeno peppers, chopped
- ¼ cup cilantro, chopped
- 3 tablespoons lime juice

Directions:

1. 1.In a bowl, mix tomatoes with watermelon, onion and jalapeno.
2. 2.Add cilantro, lime juice and pepper, toss, divide between plates and serve as a side dish.
3. Enjoy!

Nutrition Value: calories 87, fat 1, fiber 2, carbs 4, protein 7

111. Sprouts Side Salad

Preparation time: ten minutes
Cooking time: 0 minutes
Servings: 4

Ingredients:

- 2 zucchinis, cut employing a spiralizer
- 2 cups bean sprouts
- 4 green onions, chopped
- 1 red bell pepper, chopped
- Juice of a single lime
- 1 tablespoon organic essential olive oil
- ½ cup cilantro, chopped
- ¾ cup almonds, chopped
- Black pepper for that taste

Directions:

1. 1.In a salad bowl, mix zucchinis with bean sprouts, onions and bell pepper.
2. 2.Add black pepper, lime juice, almonds, cilantro and essential essential olive oil, toss everything, divide between plates and serve as as being a side dish.
3. Enjoy!

Nutrition Value: calories 120, fat 4, fiber 2, carbs 7, protein 12

112. Cabbage Slaw

Preparation time: ten mins
Cooking time: 0 minutes
Servings: 4

Ingredients:

- 1 green cabbage head, shredded
- 1/3 cup coconut, shredded
- ¼ cup essential extra virgin olive oil
- 2 tablespoons lemon juice
- ¼ cup coconut aminos
- 3 tablespoons sesame seeds
- ½ teaspoon curry powder
- 1/3 teaspoon turmeric powder
- ½ teaspoon cumin, ground

Directions:

1. 1.In a bowl, mix cabbage with coconut and fresh lemon juice and stir.
2. 2.Add oil, aminos, sesame seeds, curry powder, turmeric and cumin, toss to coat and serve being a side dish.
3. Enjoy!

Nutrition Value: calories 130, fat 4, fiber 5, carbs 8, protein 6

113. Edamame Side Salad

Preparation time: 10 mins
Cooking time: 0 minutes
Servings: 4

Ingredients:

- 1 tablespoon ginger, grated
- 2 green onions, chopped
- 3 cups edamame, blanched
- 2 tablespoons rice vinegar
- 1 tablespoon sesame seeds

Directions:

1. 1.In a bowl, combine the ginger while using the onions, edamame, vinegar and sesame seeds, toss, divide between plates and serve like a side dish.
2. Enjoy!

Nutrition Value: calories 120, fat 3, fiber 2, carbs

5, protein 9

114. Flavored Beets Side Salad

Preparation time: ten minutes
Cooking time: 0 minutes
Servings: 4

Ingredients:

- 4 carrots, sliced
- 12 radishes, sliced
- 1 beet, peeled and grated
- 2 tablespoons raisins
- Juice of 2 lemons
- 1 sugar beet, peeled and chopped
- 1 tablespoon chives, chopped
- 1 tablespoon parsley, chopped
- 1 tablespoon lemon thyme, chopped
- 1 tablespoon white sesame seeds
- 4 handfuls spinach leaves
- 4 tablespoons extra virgin extra virgin olive oil
- Black pepper for the taste

Directions:

1. 1.In a salad bowl, mix carrots, radishes, beets, sugar beet, raisins, chives, parsley, spinach, thyme and sesame seeds.
2. 2.Add fresh lemon juice, oil and black pepper, toss well and serve as being a side dish.
3. Enjoy!

Nutrition Value: calories 110, fat 2, fiber 2, carbs 4, protein 7

115. Tomato and Avocado Salad

Preparation time: ten mins
Cooking time: 0 minutes
Servings: 4

Ingredients:

- 1 cucumber, chopped
- 1 pound tomatoes, chopped
- 2 avocados, pitted, peeled and chopped
- 1 small red onion, sliced
- 2 tablespoons extra virgin olive oil
- 2 tablespoons fresh freshly squeezed lemon juice

- ¼ cup cilantro, chopped
- Black pepper for the taste

Directions:

1. 1.In a salad bowl, mix tomatoes with onion, avocado, cucumber and cilantro.
2. 2.In a lesser bowl, mix oil with lemon juice and black pepper, whisk well, pour this around the salad, toss and serve like a side dish.
3. Enjoy!

Nutrition Value: calories 120, fat 2, fiber 2, carbs 3, protein 4

116. Greek Side Salad

Preparation time: ten mins
Cooking time: 0 minutes
Servings: 4

Ingredients:

- 4 pounds heirloom tomatoes, sliced
- 1 yellow bell pepper, thinly sliced
- 1 green bell pepper, thinly sliced
- 1 red onion, thinly sliced
- Black pepper for the taste
- ½ teaspoon oregano, dried
- 2 tablespoons mint leaves, chopped
- A drizzle of organic essential olive oil

Directions:

1. 1.In a salad bowl, mix tomatoes with yellow and green peppers, onion, salt and pepper, toss to coat as well as leaving aside for 10 mins.
2. 2.Add oregano, mint and essential organic olive oil, toss to coat and serve as a side salad.
3. Enjoy!

Nutrition Value: calories 100, fat 2, fiber 2, carbs 3, protein 6

117. Cucumber Salad

Preparation time: 10 minutes
Cooking time: 0 minutes
Servings: 4

Ingredients:

- 2 English cucumbers, chopped

- 8 dates, pitted and sliced
- ¾ cup fennel, sliced
- 2 tablespoons chives, chopped
- ½ cup walnuts, chopped
- 2 tablespoons fresh lemon juice
- 4 tablespoons organic olive oil
- Black pepper to the taste

Directions:

1. 1.In a salad bowl, combine the cucumbers with dates, fennel, chives, walnuts, freshly squeezed lemon juice, oil and black pepper, toss, divide between plates and serve as a side dish.
2. Enjoy!

Nutrition Value: calories 100, fat 1, fiber 1, carbs 7, protein 6

118. Black Beans and Veggies Side Salad

Preparation time: ten mins
Cooking time: 0 minutes
Servings: 4

Ingredients:

- 1 big cucumber, cut into chunks
- 15 ounces canned black beans, no-salt-added, drained and rinsed
- 1 cup corn
- 1 cup cherry tomatoes, halved
- 1 small red onion, chopped
- 3 tablespoons essential organic olive oil
- 4 and ½ teaspoons orange marmalade
- Black pepper on the taste
- ½ teaspoon cumin, ground
- 1 tablespoon fresh freshly squeezed lemon juice

Directions:

1. 1.In a bowl, mix beans with cucumber, corn, onion and tomatoes.
2. 2.In another bowl, mix marmalade with oil, fresh lemon juice, black pepper around the taste and cumin, whisk, pour inside the salad, toss and serve as as a side dish.
3. Enjoy!

Nutrition Value: calories 110, fat 0, fiber 3, carbs

6, protein 8

119. Endives and Escarole Side Salad

Preparation time: 10 minutes
Cooking time: 0 minutes
Servings: 4

Ingredients:

- 1 teaspoon shallot, minced
- ¼ cup using apple cider vinegar
- 1 teaspoon Dijon mustard
- 3 Belgian endives, roughly chopped
- ¾ cup organic olive oil
- 1 cup escarole leaves, torn

Directions:

1. In a bowl, mix escarole leaves with endives, shallot, vinegar, mustard and oil, toss, divide between plates and serve as a side salad.
2. Enjoy!

Nutrition Value: calories 100, fat 1, fiber 3, carbs 6, protein 7

120. Marinated Veggie Mix

Preparation time: 10 minutes
Cooking time: 4 hours
Servings: 4

Ingredients:

- 1 zucchini, sliced
- 1 red bell pepper, cut into strips
- 1 red onion, cut into rings
- 1 cup mushrooms, halved
- 1 cup grape tomatoes
- 1 eggplant, cubed
- ¼ cup olive oil
- 2 tablespoons balsamic vinegar
- 1 teaspoon basil, dried
- Juice of 1 lemon
- 1 teaspoon garlic powder
- A pinch of salt and black pepper

Directions:

1. In your slow cooker, mix the zucchinis with the bell pepper, onion, mushrooms, tomatoes, eggplant, oil, vinegar, basil, lemon juice, garlic powder, salt and pepper, cover, cook on Low for 4 hours, toss, divide between plates and serve as a side dish.
2. Enjoy!

Nutrition Value: calories 200, fat 3, fiber 6, carbs 17, protein 5

121. Chipotle Butternut Squash Mix

Preparation time: 10 minutes
Cooking time: 5 hours
Servings: 4

Ingredients:

- 2 pounds butternut squash, cubed
- 2 tablespoons olive oil
- 2 teaspoons chipotle powder
- A pinch of salt and black pepper
- Zest of 2 limes, grated
- Juice of 2 limes
- 1/3 cup cilantro, chopped
- ½ cup veggie stock

Directions:

1. In your slow cooker, mix the butternut squash with the oil, chipotle powder, salt, pepper, limejuice, lime zest, cilantro and stock, toss, cover and cook on Low for 5 hours.
2. Toss everything one more time, divide between plates and serve as a side dish.
3. Enjoy!

Nutrition Value: calories 251, fat 4, fiber 7, carbs 17, protein 4

122. Easy Potatoes and Cauliflower Mash

Preparation time: 10 minutes
Cooking time: 5 hours
Servings: 4

Ingredients:

- 2 pounds potatoes, peeled and sliced
- 1 and ½ cups water
- 8 ounces cauliflower florets
- 1 garlic clove, minced
- A pinch of salt and black pepper

Directions:

1. In your slow cooker, mix potatoes with water, cauliflower, salt and pepper, cover, cook on Low for 5 hours, drain, add garlic, mash well, divide between plates and serve as a side dish.
2. Enjoy!

Nutrition Value: calories 247, fat 1, fiber 7, carbs 15, protein 8

123. Hot Sweet Potatoes

Preparation time: 10 minutes
Cooking time: 5 hours
Servings: 4

Ingredients:

- 4 sweet potatoes, cut into wedges

- 1 cup veggie stock
- A pinch of salt and black pepper
- ¼ teaspoon cumin, ground
- 1 teaspoon hot paprika

Directions:

1. In your slow cooker, mix potato wedges with stock, salt, pepper, cumin and paprika, toss, cover and cook on Low for 5 hours.
2. Divide between plates and serve as a side dish
3. Enjoy!

Nutrition Value: calories 210, fat 4, fiber 7, carbs 12, protein 8

124. Orange Brussels Sprouts

Preparation time: 10 minutes
Cooking time: 2 hours and 30 minutes
Servings: 8

Ingredients:

- 2 pounds Brussels sprouts, halved
- 1 tablespoon olive oil
- 1 teaspoon orange zest, grated
- ¼ cup orange juice
- A pinch of salt and black pepper

Directions:

1. Grease your slow cooker with the oil, add Brussels sprouts, orange zest, orange juice, salt and pepper, toss, cover, cook on High for 2 hours and 30 minutes, divide between plates and serve as a side dish.
2. Enjoy!

Nutrition Value: calories 203, fat 4, fiber 1, carbs 8, protein 7

125. Easy Potato Wedges

Preparation time: 10 minutes
Cooking time: 5 hours
Servings: 4

Ingredients:

- 1 and ½ pounds potatoes, cut into wedges
- ¼ cup avocado oil
- A pinch of salt and black pepper
- ½ teaspoon onion powder
- ¼ teaspoon sweet paprika

- 1 cup veggie stock
- 1 teaspoon garlic powder

Directions:

1. Grease your slow cooker with the oil, add potatoes, salt, pepper, onion powder, paprika, stock and garlic powder, toss, cover and cook on Low for 5 hours.
2. Toss the potatoes one more time, divide them between plates and serve as a side dish.
3. Enjoy!

Nutrition Value: calories 260, fat 6, fiber 8, carbs 16, protein 9

126. Chili Cauliflower Mix

Preparation time: 10 minutes
Cooking time: 5 hours
Servings: 4

Ingredients:

- 1 cup yellow onion, chopped
- 3 tablespoons olive oil
- 3 cups cauliflower florets
- 1 cup tomatoes, crushed
- 2 garlic cloves, minced
- 2 cups veggie stock
- ¼ cup cilantro, chopped
- ½ teaspoon chili powder

Directions:

1. Grease your slow cooker with the oil, add onion, cauliflower, tomatoes, garlic, stock, cilantro and chili powder, toss, cover, cook on Low for 5 hours, divide between plates and serve as a side dish.
2. Enjoy!

Nutrition Value: calories 200, fat 4, fiber 3, carbs 15, protein 8

127. Green Bell Peppers Mix

Preparation time: 10 minutes
Cooking time: 4 hours
Servings: 6

Ingredients:

- 1 teaspoon olive oil
- 22 ounces green bell pepper, chopped

- 12 ounces sweet onion, chopped
- 4 garlic cloves, minced
- 2 and ½ teaspoons cumin, ground
- 2 tablespoons tomato paste
- 2 cups veggie stock
- A pinch of salt and black pepper

Directions:

1. Grease your slow cooker with the oil, add green bell peppers, onion, garlic, cumin, tomato paste, stock, salt and pepper, toss, cover and cook on Low for 4 hours.
2. Divide the mix between plates and serve as a side dish.
3. Enjoy!

Nutrition Value: calories 261, fat 5, fiber 4, carbs 19, protein 8

128. Citrus Yam Mix

Preparation time: 10 minutes
Cooking time: 4 hours
Servings: 4

Ingredients:

- 2 pounds yams, peeled and cut into quarters
- 3 tablespoons olive oil
- 6 garlic cloves, minced
- A pinch of salt and black pepper
- ½ cup orange juice
- ½ cup lime juice
- ¼ cup yellow onion, chopped

Directions:

1. In your slow cooker, mix the yams with the oil, garlic, salt, pepper, orange juice, lime juice and onion, toss, cover, cook on Low for 4 hours, divide between plates and serve as a side dish.
2. Enjoy!

Nutrition Value: calories 251, fat 4, fiber 2, carbs 7, protein 9

129. Mashed Cauliflower

Preparation time: 10 minutes
Cooking time: 3 hours
Servings: 4

Ingredients:

- 1 and ½ cups water
- 1 cauliflower head, florets separated
- 2 teaspoons olive oil
- A pinch of salt and black pepper
- ½ teaspoon turmeric powder
- 3 chives, chopped

Directions:

1. In your slow cooker, mix the water with the cauliflower, salt and pepper, cover, cook on High for 3 hours, drain, add oil, turmeric and chives, mash using a potato masher, whisk well, divide between plates and serve as a side dish.
2. Enjoy!

Nutrition Value: calories 240, fat 4, fiber 4, carbs 14, protein 10

130. Wild Mushrooms Mix

Preparation time: 10 minutes
Cooking time: 3 hours
Servings: 6

Ingredients:

- 2 tablespoons olive oil
- 4 ounces wild mushrooms, sliced
- 3 shallots, chopped
- 8 ounces cremini mushrooms, sliced
- 1 cup veggie stock
- 1 teaspoon fennel seeds
- A pinch of salt and black pepper
- 2 tablespoons cilantro, chopped

Directions:

1. Grease your slow cooker with the oil, add mushrooms, shallots, cremini mushrooms, stock, fennel seeds, salt, pepper and cilantro, toss, cover and cook on High for 3 hours.
2. Divide between plates and serve as a side dish.
3. Enjoy!

Nutrition Value: calories 209, fat 3, fiber 4, carbs 11, protein 8

131. Easy Artichokes

Preparation time: 10 minutes
Cooking time: 4 hours

Servings: 2

Ingredients:

- ½ cup veggie stock
- 2 teaspoons garlic, minced
- 4 artichokes, trimmed and halved
- 4 teaspoons olive oil
- A pinch of salt and black pepper

Directions:

1. Put the artichokes in your slow cooker, add garlic, salt, pepper and stock, cover, cook on Low for 4 hours, divide between plates and serve as a side dish.
2. Enjoy!

Nutrition Value: calories 253, fat 6, fiber 2, carbs 16, protein 9

132. Easy Baby Mushroom Mix

Preparation time: 10 minutes
Cooking time: 3 hours
Servings: 2

Ingredients:

- 2 green onions, chopped
- 1 garlic clove, minced
- 1 pound baby Portobello mushrooms, sliced
- 1 cup beef stock

Directions:

1. In your slow cooker, mix onions, garlic, mushrooms and stock, stir, cover, cook on Low for 3 hours, divide between plates and serve as a side dish.
2. Enjoy!

Nutrition Value: calories 200, fat 6, fiber 4, carbs 17, protein 7

133. Creamy Mushroom Mix

Preparation time: 10 minutes
Cooking time: 4 hours
Servings: 2

Ingredients:

- 1 pound mushrooms, halved
- 1 yellow onion, chopped
- 3 garlic cloves, minced
- 1 cup veggie stock

- 1 tablespoon coconut cream
- 2 teaspoons smoked paprika
- Salt and black pepper to the taste
- 2 tablespoons parsley, chopped

Directions:

1. In your slow cooker, mix mushrooms with garlic, onion, stock, salt, pepper and paprika, stir, cover, cook on High for 4 hours, add cream and parsley, toss, divide between plates and serve as a side dish.
2. Enjoy!

Nutrition Value: calories 260, fat 6, fiber 12, carbs 16, protein 8

134. Bell Peppers and Mushroom Salad

Preparation time: 10 minutes
Cooking time: 4 hours
Servings: 2

Ingredients:

- 1 cup green bell peppers, chopped
- 1 small yellow onion, chopped
- 1 garlic clove, minced
- ½ pound mushrooms, chopped
- 12 ounces tomato sauce
- A pinch of salt and black pepper

Directions:

1. In your slow cooker, mix bell peppers with onion, garlic, mushrooms, tomato sauce, salt and pepper, stir, cover, cook on Low for 4 hours, divide between plates and serve as a side dish.
2. Enjoy!

Nutrition Value: calories 265, fat 4, fiber 7, carbs 12, protein 4

135. Tomato Green Beans

Preparation time: 10 minutes
Cooking time: 8 hours
Servings: 2

Ingredients:

- ½ pound green beans
- 1 celery ribs, chopped
- 1 tablespoon olive oil

- 1 yellow onions, chopped
- 1 carrot, chopped
- 2 tablespoons tomato paste
- 1 garlic cloves, minced
- A pinch of salt and black pepper
- 1 cup water
- ½ teaspoon oregano, dried
- ¼ teaspoon thyme, dried
- A pinch of red pepper, crushed
- 2 tablespoons parsley, chopped

Directions:

1. In your slow cooker, mix oil with onions, garlic, celery, carrots, salt, pepper, green beans, tomato paste, water, oregano, thyme and red pepper, stir, cover and cook on Low for 8 hours.
2. Add parsley, stir, divide between plates and serve as a side dish.
3. Enjoy!

Nutrition Value: calories 200, fat 3, fiber 7, carbs 14, protein 8

136. Squash and Spinach

Preparation time: 10 minutes
Cooking time: 7 hours
Servings: 2

Ingredients:

- 1 butternut squash, peeled and cubed
- 1 small yellow onion, cut into medium wedges
- 3 ounces spinach
- 1 cup veggie stock
- A pinch of salt and black pepper
- 1 garlic clove, minced

Directions:

1. Put squash in your slow cooker, add spinach, stock, onion, garlic, salt and pepper, stir, cover, cook on Low for 7 hours, divide between plates and serve as a side dish.
2. Enjoy!

Nutrition Value: calories 210, fat 3, fiber 7, carbs 13, protein 7

137. Cabbage, Zucchini and

Carrots Mix

Preparation time: 10 minutes
Cooking time: 3 hours
Servings: 4

Ingredients:

- 3 cups carrots, shredded
- 1 celery stalk, chopped
- ½ green cabbage head, shredded
- 2 zucchinis, chopped
- 1 sweet onion, chopped
- 4 tomatoes, chopped
- 2 tablespoons tomato paste
- 5 garlic cloves, minced
- 2 jalapenos, chopped
- 1 cup cilantro, chopped
- 3 cups chicken stock
- 1 tablespoon cumin, ground
- 1 tablespoon chili powder
- A drizzle of olive oil
- A pinch of salt and black pepper

Directions:

1. Grease your slow cooker with the oil, add carrots, celery, cabbage, zucchinis, onion, tomatoes, tomato paste, garlic, jalapenos, cilantro, stock, cumin, chili powder, salt and pepper, cover, cook on Low for 3 hours, divide between plates and serve as a side dish.
2. Enjoy!

Nutrition Value: calories 211, fat 3, fiber 3, carbs 13, protein 8

138. Okra and Cherry Tomatoes

Preparation time: 10 minutes
Cooking time: 3 hours
Servings: 4

Ingredients:

- 2 cups okra, sliced
- 1 and ½ cups red onion, roughly chopped
- 3 cups cherry tomatoes, halved
- 2 cups red and yellow bell peppers, sliced
- 1 cup white mushrooms, sliced
- ½ cup olive oil
- ½ cup balsamic vinegar

- 2 tablespoons basil, chopped

Directions:

1. In your slow cooker, mix okra with onion, tomatoes, bell peppers, mushrooms, basil, oil and vinegar, toss, cover and cook on High for 3 hours.
2. Divide between plates and serve as a side dish.
3. Enjoy!

Nutrition Value: calories 203, fat 12, fiber 4, carbs 14, protein 5

139. Marjoram Cauliflower Rice

Preparation time: 10 minutes
Cooking time: 6 hours
Servings: 8

Ingredients:

- 2 cups veggie stock
- 2 and ½ cups cauliflower rice
- 4 ounces mushrooms, sliced
- 2 tablespoons olive oil
- 2 teaspoons marjoram, dried and crushed
- A pinch of salt and black pepper
- 2/3 cup dried cherries
- 2/3 cup green onions, chopped

Directions:

1. In your slow cooker, mix stock with cauliflower, mushrooms, oil, marjoram, salt, pepper, cherries and green onions, toss, cover, cook on Low for 6 hours, divide between plates and serve as a side dish.
2. Enjoy!

Nutrition Value: calories 209, fat 5, fiber 3, carbs 8, protein 5

140. Coconut Cauliflower Rice

Preparation time: 10 minutes
Cooking time: 4 hours
Servings: 6

Ingredients:

- 6 garlic cloves, minced
- 1 big cauliflower head, riced
- 1 cup coconut milk

- 1 cup veggie stock
- 1 tablespoons olive oil
- Salt and black pepper to the taste

Directions:

1. In your slow cooker, mix cauliflower with stock, garlic, salt and pepper, cover and cook on High for 3 hours.
2. Add oil and coconut milk, toss, cover and cook on High for 1 more hour.
3. Divide between plates and serve as a side dish.
4. Enjoy!

Nutrition Value: calories 195, fat 5, fiber 6, carbs 17, protein 6

141. Eggplant Salad

Preparation time: 10 minutes
Cooking time: 2 hours
Servings: 6

Ingredients:

- 14 ounces canned roasted tomatoes, chopped
- 4 cups eggplant, cubed
- 1 yellow bell pepper, chopped
- 1 red onion, cut into medium wedges
- 2 tablespoons olive oil
- 1 teaspoon mustard
- 3 tablespoons red vinegar
- 1 garlic clove, minced
- A pinch of salt and black pepper
- ½ cup basil, chopped

Directions:

1. In your slow cooker, mix the eggplant with tomatoes, bell pepper and onion, toss, cover and cook on High for 2 hours.
2. Meanwhile, in a bowl, mix oil with vinegar, mustard, basil, garlic, salt and pepper, whisk well, add to the slow cooker, toss, transfer to plates and serve as a side dish.
3. Enjoy!

Nutrition Value: calories 301, fat 9, fiber 6, carbs 15, protein 7

142. Spinach Mash

Preparation time: 10 minutes

Cooking time: 3 hours
Servings: 2

Ingredients:

- 2 garlic cloves, minced
- 10 ounces spinach leaves
- A drizzle of olive oil
- Salt and black pepper to the taste
- 4 tablespoons coconut cream

Directions:

1. Grease your slow cooker with the oil, add garlic, spinach, salt, pepper and coconut cream, toss, cover and cook on Low for 3 hours.
2. Mash using an immersion blender, divide between plates and serve as a side dish.
3. Enjoy!

Nutrition Value: calories 263, fat 10, fiber 4, carbs 15, protein 7

143. Minty Okra

Preparation time: 10 minutes
Cooking time: 3 hours
Servings: 4

Ingredients:

- 1 pound okra, sliced
- Salt and black pepper to the taste
- 1 tablespoon mint, chopped
- 2 teaspoons olive oil
- 2 tablespoons chicken stock
- 3 green onions, chopped
- 1 garlic clove, minced

Directions:

1. Grease your slow cooker with the oil, add okra, salt, pepper, mint, stock, garlic and green onions, toss, cover, cook on Low for 3 hours, divide between plates and serve as a side dish.
2. Enjoy!

Nutrition Value: calories 180, fat 1, fiber 1, carbs 8, protein 7

144. Swiss Chard Mix

Preparation time: 10 minutes
Cooking time: 2 hours

Servings: 4

Ingredients:

- 2 tablespoons olive oil
- 3 tablespoons lemon juice
- ½ cup veggie stock
- 4 garlic cloves, minced
- A pinch of salt and black pepper
- 4 bacon slices, chopped
- 2 bunches Swiss chard, roughly torn

Directions:

1. In your slow cooker, mix oil with chard, bacon, stock, lemon juice, garlic, salt and pepper, toss, cover, cook on High for 2 hours, divide between plates and serve as a side dish.
2. Enjoy

Nutrition Value: calories 250, fat 7, fiber 3, carbs 12, protein 4

145. Swiss Chard and Capers Salad

Preparation time: 10 minutes
Cooking time: 2 hours
Servings: 4

Ingredients:

- 2 tablespoons olive oil
- 2 bunches Swiss chard, torn
- 3 tablespoons veggie stock
- 2 tablespoons capers
- 1 yellow onion, chopped
- Juice of 1 lemon
- Salt and black pepper to the taste
- ¼ cup black olives, pitted and sliced

Directions:

1. Grease your slow cooker with the oil, add chard, stock, onion, lemon juice, salt, pepper, capers and olives, toss a bit, cover, cook on High for 2 hours, divide between plates and serve as a side dish.
2. Enjoy!

Nutrition Value: calories 223, fat 4, fiber 3, carbs 14, protein 8

146. Garlic Chili Brussels Sprouts

Preparation time: 10 minutes
Cooking time: 30 minutes
Servings: 3

Ingredients:

- Brussels sprouts halved -1 lb.
- Olive oil -1 tbsp
- Salt and black pepper, to taste
- Sesame oil -½ tsp
- Garlic clove, minced-1
- Coconut aminos -¼ cup
- Water -¼ cup
- Apple cider vinegar -1 tsp
- Ste via -½ tbsp
- Garlic chili sauce -1 tsp
- Red pepper flakes-½ pinch

Directions:

1. Place the sprouts in a greased baking sheet.
2. Toss them with oil, salt, and pepper for seasoning.
3. Roast these sprouts for 20 minutes at 425 degrees F in a preheated oven.
4. Meanwhile, heat sesame oil in a pan over medium heat.
5. Toss in the garlic and sauté for a minute.
6. Stir in water, coconut aminos, stevia, chili paste, vinegar, salt, pepper flakes, and pepper.
7. Stir cook for 3 minutes then toss in baked sprouts.
8. Transfer the pan to the oven and broil it for 6 minutes on boiler settings.
9. Enjoy warm.

Nutrition Value: Calories: 271, Fat: 4, Fiber: 7, Carbs: 13, Protein: 11

147. Garlicky Cauliflower Florets

Preparation time: 10 minutes
Cooking time: 35 minutes
Servings: 4

Ingredients:

- Olive oil-3 tbsp
- Juice of 1 lime
- Sweet chili sauce -2 tbsp
- Salt and black pepper - 1 pinch
- Cilantro, chopped-1 tsp
- Garlic cloves, minced-3
- Cauliflower head, florets separated-1

Directions:

1. Mix chili sauce with garlic, oil, lime juice, salt, pepper, cauliflower and cilantro in a bowl.
2. Spread this lime mixture on a baking sheet lined with wax paper.
3. Bake the cauliflower for 35 minutes at 425 degrees F.
4. Serve and enjoy.

Nutrition Value: Calories: 271, Fat: 4, Fiber: 7, Carbs: 11, Protein: 7

148. Brussels Sprouts Cheese Bake

Preparation time: 10 minutes
Cooking time: 30 minutes
Servings: 3

Ingredients:

- Olive oil-1 tbsp
- Brussels sprouts-1 lb.
- Garlic clove, minced-1
- Thyme, chopped-½ tsp
- Salt and black pepper- to taste
- Mozzarella, shredded-½ cup
- Parmesan, grated- 2 tbsp
- Parsley, chopped-½ tbsp

Directions:

1. Fill 2/3 of a cooking pot with water and boil it to cook the sprouts.
2. Add the sprouts and cook them for 10 minutes.
3. Drain and immediately transfer the sprouts to ice cold water.
4. Drain again and toss them with salt, oil, pepper, thyme, and garlic in a bowl.
5. Smash the sprouts a little using a spoon then spread them in a baking sheet.
6. Top them with parmesan and mozzarella.
7. Bake those sprouts for 20 minutes at 425 degrees F in the preheated oven.
8. Garnish with parsley.
9. Enjoy fresh.

Nutrition Value: Calories: 288, Fat: 4, Fiber: 6,

Carbs: 12, Protein: 8

149. Creamy Broccoli Florets

Preparation time: 10 minutes
Cooking time: 15 minutes
Servings: 8

Ingredients:

- Olive oil -4 tbsp
- Broccoli heads, florets separated-2
- Garlic cloves, minced-4
- Mozzarella, shredded- 1 cup
- Parmesan, grated-½ cup
- Coconut cream -1 cup
- Parsley, chopped -2 tbsp

Directions:

1. Add oil to a pan and place it over medium-high heat.
2. Toss in broccoli along with garlic, salt, and pepper.
3. Sauté it for 6 minutes then add cream, parmesan, and mozzarella.
4. Mix gently then transfer the pan to the oven.
5. Bake it for 10 minutes at 375 degrees F in the preheated oven.
6. Garnish with parsley.
7. Serve fresh.

Nutrition Value: Calories: 261, Fat: 3, Fiber: 4, Carbs: 11, Protein: 8

150. Cranberry Brussels Sprouts Mix

Preparation time: 10 minutes
Cooking time: 20 minutes
Servings: 8

Ingredients:

- Brussels sprouts halved - 2 lbs.
- Olive oil- 4 tbsp
- Rosemary, chopped- 2 tsp
- Balsamic vinegar- 2 tbsp
- Thyme, chopped- 2 tsp
- Cranberries, dried- 1 cup

Directions:

1. Toss the sprouts with rosemary, oil, thyme,

and vinegar in a suitable bowl.
2. Spread these sprouts in a baking sheet lined with parchment paper.
3. Roast them for 20 minutes at 400 degrees F in a preheated oven.
4. Dish out and serve.

Nutrition Value: Calories: 199, Fat: 2, Fiber: 5, Carbs: 11, Protein: 7

151. Cilantro Cauliflower Rice

Preparation time: 10 minutes
Cooking time: 15 minutes
Servings: 2

Ingredients:

- Ghee, melted- ½ tbsp
- Juice of 1 lime
- Salt and black pepper- to taste
- Cauliflower rice- ½ cup
- Veggie stock- 2/3 cup
- Cilantro, chopped - ½ tbsp

Directions:

1. Add ghee to a pan and place it over medium-high heat.
2. Spread cauliflower in the pan and stir cook for 5 minutes.
3. Stir in salt, pepper, stock, and lime juice.
4. Let it simmer for 10 minutes then add cilantro.
5. Serve warm.

Nutrition Value: Calories: 181, Fat: 2, Fiber: 5, Carbs: 9, Protein: 6

152. Tomato Zoodle Salad

Preparation time: 10 minutes
Cooking time: 0 minutes
Servings: 2

Ingredients:

- Zucchinis, cut with a spiralizer- 2
- Olive oil- 1 tbsp
- Salt and black pepper- to taste
- Mozzarella, shredded- ½ cup
- Cherry tomatoes, halved- 1 cup
- Basil, torn- 2 tbsp
- Balsamic vinegar - 1 tbsp

Directions:

1. Toss zucchini noodles (zoodles) with oil, salt, and pepper in a suitable bowl.
2. Let these noodles sit for 10 minutes at room temperature then stir in tomatoes, basil, vinegar, and mozzarella.
3. Serve fresh.

Nutrition Value: Calories: 188, Fat: 6, Fiber: 8, Carbs: 8, Protein: 6

153. Spicy tomato jumble

Preparation time: 10 minutes
Servings: 6

Ingredients:

- Chopped scallions- 1 cup
- Chopped cilantro- 1 cup
- Dark plums: cut into wedges- 2
- Tomatoes: cut into wedges- 1½ Ib.
- Coconut aminos – 2 tsp.
- Grated ginger- 3 tbsp.
- Olive oil- 2 tbsp.
- Red vinegar- 2 tbsp.
- Garlic clove: minced- 1
- Stevia- 2 tsp.
- Black sesame seeds- 2 tsp.
- Grated orange zest- ¼ tsp.
- Crushed red pepper- ½ tsp.
- Salt
- Black pepper

Directions:

1. Whisk oil, aminos, ginger, stevia, zest, vinegar and garlic together in a bowl.
2. Mix plums, cilantro, scallions, tomatoes, salt, and pepper together in a salad bowl.
3. Mix in the sesame seeds and the dressing.
4. Serve

Nutrition Value: Calories 199, carbs 11, protein 9, fiber 3, fats 3

154. Dill topped squash and cucumber mix

Preparation time: 30 minutes
Servings: 4

Ingredients:

- Yellow summer squash: sliced – 1
- Cherry tomatoes: halved- 1 cup
- Minced garlic clove- 1
- Chopped dill- 1 tbsp.
- Cucumber: sliced- 1
- Cider vinegar- ⅓ cup
- Stevia- 2 tsp.
- Salt
- Black pepper

Directions:

1. Mix squash, cucumber, tomatoes, stevia, salt, pepper, garlic, and vinegar in a bowl.
2. Cover and let it chill in the fridge for 30 minutes.
3. Flip with the chopped dill.
4. Serve.

Nutrition Value: Calories 188, carbs 9, protein 8, fiber 2, fat 1

155. Seasoned okra with tomatoes

Preparation time: 25 minutes
Servings: 6

Ingredients:

- Okra pods: quartered- 15
- Sliced tomatoes- 3
- Crushed red pepper- ½ tsp.
- Grated parmesan- ¼ cup
- Chopped tarragon- 2 tsp.
- Chopped scallion- 1
- Coconut cream- ¼ cup
- Avocado mayonnaise- ¼ cup
- Almond milk- 3 tbsp.
- Sliced red onion- 1
- Olive oil- 3 tbsp.
- Lemon juice- 2 tsp.
- Grated lemon zest- 1 tsp.
- Salt and black pepper

Directions:

1. Combine okra, a pinch of salt, pepper, 2 tbsp. of olive oil together in a bowl and spread on a lined baking sheet.
2. Bake in the oven for 15 minutes at 400°F.
3. Pour the remaining oil into the pan over

medium-high and fry the onion for 3 minutes, remove and set aside.

4. Mix tomatoes with the fried onions together with red pepper, roasted okra and salt, and pepper.

5. Combine coconut cream, almond milk, tarragon, mayonnaise, Parmesan, scallions, onion, zest and juice and mix well in a bowl.

6. Add the cream mix to the okra and tomatoes mix and serve.

Nutrition Value: Calories 221, carbs 14, protein 8, fiber 3, fats 4

156. Mint watermelon and tomato shuffle

Preparation time: 10 minutes
Servings: 4

Ingredients:

- Tomatoes: cubed- 1½ cups
- Black sesame seeds- 2 tsp.
- Half Chopped jalapeño
- Cubed watermelon- 1½ cups
- Chopped mint- 2 tbsp.
- Lime juice- 3 tbsp.
- Avocado: cubed- 1
- Ginger: grated- 2 tbsp.
- Olive oil- ½ tsp.
- Tomatoes: cubed- 1 ½ cups
- Salt
- Black pepper

Directions:

1. Mix the watermelon, avocado oil, ginger, black seeds, lime zest, jalapeño, oil, lime juice, tomatoes together in a salad bowl.
2. Serve.

Nutrition Value: Calories 199, carbs 9, protein 5, fiber 5, fats 2

157. Tasty Mexican Breakfast

Preparation Time: 40 minutes
Servings: 8

Ingredients:

- Chopped avocado, 1
- Garlic powder, ½ tsp.
- Dried basil, 1 tsp.
- Black pepper
- Dried oregano, 1 tsp.
- Chili powder, 2 tsps.
- Tomato paste, ½ c.
- Cumin, 1 tsp.
- Chopped chorizo, 1 lb.
- Salt
- Medium eggs, 8
- Chopped tomato, 1
- Ground pork, 1 lb.
- Butter, 3 tbsps.
- Chopped onion, ½ c.

Directions:

1. Set 2 mixing bowls in a clean working surface.
2. In the first bowl, mix the enchilada sauce while in another bowl combine chorizo and pork then spread on a well-lined baking tray topped with the sauce
3. Set the oven for 20 minutes at 3500F, allow to bake
4. Set the pan over medium heat then scramble the eggs on the pan
5. Remove the pork mixture from oven and spread the eggs on top
6. Top with the seasonings, onion, tomato, and avocado
7. Enjoy

Nutrition Value:

Calories: 513, Fat: 37.6, Fiber: 2.8, Carbs: 8.4, Protein: 35.6

158. Almond Breakfast Pie

Preparation Time: 55 minutes
Servings: 8

Ingredients:

- Coconut oil, 1 Tsp.
- Medium eggs, 8
- Chopped red bell pepper, ½
- Black pepper
- Ground beef, ¾ lbs.
- Salt
- Taco seasoning, 3 tbsps.
- Chopped onion, ½

- Chopped cilantro, ½ c.
- For the pie crust:
- Baking soda, 1 tsp.
- Coconut flour, 2 oz.
- Xanthan gum, ½ tsp.
- Cold butter, 6 oz.
- Almond flour, 7 oz.
- Baking powder, ½ tsp.

Directions:

1. Set the pan over medium heat with oil to brown the beef then add the taco seasoning, pepper, and salt. Gently stir then reserve in a bowl.
2. Using the same pan, fry the onions and bell peppers with juices from the meat for about four minutes
3. Stir in baking soda, eggs, and some salt
4. Combine the chopped cilantro and get off heat and reserve
5. Set a large mixing bowl in position to make the pie crust ingredients.
6. Refrigerate the pie crust mixture for an hour
7. Roll the pastry then place the baking tray on top of the pastry and turn them both up to the right way.
8. Set the beef mixture in pie crust then adds veggies mixture, spread over meat.
9. Set the oven for 45 minutes at 3500F, allow to bake
10. Allow the pie to cool before slicing.
11. Enjoy with slices of papaya.

Nutrition Value:

Calories: 421, Fat: 34.8, Fiber: 2.7, Carbs: 6.3, Protein: 23.3

159. Savory celery stir-fry

Preparation time: 15 minutes
Servings: 6

Ingredients:

- Celery: julienned- 4 cups
- Chili peppers: dried and crushed- 3
- Coconut aminos- 2 tbsp.
- Olive oil- 2 tbsp.

Directions:

1. Pour oil on a pan over medium-high and add the peppers to cook for 2 minutes.
2. Stir in the coconut aminos and the celery and let it cook for 3 minutes.
3. Serve.

Nutrition Value: Calories 162, carbs 12, protein 7, fiber 7, fats 2

160. Easy celery and squash jumble

Preparation time: 22 minutes
Servings: 2

Ingredients:

- Chopped celery- 4 oz.
- Veggie stock- 2 cups
- Squash: seeded and chopped roughly- 7 oz.
- Salt and black pepper

Directions:

1. Pour the veggie stock in a pot and let simmer over medium heat.
2. Add the celery, salt, pepper, squash and let it cook for 12 minutes.
3. Remove the liquid and serve.

Nutrition Value: Calories 80, carbs 11, protein 2, fiber 4, fats 2

161. Creamy cauliflower rice

Preparation time: 30 minutes
Servings: 4

Ingredients:

- Cauliflower heads: grated- 2
- Chopped yellow onion- 1
- Veggie stock -1 cup
- Olive oil- ¼ cup
- Minced garlic cloves: 2
- Chopped asparagus- 1 bunch
- Grated parmesan- ½ cup
- Chopped parsley- 2 tbsp.
- Coconut cream- ½ cup
- Zest of 1 lemon
- pesto:
- Olive oil- ⅓ cup
- Grated parmesan- ⅓ cup
- Lemon juice- 1 tbsp.

- Chopped cilantro- 1 cup
- Basil: torn- 1 cup
- Garlic clove: minced- 1
- Hemp seeds- ½ cup
- Salt and black pepper

Directions:

1. Pour ¼ cup of olive oil in a pan over medium-high.
2. Add the 2 garlic cloves and onions and let it cook for 2 minutes.
3. Stir in the grated cauliflower, parsley, ½ cup of parmesan, stock, asparagus, cream, and lemon zest and let it cook for 10 minutes.
4. Put cilantro, basil, hemp seeds, ⅓ cup olive oil, garlic clove, ⅓ cup parmesan, salt, pepper, and lemon juice in a food processor and pulse until smooth.
5. Mix and let it cook for 8 minutes.
6. Serve.

Nutrition Value: Calories 223, carbs 13, protein 8, fiber 6, fats 4

162. Whole30 Cheddar Soufflés

Preparation time: 35 minutes
Servings: 8

Ingredients:

- 2 cups cheddar cheese, shredded
- 3/4 cup heavy cream
- 6 eggs
- 1/4 cup chives, chopped.
- 1/2 cup almond flour
- 1/4 teaspoon cream of tartar
- A pinch of cayenne pepper
- 1/2 teaspoon xanthan gum
- 1 teaspoon mustard powder
- Cooking spray
- Salt and black pepper to the taste.

Directions:

1. In a bowl, mix almond flour with salt, pepper, mustard, xanthan gum and cayenne and whisk well.
2. Add cheese, cream, chives, eggs and cream of tartar and whisk well again.
3. Grease 8 ramekins with cooking spray,

pour cheddar and chives mix, introduce in the oven at 350 degrees F and bake for 25 minutes
4. Serve your soufflés with a tasty Whole30 steak.

Nutrition Values: Calories: 288; Fat : 23; Fiber : 1; Carbs : 3. 3; Protein : 14

163. Tasty Twice Baked Zucchinis

Preparation time: 40 minutes
Servings: 4

Ingredients:

- 2 zucchinis, cut into halves and each half in half lengthwise
- 2 ounces cream cheese, soft
- 1 tablespoon jalapeno pepper, chopped.
- 2 tablespoons ghee
- 1/4 cup sour cream
- 1/4 cup yellow onion, chopped.
- 1/2 cup cheddar cheese, shredded
- 4 bacon strips, cooked and crumbled
- Salt and black pepper to the taste.

Directions:

1. Scoop zucchini insides, place flesh in a bowl and arrange zucchini cups in a baking dish.
2. Add onion, cheddar cheese, bacon crumbles, jalapeno, salt, pepper, sour cream, cream cheese and ghee to the bowl.
3. Whisk very well, fill zucchini quarters with this mix, introduce in the oven at 350 degrees F and bake for 30 minutes
4. Divide zucchinis between plates and serve with some lamb chops on the side

Nutrition Values: Calories: 260; Fat : 22; Fiber : 4; Carbs : 3; Protein : 10

164. Delicious Asian Salad

Preparation time: 15 minutes
Servings: 6

Ingredients:

- 3 carrots, finely grated
- 1/2 red onion, chopped.
- 6 mint leaves, roughly chopped.
- A bunch of radishes, finely sliced

- 2 courgettes, finely sliced
- For the salad dressing:
- 1 tablespoons balsamic vinegar
- 1 tablespoons homemade mayo
- 2 tablespoons extra virgin olive oil
- 1 teaspoon mustard
- Salt and black pepper to the taste.

Directions:
1. In a bowl, mix mustard with mayo, vinegar, salt and pepper to the taste. and stir well.
2. Add oil gradually and whisk everything.
3. In a salad bowl, mix carrots with radishes, courgettes and mint leaves
4. Add salad dressing, toss to coat and keep in the fridge until you serve it.

Nutrition Values: Calories: 140; Fat : 1; Fiber : 2; Carbs : 1; Protein : 7

165. Whole30 Eggplant Salad

Preparation time: 20 minutes
Servings: 4

Ingredients:
- 1 eggplant, sliced
- 1 avocado, pitted and chopped.
- 1 teaspoon mustard
- 1 tablespoon balsamic vinegar
- Zest from 1 lemon
- 1 red onion, sliced
- A drizzle of canola oil
- Some parsley sprigs, chopped for serving
- 1 tablespoon fresh oregano, chopped.
- A drizzle of olive oil
- Salt and black pepper to the taste.

Directions:
1. Brush red onion slices and eggplant ones with a drizzle of canola oil, place them on heated kitchen grill and cook them until they become soft.
2. Transfer them to a cutting board, leave them to cool down, chop them and put them in a bowl.
3. Add avocado and stir gently.
4. In a bowl, mix vinegar with mustard, oregano, olive oil, salt and pepper to the taste.

5. Add this to eggplant, avocado and onion mix, toss to coat, add lemon zest and parsley on top and serve

Nutrition Values: Calories: 120; Fat : 3; Fiber : 2; Carbs : 1; Protein : 8

166. Mushroom Salad

Preparation time: 20 minutes
Servings: 4

Ingredients:
- 2 tablespoons ghee
- 1 pound cremini mushrooms, chopped.
- 8 slices prosciutto
- 2 tablespoons apple cider vinegar
- 8 sun-dried tomatoes in oil, drained and chopped.
- 4 tablespoons extra virgin olive oil
- 4 bunches arugula
- Some parmesan shavings
- Some parsley leaves, chopped.
- Salt and black pepper to the taste.

Directions:
1. Heat up a pan with the ghee and half of the oil over medium high heat.
2. Add mushrooms, salt and pepper; stir and cook for 3 minutes
3. Reduce heat; stir again and cook for 3 more minutes
4. Add the rest of the oil and the vinegar; stir and cook 1 minute more
5. Place arugula on a serving platter, add prosciutto on top, add mushroom mix, sun dried tomatoes, more salt and pepper, parmesan shavings and parsley and serve

Nutrition Values: Calories: 160; Fat : 4; Fiber : 2; Carbs : 2; Protein : 6

167. Sautéed Broccoli

Preparation time: 32 minutes
Servings: 4

Ingredients:
- 1 pound broccoli florets
- 1 garlic clove, minced
- 1 tablespoon parmesan, grated
- 5 tablespoons olive oil

- Salt and black pepper to the taste.

Directions:

1. Put water in a pot, add salt, bring to a boil over medium high heat; add broccoli, cook for 5 minutes and drain.
2. Heat up a pan with the oil over medium high heat; add garlic; stir and cook for 2 minutes
3. Add broccoli; stir and cook for 15 minutes
4. Take off heat; sprinkle parmesan, divide between plates and serve

Nutrition Values: Calories: 193; Fat : 14; Fiber : 3; Carbs : 6; Protein : 5

168. Avocado Fries

Preparation time: 15 minutes
Servings: 3
Ingredients:

- 3 avocados, pitted, peeled, halved and sliced
- 1½ cups almond meal
- A pinch of cayenne pepper
- 1½ cups sunflower oil
- Salt and black pepper to the taste.

Directions:

1. In a bowl mix almond meal with salt, pepper and cayenne and stir.
2. In a second bowl, whisk eggs with a pinch of salt and pepper.
3. Dredge avocado pieces in egg and then in almond meal mix.
4. Heat up a pan with the oil over medium high heat; add avocado fries and cook them until they are golden.
5. Transfer to paper towels, drain grease and divide between plates
6. Serve as a side dish.

Nutrition Values: Calories: 450; Fat : 43; Fiber : 4; Carbs : 7; Protein : 17

169. Yummy Creamy Spaghetti Pasta

Preparation time: 50 minutes
Servings: 4

Ingredients:

- 1 spaghetti squash

- 2 tablespoons ghee
- 2 cups heavy cream
- 1 teaspoon Cajun seasoning
- A pinch of cayenne pepper
- Salt and black pepper to the taste.

Directions:

1. Prick spaghetti with a fork, place on a lined baking sheet, introduce in the oven at 350 degrees F and bake for 15 minutes
2. Take spaghetti squash out of the oven, leave aside to cool down a bit and scoop squash noodles
3. Heat up a pan with the ghee over medium heat; add spaghetti squash; stir and cook for a couple of minutes
4. Add salt, pepper, cayenne pepper and Cajun seasoning; stir and cook for 1 minute
5. Add heavy cream; stir, cook for 10 minutes more, divide between plates and serve as a Whole30 side dish.

Nutrition Values: Calories: 200; Fat : 2; Fiber : 1; Carbs : 5; Protein : 8

170. Green Beans Side Dish

Preparation time: 20 minutes
Servings: 4

Ingredients:

- 12 ounces green beans
- 1/2 teaspoon garlic powder
- 1/4 teaspoon paprika
- 2/3 cup parmesan, grated
- 1 egg
- Salt and black pepper to the taste.

Directions:

1. In a bowl, mix parmesan with salt, pepper, garlic powder and paprika and stir.
2. In another bowl, whisk the egg with salt and pepper.
3. Dredge green beans in egg and then in parmesan mix.
4. Place green beans on a lined baking sheet, introduce in the oven at 400 degrees F for 10 minutes
5. Serve hot as a side dish.

Nutrition Values: Calories: 114; Fat : 5; Fiber : 7; Carbs : 3; Protein : 9

171. Greek Style Salad

Preparation time: 17 minutes

Servings: 6

Ingredients:

- 1/2 pounds mushrooms, sliced
- 1 tablespoon extra-virgin olive oil
- 1 tomato, diced
- 3 tablespoons lemon juice
- 1/2 cup water
- 3 garlic cloves, minced
- 1 teaspoon basil, dried
- 1 tablespoons coriander, chopped.
- Salt and black pepper to the taste.

Directions:

1. Heat up a pan with the oil over medium heat; add mushrooms; stir and cook for 3 minutes
2. Add basil and garlic; stir and cook for 1 minute more
3. Add water, salt, pepper, tomato and lemon juice; stir and cook for a few minutes more
4. Take off heat; transfer to a bowl, leave aside to cool down, sprinkle coriander and serve

Nutrition Values: Calories: 200; Fat : 2; Fiber : 2; Carbs : 1; Protein : 10

172. Healthy Whole30 Cucumber And Dates Salad

Preparation time: 10 minutes

Servings: 4

Ingredients:

- 2 English cucumbers, chopped.
- 1/2 cup walnuts, chopped.
- 2 tablespoons lemon juice
- 4 tablespoons fruity olive oil
- 8 dates, pitted and sliced
- 3/4 cup fennel, thinly sliced
- 2 tablespoons chives, finely chopped.
- Salt and black pepper to the taste.

Directions:

1. Put cucumber pieces on a paper towel, press well and transfer to a salad bowl.
2. Crush them a bit using a fork.

3. Add dates, fennel, chives and walnuts and stir gently.
4. Add salt, pepper to the taste., lemon juice and the oil, toss to coat and serve right away.

Nutrition Values: Calories: 80; Fat : 0.2; Fiber : 1; Carbs : 0.4; Protein : 5

173. Roasted Cauliflower

Preparation time: 35 minutes

Servings: 6

Ingredients:

- 1 cauliflower head, florets separated
- 1/3 cup parmesan, grated
- 3 tablespoons olive oil
- 2 tablespoons extra virgin olive oil
- 1 tablespoon parsley, chopped.
- Salt and black pepper to the taste.

Directions:

1. In a bowl, mix oil with garlic, salt, pepper and cauliflower florets
2. Toss to coat well, spread this on a lined baking sheet, introduce in the oven at 450 degrees F and bake for 25 minutes; stirring halfway.
3. Add parmesan and parsley; stir and cook for 5 minutes more
4. Divide between plates and serve as a Whole30 side dish.

Nutrition Values: Calories: 118; Fat : 2; Fiber : 3; Carbs : 1; Protein : 6

174. Summer Kale Side Dish

Preparation time: 55 minutes

Servings: 4

Ingredients:

- 1 bunch kale, steamed and chopped.
- 1 small yellow onion, chopped.
- 1 tablespoon balsamic vinegar
- 1/3 cup almonds, toasted
- 2 tablespoons olive oil
- 2 cups water
- 3 garlic cloves, minced

Directions:

1. Heat up a pan with the oil over medium heat; add onion; stir and cook for 10 minutes
2. Add garlic; stir and cook for 1 minute
3. Add water and kale, cover pan and cook for 30 minutes
4. Add salt, pepper, balsamic vinegar and almonds, toss to coat, divide between plates and serve as a side

Nutrition Values: Calories: 170; Fat : 11; Fiber : 3; Carbs : 7; Protein : 7

175. Endives And Watercress Side Salad

Preparation time: 15 minutes
Servings: 4

Ingredients:

- 4 medium endives, roots and ends cut and thinly sliced crosswise
- 1 tablespoon lemon juice
- 1 shallot finely, chopped.
- 1 apple, thinly sliced
- 1 tablespoon chervil, chopped.
- 1 tablespoon tarragon, chopped.
- 1 tablespoon chives, chopped.
- 1/3 cup almonds, chopped.
- 1 tablespoon balsamic vinegar
- 2 tablespoons extra virgin olive oil
- 6 tablespoons heavy cream
- 4 ounces watercress, cut in medium springs
- 1 tablespoon parsley, chopped.
- Salt and black pepper to the taste.

Directions:

1. In a bowl, mix lemon juice with vinegar, salt and shallot; stir and leave a side for 10 minutes
2. Add olive oil, pepper; stir and leave aside for another 2 minutes
3. Put endives, apple, watercress, chives, tarragon, parsley and chervil in a salad bowl.
4. Add salt and pepper to the taste. and toss to coat.
5. Add heavy cream and vinaigrette; stir gently and serve as a side dish with almonds on top.

Nutrition Values: Calories: 200; Fat : 3; Fiber : 5; Carbs : 2; Protein : 10

176. Italian Whole30 Salad

Preparation time: 3 hours 40 minutes
Servings: 12

Ingredients:

- 6 eggplants
- 1 garlic clove, crushed.
- 1 teaspoon parsley, dried
- 1 tablespoon balsamic vinegar
- 1/4 teaspoon basil, dried
- 3 tablespoons extra virgin olive oil
- 1 teaspoon oregano, dried
- 2 tablespoons stevia
- Salt and black pepper to the taste.

Directions:

1. Prick eggplants with a fork, arrange them on a baking sheet, introduce in the oven at 350 degrees F, bake for 1 hour and 30 minutes, take them out of the oven, leave them to cool down, peel, chop them and transfer to a salad bowl.
2. Add garlic, oil, parsley, stevia, oregano, basil, salt and pepper to the taste., toss to coat, keep in the fridge for 2 hours and then serve

Nutrition Values: Calories: 150; Fat : 1; Fiber : 2; Carbs : 1,protein 8

177. Perfect Sautéed Zucchinis

Preparation time: 25 minutes
Servings: 6

Ingredients:

- 4 zucchinis, sliced
- 1/2 pound tomatoes, chopped.
- 1 garlic clove, minced
- 1 garlic clove, minced
- 1 teaspoon Italian seasoning
- 1 red onion, chopped.
- 1 tomato, chopped.
- Salt and black pepper to the taste.

Directions:

1. Heat up a pan with the oil over medium

heat; add onion, salt and pepper; stir and cook for 2 minutes

2. Add mushrooms and zucchinis; stir and cook for 5 minutes

3. Add garlic, tomatoes and Italian seasoning; stir, cook for 6 minutes more

4. Take off heat; divide between plates and serve as a side dish.

Nutrition Values: Calories: 70; Fat : 3; Fiber : 2; Carbs : 6; Protein : 4

178. Delicious Roasted Olives

Preparation time: 30 minutes
Servings: 6

Ingredients:

- 1 cup kalamata olives, pitted
- 1 cup black olives, pitted
- 10 garlic cloves
- 1 tablespoon herbes de Provence
- 1 teaspoon lemon zest, grated
- 1 cup green olives, stuffed with almonds and garlic
- 1/4 cup olive oil
- Black pepper to the taste.
- Some chopped thyme for serving

Directions:

1. Place black, kalamata and green olives on a lined baking sheet, drizzle oil, garlic and herbes de Provence, toss to coat, introduce in the oven at 425 degrees F and bake for 10 minutes

2. Stir olives and bake for 10 minutes more

3. Divide olives on plates, sprinkle lemon zest, black pepper and thyme on top, toss to coat and serve warm.

Nutrition Values: Calories: 200; Fat : 20; Fiber : 4; Carbs : 3; Protein : 1

179. Brussels Sprouts Dish

Preparation time: 20 minutes
Servings: 4

Ingredients:

- 1 pound Brussels sprouts, trimmed and halved
- 1 teaspoon sesame seeds

- 1 tablespoon coconut aminos
- 2 tablespoons sesame oil
- 1 tablespoon sriracha
- 1 tablespoon green onions, chopped.
- 1½ tablespoons sukrin gold syrup
- Salt and black pepper to the taste.

Directions:

1. In a bowl, mix sesame oil with coconut aminos, sriracha, syrup, salt and black pepper and whisk well.

2. Heat up a pan over medium high heat; add Brussels sprouts and cook them for 5 minutes on each side

3. Add sesame oil mix, toss to coat, sprinkle sesame seeds and green onions; stir again and serve as a side dish.

Nutrition Values: Calories: 110; Fat : 4; Fiber : 4; Carbs : 6; Protein : 4

180. Mushroom And Hemp Pilaf

Preparation time: 30 minutes
Servings: 4

Ingredients:

- 1 cup hemp seeds
- 2 tablespoons ghee
- 1/2 teaspoon garlic powder
- 1/2 cup chicken stock
- 1/4 teaspoon parsley, dried
- 1/4 cup almonds, sliced
- 3 mushrooms, roughly chopped.
- Salt and black pepper to the taste.

Directions:

1. Heat up a pan with the ghee over medium heat; add almonds and mushrooms; stir and cook for 4 minutes

2. Add hemp seeds and stir.

3. Add salt, pepper, parsley, garlic powder and stock; stir, reduce heat; cover pan and simmer until stock is absorbed.

4. Divide between plates and serve as a side dish.

Nutrition Values: Calories: 324; Fat : 24; Fiber : 15; Carbs : 2; Protein : 15

181. Perfect Asian Side Salad

Preparation time: 40 minutes
Servings: 4

Ingredients:

- 1 packet Asian noodles
- 1 big cucumber, thinly sliced
- 1 tablespoon sesame oil
- 1/4 teaspoon red pepper flakes
- 1 teaspoon sesame seeds
- 1 spring onion, chopped.
- 2 tablespoons coconut oil
- 1 tablespoon balsamic vinegar
- Salt and black pepper to the taste.

Directions:

1. Cook noodles according to package instructions, drain and rinse them well.
2. Heat up a pan with the coconut oil over medium high heat; add noodles, cover pan and fry them for 5 minutes until they are crispy enough.
3. Transfer them to paper towels and drain grease
4. In a bowl, mix cucumber slices with spring onion, pepper flakes, vinegar, sesame oil, sesame seeds, salt, pepper and noodles
5. Toss to coat well, keep in the fridge for 30 minutes and serve as a side for some grilled shrimp.

Nutrition Values: Calories: 400; Fat : 34; Fiber : 2; Carbs : 4; Protein : 2

182. Whole30 Mushrooms

Preparation time: 40 minutes
Servings: 4

Ingredients:

- 16 ounces baby mushrooms
- 3 tablespoons onion, dried
- 3 tablespoons parsley flakes
- 1 teaspoon garlic powder
- 4 tablespoons ghee
- Salt and black pepper to the taste.

Directions:

1. In a bowl, mix parsley flakes with onion, salt, pepper and garlic powder and stir.
2. In another bowl, mix mushroom with melted ghee and toss to coat.

3. Add seasoning mix, toss well, spread on a lined baking sheet, introduce in the oven at 300 degrees F and bake for 30 minutes
4. Serve as a side dish for a tasty Whole30 roast.

Nutrition Values: Calories: 152; Fat : 12; Fiber : 5; Carbs : 6; Protein : 4

183. Special Side Dish

Preparation time: 4 hours 30 minutes
Servings: 8

Ingredients:

- 2 cups almond flour
- 1/4 cup coconut flour
- 2 tablespoons whey protein powder
- 1¼ cups cheddar cheese, shredded
- 1/2 teaspoon garlic powder
- 2 teaspoons baking powder
- 2 eggs
- 1/4 cup melted ghee
- ¾ cup water
- For the stuffing:
- 1/2 cup yellow onion, chopped.
- 2 tablespoons ghee
- 1 red bell pepper, chopped.
- 1/4 cup whipping cream
- 1 jalapeno pepper, chopped.
- 12 ounces sausage, chopped.
- 2 eggs
- ¾ cup chicken stock
- Salt and black pepper to the taste.

Directions:

1. In a bowl, mix coconut flour with whey protein, almond flour, garlic powder, baking powder and 1 cup cheddar cheese and stir everything.
2. Add water, 2 eggs and 1/4 cup ghee and stir well.
3. Transfer this to a greased baking pan, sprinkle the rest of the cheddar cheese, introduce in the oven at 325 degrees F and bake for 30 minutes
4. Leave the bread to cool down for 15 minutes and cube it.
5. Spread bread cubes on a lined baking sheet,

introduce in the oven at 200 degrees F and bake for 3 hours

6. Take bread cubes out of the oven and leave aside for now.
7. Heat up a pan with 2 tablespoons ghee over medium heat; add onion; stir and cook for 4 minutes
8. Add jalapeno and red bell pepper; stir and cook for 5 minutes
9. Add salt and pepper; stir and transfer everything to a bowl.
10. Heat up the same pan over medium heat; add sausage; stir and cook for 10 minutes
11. Transfer to the bowl with the veggies, also add stock, bread and stir everything.
12. In a separate bowl, whisk 2 eggs with some salt, pepper and whipping cream.
13. Add this to sausage and bread mix; stir, transfer to a greased baking pan, introduce in the oven at 325 degrees F and bake for 30 minutes
14. Serve hot as a side

Nutrition Values: Calories: 340; Fat : 4; Fiber : 6; Carbs : 3. 4; Protein : 7

184. Green Beans And Avocado

Preparation time: 15 minutes
Servings: 4

Ingredients:

- 2 avocados, pitted and peeled
- 2/3 pound green beans, trimmed
- 5 scallions, chopped.
- 3 tablespoons olive oil
- A handful cilantro, chopped.
- Salt and black pepper to the taste.

Directions:

1. Heat up a pan with the oil over medium heat; add green beans; stir and cook for 4 minutes
2. Add salt and pepper; stir, take off heat and transfer to a bowl.
3. In another bowl, mix avocados with salt and pepper and mash with a fork.
4. Add onions and stir well.
5. Add this over green beans, toss to coat and serve with chopped cilantro on top.

Nutrition Values: Calories: 200; Fat : 5; Fiber : 3;

Carbs : 4; Protein : 6

185. Special Tomato And Bocconcini

Preparation time: 6 minutes
Servings: 4

Ingredients:

- 8 ounces baby bocconcini, drain and torn
- 1 cup basil leaves, roughly chopped.
- 20 ounces tomatoes, cut in wedges
- 1 teaspoon stevia
- 1 garlic clove, finely minced
- 2 tablespoons extra virgin olive oil
- 1½ tablespoons balsamic vinegar
- Salt and black pepper to the taste.

Directions:

1. In a bowl, mix stevia with vinegar, garlic, oil, salt and pepper and whisk very well.
2. In a salad bowl, mix bocconcini with tomato and basil.
3. Add dressing, toss to coat and serve right away as a Whole30 side dish.

Nutrition Values: Calories: 100; Fat : 2; Fiber : 2; Carbs : 1; Protein : 9

186. Whole30 Veggie Noodles

Preparation time: 30 minutes
Servings: 6

Ingredients:

- 1 zucchini, cut with a spiralizer
- 1 summer squash, cut with a spiralizer
- 6 ounces yellow, orange and red bell peppers, cut into thin strips
- 4 tablespoons bacon fat
- 3 garlic cloves, minced
- 1 carrot, cut with a spiralizer
- 1 sweet potato, cut with a spiralizer
- 4 ounces red onion, chopped.
- Salt and black pepper to the taste.

Directions:

1. Spread zucchini noodles on a lined baking sheet.
2. Add squash, carrot, sweet potato, onion and all bell peppers

3. Add salt, pepper and garlic and toss to coat.
4. Add bacon fat, toss again all noodles, introduce in the oven at 400 degrees F and bake for 20 minutes
5. Transfer to plates and serve right away as a Whole30 side dish.

Nutrition Values: Calories: 50; Fat : 1; Fiber : 1; Carbs : 6; Protein : 2

187. Easy Fried Cabbage

Preparation time: 25 minutes
Servings: 4

Ingredients:

- 1½ pound green cabbage, shredded
- ounces ghee
- A pinch of sweet paprika
- Salt and black pepper to the taste.

Directions:

1. Heat up a pan with the ghee over medium heat.
2. Add cabbage and cook for 15 minutes stirring often.
3. Add salt, pepper and paprika; stir, cook for 1 minute more, divide between plates and serve

Nutrition Values: Calories: 200; Fat : 4; Fiber : 2; Carbs : 3; Protein : 7

188. Delicious Caramelized Bell Peppers

Preparation Time: 42 minutes
Servings: 4

Ingredients:

- 2 red bell peppers, cut into thin strips
- 2 red onions, cut into thin strips
- 1 teaspoon ghee
- 1 teaspoon basil, dried
- 1 tablespoon olive oil
- Salt and black pepper to the taste.

Directions:

1. Heat up a pan with the ghee and the oil over medium heat; add onion and bell peppers; stir and cook for 2 minutes
2. Reduce temperature and cook for 30

minutes more stirring often.
3. Add salt, pepper and basil; stir again, take off heat and serve as a Whole30 side dish.

Nutrition Values: Calories: 97; Fat : 4; Fiber : 2; Carbs : 6; Protein : 2

189. Grilled Asparagus

Preparation time: 30 minutes
Cooking time: 15 minutes
Servings: 4

Ingredients:

- 5 tablespoons olive oil
- 1 garlic head
- 2 tablespoons shallot, chopped
- Salt
- Black pepper to taste
- 1 and ½ teaspoons white wine vinegar
- 1 and ½ pound asparagus
- 2 slices ciabatta bread
- ½ teaspoon red wine vinegar

Directions:

1. Season garlic with salt, pepper and 1 tablespoon olive oil, arrange on a baking tray and bake at 350 degrees F for 40 minutes.
2. Squeeze garlic into a bowl, add salt, pepper and 2 tablespoons of oil and leave aside.
3. In a bowl, mix shallot with the white and red vinegar, stir well and leave aside for 30 minutes.
4. Add remaining oil, salt and pepper and the asparagus.
5. Preheat your grill pan over medium high heat, add asparagus in and cook for 10 minutes.
6. Meanwhile, spread roasted garlic mix over bread and grill it for a few minutes.
7. Divide asparagus on plates, drizzle vinegar mix and garlic all over and serve as a side dish.

Nutrition Value: calories 132, fat 1, fiber 2, carbs 4, protein 4, carbs 3

190. Cucumber Side Dish

Preparation time: 1 hour
Cooking time: 0 minutes

Servings: 12

Ingredients:

- 2 cucumbers, chopped
- 2 tomatoes, chopped
- ½ cup green bell pepper, chopped
- 1 yellow onion, chopped
- 1 jalapeno pepper, chopped
- 1 garlic clove, minced
- 1 teaspoon parsley, chopped
- 2 tablespoons lime juice
- 2 teaspoons cilantro, chopped
- ½ teaspoon dill weed, dried
- Salt to taste

Directions:

1. In a large salad bowl, mix cucumbers with tomatoes and jalapeno pepper.
2. Add green pepper, onion, garlic, salt and stir.
3. Add dill weed, parsley, cilantro and lime juice and toss to coat.
4. Place in the fridge about 1 hour before serving. Serve as a side dish.

Nutrition Value: calories 132, fat 3, fiber 1, carbs 2, protein 4

191. Cucumber and Peanut Salad

Preparation time: 10 minutes
Cooking time: 5 minutes
Servings: 2

Ingredients:

- 1 large cucumber, chopped
- 1 tablespoon butter
- Salt to taste
- 1 red chili pepper, dried
- ½ teaspoon cumin, ground
- 1 tablespoon lemon juice
- 3 tablespoons peanuts, chopped
- 1 teaspoon cilantro, chopped

Directions:

1. In a bowl, mix cucumber with salt, leave aside for 10 minutes, drain well, pat dry and transfer to a bowl.
2. Heat a pan with the butter over medium heat, add chili pepper and cumin, stir well

and cook for 30 seconds.
3. Add peanuts, stir, add to the bowl with the cucumber, also add lemon juice, sprinkle cilantro on top and serve as a side dish.

Nutrition Value: calories 142, fat 6, fiber 5, carbs 12, protein 5

192. Easy Beet Salad

Preparation time: 10 minutes
Cooking time: 1 hour
Servings: 4

Ingredients:

- 4 fresh beets
- Salt and black pepper to taste
- ½ cup olive oil + a drizzle
- ¼ cup lemon juice
- 8 slices goats cheese, crumbled
- 1/3 cup walnuts, chopped
- 8 lettuce leaves

Directions:

- Arrange beets on a lined, baking sheet, add a drizzle of oil, season with some salt and pepper, place in the oven at 400 degrees F and bake for 1 hour.
- Peel beets, cut them and transfer to a bowl. In a small bowl mix lemon juice with ½ cup olive oil, salt and black pepper to taste and whisk.
- Add this to beets, also add lettuce and cheese, toss to coat, divide between plates and serve.

Nutrition Value: calories 121, fat 1, fiber 2, carbs 3, protein 3

193. Grilled Beets

Preparation time: 10 minutes
Cooking time: 30 minutes
Servings: 6

Ingredients:

- 3 medium beets, sliced
- 1/3 cup balsamic vinegar
- 1 teaspoon rosemary, chopped
- 1 garlic clove, minced
- ½ teaspoon Italian seasoning
- A drizzle of olive oil

Directions:

1. In a bowl, mix rosemary with vinegar, garlic and Italian seasoning and whisk.
2. Add beets, toss and leave aside for 10 minutes.
3. Place beets and the marinade on aluminum foil pieces, add a drizzle of oil, seal edges, place on preheated grill pan over medium heat and cook for 25 minutes.
4. Unwrap beets, peel and cube them.
5. Arrange beets and the marinade on serving plates and serve right away as a side dish.

Nutrition Value: calories 100, fat 2, fiber 2, carbs 2, protein 4

194. Grilled Squash

Preparation time: 10 minutes
Cooking time: 10 minutes
Servings: 6

Ingredients:

- 4 medium assorted squash, thinly sliced
- ¼ teaspoon red pepper flakes, crushed
- 2 tomatoes, chopped
- 2 tablespoons feta cheese, crumbled
- ¼ cup Greek yogurt
- 1 tablespoon olive oil
- 1 tablespoon cilantro, chopped

Directions:

1. Arrange the squash slices on a preheated grill.
2. Brush them with the oil, and cook over medium heat for 6 minutes on each side.
3. In a bowl, mix the grilled squash with pepper flakes, tomatoes, cheese, yogurt and cilantro, toss and serve.

Nutrition Value: calories 170, fat 7, fiber 1, carbs 8, protein 6

195. Grilled Eggplant

Preparation time: 10 minutes
Cooking time: 5 minutes
Servings: 6

Ingredients:

- 1/3 cup homemade mayonnaise
- 2 tablespoons balsamic vinegar
- A pinch of salt and black pepper
- 1 tablespoon lime juice
- 2 big eggplants, sliced
- ¼ cup cilantro, chopped
- ¼ cup olive oil

Directions:

1. In a small bowl, mix mayonnaise with vinegar, lime juice and black pepper, stir well and leave aside.
2. Brush each eggplant slice with some olive oil, season with salt and pepper, place on preheated grill pan over medium high heat, cook for 5 minutes on each side and divide between plates.
3. Drizzle the mayo mix all over, sprinkle cilantro and serve as a side dish.

Nutrition Value: calories 100, fat 1, fiber 2, carbs 2, protein 2

196. Barley Risotto

Preparation time: 10 minutes
Cooking time: 1 hour
Servings: 4

Ingredients:

- 1 tablespoon butter
- 1 yellow onion, chopped
- 4 parsnips, roughly chopped
- 10 sage leaves, chopped
- 1 garlic clove, minced
- 14 ounces barley
- ½ tablespoon parmesan, grated
- 6 cups hot veggie stock
- Salt and black pepper

Directions:

1. Heat a pan with the butter over medium high heat, add onion, some salt and pepper, stir and cook for 5 minutes.
2. Add parsnips and cook for 10 more minutes.
3. Add sage, garlic, barley and stock, stir well, bring to a simmer and cook for 40 minutes.
4. Add parmesan, stir, divide between plates and serve with sage on top.

Nutrition Value: calories 132, fat 1, fiber 1, carbs 2, protein 2

197. Lentil Side Salad

Preparation time: 15 minutes
Cooking time: 30 minutes
Servings: 4

Ingredients:

- 7 ounces lentils
- 3 tablespoons capers, chopped
- Juice of 1 lemon
- Zest and juice from 1 lemon
- 1 red onion, chopped
- 3 tablespoons olive oil
- 14 ounces canned chickpeas, drained
- 8 ounces already cooked beetroot, chopped
- 1 small handful parsley, chopped
- Salt and pepper to taste

Directions:

1. Put lentils in a saucepan, add water to cover, bring to a simmer over medium heat, boil for 20 minutes, drain and leave aside.
2. Put lemon juice from 1 lemon in a bowl, add onion, salt and pepper, whisk and leave aside.
3. Put the juice and zest from the second lemon in a bowl, add oil, salt, pepper and the capers, whisk well and leave aside.
4. Add chickpeas to lentils, then add beets, parsley, pickled onion mix and toss to coat. Add capers mix, toss well and serve.

Nutrition Value: calories 132, fat 1, fiber 2, carbs 2, protein 3

198. Sweet Potato Side Dish

Preparation time: 10 minutes
Cooking time: 1 hour
Servings: 4

Ingredients:

- 4 tablespoons olive oil
- 1 garlic clove, minced
- 4 medium sweet potatoes
- 1 shallot, chopped
- 14 ounces canned chickpeas, drained
- 3 ounces baby spinach
- Zest and juice from 1 lemon
- A small bunch dill, chopped

For the tahini yogurt:

- 1 ½ tablespoons Greek yogurt
- ½ tablespoon pine nuts
- 2 tablespoons tahini paste
- 4 ounces pomegranate seeds
- Salt and pepper to taste

Directions:

1. Wrap potatoes in foil, arrange them on a lined baking sheet, place in the oven at 350 degrees F and cook them for 1 hour.
2. Meanwhile, heat a pan with 1 tablespoon olive oil over medium high heat, add shallot and garlic, stir and cook for 3 minutes.
3. Add chickpeas, stir and cook for 1 more minute.
4. Add spinach and dill, stir, take off heat and leave aside.
5. In a bowl, mix remaining oil with lemon zest and juice and whisk.
6. Add to chickpeas mix and mash everything with a potato masher.
7. In another bowl, mix yogurt with tahini, salt and pepper and stir well.
8. Take potatoes out of oven, unwrap, split them lengthwise, divide between plates, stuff with chickpeas mix, drizzle tahini mix all over and serve with pine nuts and pomegranate seeds on top.

Nutrition Value: calories 120, fat 1, fiber 1, carbs 2, protein 2

199. Warm Cabbage Mix

Preparation time: 10 minutes
Cooking time: 20 minutes
Servings: 2

Ingredients:

- 2 tablespoons olive oil
- 1 yellow potato, cubed
- 2 garlic cloves, minced
- 1 green cabbage, shredded
- 1 cup canned chickpeas, drained
- 1 teaspoon sweet paprika
- A pinch of salt and black pepper

Directions:

1. Heat a pan with the oil over medium heat, add the potatoes, salt and pepper, stir and sauté for 10 minutes.
2. Add the garlic, chickpeas, cabbage and the paprika, stir, cook for 10 minutes more, divide between plates and serve as a side dish.

Nutrition Value: calories 182, fat 6, fiber 6, carbs 11, protein 6

200. Mushroom Pilaf

Preparation time: 10 minutes
Cooking time: 30 minutes
Servings: 4

Ingredients:

- 2 cups chicken stock
- 1 yellow onion, chopped
- 10 ounces mixed mushrooms, sliced
- 2 garlic cloves, minced
- 8 ounces wild and basmati rice
- Juice and zest of 1 lemon
- A small bunch of chives, chopped
- 6 tablespoons light goats cheese with herbs, crumbled
- Salt and black pepper to taste

Directions:

1. Heat a pot with 2 tablespoons of stock over medium high heat, add onion, stir and cook for 5 minutes.
2. Add stock, mushrooms and garlic and cook for further 2 minutes.
3. Add rice, lemon juice, lemon zest, salt and pepper, stir, bring to a simmer, cover and cook for 25 minutes.
4. Add half of the chives and half of the cheese and stir gently.
5. Divide between plates and serve with the rest of the chives and the cheese sprinkled on top.

Nutrition Value: calories 142, fat 1, fiber 2, carbs 2, protein 2

201. Baked Potato with Beans

Preparation time: 10 minutes
Cooking time: 1 hour and 10 minutes
Servings: 4

Ingredients:

- 4 potatoes, scrubbed and pricked with a fork
- 1 carrot, chopped
- 1 tablespoon olive oil
- 1 celery stalk, chopped
- 2 tomatoes, chopped
- A splash of water
- 1 teaspoon sweet paprika
- 14 ounces canned haricot beans, drained
- 1 teaspoon Worcestershire sauce
- Salt and black pepper to taste
- 2 tablespoons chives, chopped

Directions:

1. Place potatoes on a lined baking sheet, place in the oven and bake at 350 degrees F for 1 hour.
2. Heat a pan with the oil over medium heat.
3. Add celery and carrot, stir for 10 minutes.
4. Add beans, tomatoes, salt, pepper and sweet paprika, stir and cook for 5 minutes.
5. Add a splash of water, Worcestershire sauce, stir and cook for 5 minutes.
6. Take potatoes out of oven, split them, spoon beans mix in each, sprinkle chives on top, arrange on plates and serve as a side dish.

Nutrition Value: calories 123, fat 1, fiber 2, carbs 2, protein 1

Kale Salad

Preparation time: 10 minutes
Cooking time: 15 minutes
Servings: 6

Ingredients:

- 4 ounces bulgur wheat
- 4 ounces kale
- A bunch of mints, chopped
- A bunch of scallions, chopped
- ½ cucumber, chopped
- A pinch of cinnamon powder
- A pinch of allspice
- 6 tablespoons olive oil
- Zest and juice from ½ lemon
- 4 ounces feta cheese, crumbled

Directions:

1. Put bulgur in a bowl, cover with hot water and set aside for 10 minutes.
2. Put kale in a food processor and gently pulse.
3. Drain bulgur, transfer to another bowl and mix with kale, mint, scallions, cucumber and tomatoes.
4. Add cinnamon and allspice and stir.
5. Add olive oil and lemon juice and toss to coat.
6. Add feta cheese and lemon zest on top, toss and serve as a side dish.
7. Arrange lettuce leaves on plates and scoop salad into each.

Nutrition Value: calories 100, fat 1, fiber 2, carbs 2, protein 4

203. Spicy Beans

Preparation time: 10 minutes
Cooking time: 25 minutes
Servings: 4

Ingredients:

- 4 teaspoons olive oil
- 1 garlic clove, minced
- ½ teaspoon smoked paprika
- ¾ cup veggie stock
- 1 yellow onion, sliced
- 1 red bell pepper, chopped
- 15 ounces canned butter beans, drained
- 4 cups baby spinach
- ½ cup goats cheese, shredded
- 2 teaspoon sherry vinegar

Directions:

1. Heat a pan with the oil over medium heat, add garlic, stir and cook for 30 seconds.
2. Add onion, paprika and bell pepper and cook for 6 minutes.
3. Add beans, spinach and stock and cook for 3 minutes more.
4. Add cheese and vinegar, divide between plates and serve.

Nutrition Value: calories 140, fat 1, fiber 2, carbs 2, protein 2

204. Veggie Brown Rice

Preparation time: 10 minutes
Cooking time: 40 minutes
Servings: 4

Ingredients:

- 2 cups brown rice
- 1 shallot, chopped
- A pinch of salt and black pepper
- 1 red bell pepper, chopped
- 1 zucchini, grated
- 1 carrot, grated
- ¼ cup parsley, chopped
- ¼ cup olive oil
- ½ teaspoon oregano, dried
- ¼ teaspoon sweet paprika
- ½ teaspoon thyme, dried
- 4 cups water

Directions:

1. Heat a pan with half the olive oil over medium heat.
2. Add the shallot, bell pepper, zucchini, carrot, salt and pepper, stir and cook for 2 minutes.
3. Add oregano, paprika and thyme, stir and cook for 2 minutes more.
4. Add the rice, parsley and water, stir, bring to a simmer and cook for 35 minutes.
5. Divide the rice between plates and serve as a side dish.

Nutrition Value: calories 182, fat 11, fiber 4, carbs 8, protein 5

205. Millet with Tomato and Onion

Preparation time: 10 minutes
Cooking time: 20 minutes
Servings: 6

Ingredients:

- 4 tablespoons olive oil
- 1 cup millet
- 2 small bunches green onions, chopped
- 2 tomatoes, chopped
- ½ cup cilantro, chopped
- 5 drops hot sauce
- 6 cups cold water

- ½ cup lemon juice
- Salt and black pepper to taste

Directions:

1. Heat up a pan with 2 tablespoons oil over medium high heat, add millet, stir and cook for 4 minutes.
2. Add water, bring to a boil, cover and boil for 20 minutes.
3. Transfer millet to a bowl, add tomatoes, onions, lemon juice, cilantro, hot sauce, the rest of the oil, salt and pepper, toss and serve as a side.

Nutrition Value: calories 163, fat 1, fiber 2, carbs 5, protein 3

206. Quinoa Side Salad

Preparation time: 10 minutes
Cooking time: 0 minutes
Servings: 4

Ingredients:

- 1 cup quinoa, cooked
- 1 avocado, chopped
- 1 medium bunch collard greens, chopped
- 1 handful strawberries, sliced
- 4 tablespoons walnuts, chopped
- 2 tablespoons white wine vinegar
- 4 tablespoons tahini
- 4 tablespoons cold water
- 1 tablespoon maple syrup

Directions:

1. In a bowl, mix tahini with maple syrup, water and vinegar and pulse well.
2. In a salad bowl, mix collard green leaves with half of the salad dressing and toss to coat.
3. Add avocado, walnuts, quinoa and strawberries and toss again.
4. Add remaining dressing on top and serve.

Nutrition Value: calories 175, fat 3, fiber 3, carbs 5, protein 3

207. Herbed Corn and Radish Mix

Preparation time: 10 minutes
Cooking time: 0 minutes
Servings: 4

Ingredients:

- 1 tablespoon pumpkin seeds, roasted
- 2 tablespoons cilantro, chopped
- 4 tablespoons parsley, chopped
- 2 cups corn
- 1 cup radishes, sliced
- 2 avocados, peeled, pitted and chopped
- 3 tablespoons olive oil
- 4 tablespoons Greek yogurt
- 2 tablespoons lemon juice
- Salt and black pepper to taste

Directions:

1. In a bowl, mix the corn with radishes, avocado, pumpkin seeds, cilantro, parsley, oil, yogurt, lemon juice, salt and pepper, toss, divide between plates and serve as a side dish.

Nutrition Value: calories 170, fat 6, fiber 4, carbs 5, protein 3

208. Beet And Cheese Side Salad

Preparation time: 15 minutes
Cooking time: 0 minutes
Servings: 6

Ingredients:

- 2 pounds beets, baked, peeled and cubed
- 2 tablespoons olive oil
- 1 tablespoon lemon juice
- 2 tablespoons red wine vinegar
- 1 cup blue cheese, crumbled
- 3 small garlic cloves, minced
- 4 green onions, chopped
- 5 tablespoons dill, chopped
- Salt and black pepper to taste

Directions:

2. In a bowl, mix vinegar with oil, lemon juice, garlic, salt and pepper, whisk well and leave aside.
3. Add green onions, cheese, beets and dill and toss to coat.
4. Leave in the fridge for 15 minutes and then serve as a side dish.

Nutrition : calories 180, fat 2, fiber 3, carbs 2, protein 3

209. Broccoli Side Dish

Preparation time: 10 minutes
Cooking time: 30 minutes
Servings: 5

Ingredients:

- 2 and ½ cups quinoa
- 4 and ½ cups veggie stock
- ½ teaspoon salt
- 2 tablespoons pesto sauce
- 2 tablespoons arrowroot powder
- 12 ounces mozzarella cheese
- 2 cups spinach
- 12 ounces broccoli
- 1/3 cup parmesan
- 3 green onions, chopped

Directions:

1. Put quinoa and green onions in a baking dish.
2. Put broccoli in a heatproof bowl, place in the microwave, cook on high for 5 minutes and leave a side.
3. In a bowl, mix veggie stock with arrowroot powder, pesto sauce and some salt, stir well, transfer to a saucepan and bring to a boil over medium heat.
4. Pour over quinoa, add broccoli, spinach, parmesan and mozzarella cheese.
5. Place in the oven at 400 degrees F and bake for 30 minutes. Divide between plates and serve.

Nutrition Value: calories 210, fat 2, fiber 2, carbs 3, protein 3

210. Spicy Pea Salad

Preparation time: 10 minutes
Cooking time: 0 minutes
Servings: 8

Ingredients:

- 60 ounces peas
- 1 yellow bell pepper, chopped
- 2 ounces Cheddar cheese, grated
- ½ cup mayonnaise
- 3 tablespoon basil, dried
- 2 tablespoons red onion, chopped
- 2 teaspoons chili pepper, chopped
- 1 teaspoon apple cider vinegar
- 1 teaspoon sugar
- Salt and black pepper to taste
- 1 teaspoon garlic powder
- A drizzle of hot sauce

Directions:

1. In a salad bowl, mix bell pepper with cheese, onion, basil, chili pepper, salt and pepper and stir.
2. Add mayo, sugar, vinegar, hot sauce and garlic powder and stir.
3. Add peas, toss well, place in the fridge and serve cold as a side dish.

Nutritional value: calories 120, fat 2, fiber 1, carbs 2, protein 3

211. Mashed Potatoes

Preparation time: 10 minutes
Cooking time: 40 minutes
Servings: 10

Ingredients:

- 2 pounds gold potatoes, cut into small pieces
- 1 ½ cup fresh ricotta cheese
- Sea salt and black pepper to taste
- ½ cup low fat milk
- 3 tablespoons butter

Directions:

1. Put potatoes in a large saucepan, add water to cover, add a pinch of salt, bring to a simmer over medium heat, cook for 20 minutes then drain and mash well.
2. Add salt, pepper, milk, butter and ricotta and stir well.
3. Spoon mashed potatoes into 10 ramekins, place in a baking pan and broil them for a few minutes. Serve hot.

Nutrition Value: calories 180, fat 3, fiber 1, carbs 2, protein 3

212. Brown Rice and Tomatoes

Preparation time: 5 minutes
Cooking time: 50 minutes
Servings: 4

Ingredients:

- 1 tablespoon olive oil
- 1 cup brown rice
- 1 yellow onion, chopped
- 1 tablespoon tomato paste
- 2 tomatoes, cubed
- A pinch of salt and black pepper
- 1 tablespoon basil, chopped
- 2 cups hot water

Directions:

1. Heat a pan with the oil over medium high heat.
2. Add the onion, tomatoes, salt, pepper and the tomato paste, stir and cook for 5 minutes.
3. Add the rice and the water, stir, bring to a simmer and cook over medium heat for 45 minutes.
4. Add the basil, toss, divide the mix between plates and serve as a side dish.

Nutrition Value: calories 187, fat 7, fiber 4, carbs 7, protein 3

213. Creamy Barley Side Salad

Preparation time: 15 minutes
Cooking time: 30 minutes
Servings: 4

Ingredients:

- ½ cup barley
- 1 and ½ cup water
- ½ cup Greek yogurt
- Salt and black pepper to taste
- 2 tablespoons olive oil
- 1 teaspoon mustard
- 1 tablespoon lemon juice
- 2 celery stalks, sliced
- ¼ cup mint, chopped
- 1 apple, cored and chopped

Directions:

1. Put barley in a pan, add water and some salt, bring to a boil, cover, simmer for 25 minutes, drain, arrange on a baking sheet and leave aside.
2. In a bowl, mix yogurt with lemon juice, oil, salt, pepper and mustard and stir well.
3. Add mint, apple, celery and barley, toss to

coat and serve.

Nutrition Value: calories 132, fat 2, fiber 3, carbs 3, protein 1

214. Easy Couscous

Preparation time: 10 minutes
Cooking time: 10 minutes
Servings: 4

Ingredients:

- 10 ounces couscous
- 1 ½ cup hot water
- ½ cup pine nuts
- 2 garlic cloves, minced
- 3 tablespoons olive oil
- 15 ounces canned chickpeas, rinsed
- ½ cup raisins
- 2 bunches Swiss chard
- Salt and black pepper to taste

Directions:

1. Put couscous in a bowl, add water, stir, cover and leave aside for 10 minutes.
2. Meanwhile, heat a pan over medium high heat, add pine nuts, toast them for 4 minutes, transfer to a plate and leave aside.
3. Return pan to medium heat, add oil and heat, add garlic, stir and cook for 1 minute.
4. Add raisins, chickpeas, chard, salt, pepper, stir and cook for 5 minutes.
5. Fluff couscous, divide between plates, add chard and chickpeas mix, top with pine nuts and serve.

Nutrition Value: calories 153, fat 2, fiber 3, carbs 6, protein 4

215. Red Cabbage Mix

Preparation time: 2 hours and 10 minutes
Cooking time: 0 minutes
Servings: 4

Ingredients:

- 12 ounces red cabbage, shredded
- 1 carrot, shredded
- ¼ cup lemon juice
- ¼ cup olive oil
- A pinch of salt and black pepper
- 1 tablespoon sweet paprika

Directions:

1. In a bowl, mix the cabbage with the carrot, lemon juice, oil, salt, pepper and the paprika, toss well and keep in the fridge for 2 hours before serving as a side dish.

Nutrition Value: calories 153, fat 6, fiber 4, carbs 8, protein 5

SEAFOOD

216. Shrimp and Zucchini Salad

Preparation time: 10 minutes
Cooking time: 0 minutes
Servings: 4

Ingredients:

- 1 pound shrimp, cooked, peeled and deveined
- ½ chili pepper, chopped
- A pinch of salt and black pepper
- 2 tablespoons olive oil
- 1 zucchini, spiralized
- 1 red bell pepper, cut into thin strips
- 1 onion, peeled and chopped
- 2 tablespoons lime juice
- ¼ cup fresh cilantro, chopped

Directions:

In a salad bowl, mix the shrimp with chili pepper, zucchini, bell pepper, onion, cilantro, lime juice, salt, pepper and oil, toss and serve cold.

Nutrition Value: Calories - 140, Fat - 3, Fiber - 3, Carbs - 7, Protein - 9

217. Chinese Tuna Steaks

Preparation time: 30 minutes
Cooking time: 11 minutes
Servings: 4

Ingredients:

- ¼ cup orange juice
- 1 garlic clove, peeled and minced
- 1 tablespoon coconut aminos
- 1 tablespoon lemon juice
- 2 tablespoons olive oil
- A pinch of salt and black pepper
- 2 tablespoons fresh parsley, chopped
- 4 medium tuna steaks

Directions:

1. Heat a pan with the oil over medium high heat, add the tuna steaks, season with salt and pepper and cook for 2-3 minutes on each side. Add the garlic, the orange juice,

aminos, lemon juice, salt and pepper, toss gently, cook for 5 minutes more, divide between plates, sprinkle the parsley on top and serve.

Nutrition Value: Calories - 210, Fat - 4, Fiber - 2, Carbs - 5, Protein - 8

218. Mexican Tuna Steaks

Preparation time: 34 minutes
Cooking time: 4 minutes
Servings: 4

Ingredients:

- 4 tuna steaks
- 4 tablespoons olive oil
- 2 green onions, chopped
- 1 cucumber, chopped
- 1 tomato, cored and chopped
- ½ red chili pepper, chopped
- 2 tablespoons fresh parsley, chopped
- 1 tablespoon lemon juice
- A pinch of salt and black pepper

Directions:

1. Put the tuna steaks in a bowl, add the 3 tablespoons olive oil, toss to coat, and set aside for 30 minutes. Heat a kitchen grill pan over medium high heat, add the tuna steaks, cook them for 2 minutes on each side and divide between plates. In a bowl, mix the cucumber with onions, tomato, chili pepper, parsley, lemon juice, salt, pepper and the rest of the oil, toss well, add next to the tuna and serve.

Nutrition Value: Calories - 190, Fat - 4, Fiber - 3, Carbs - 6, Protein - 9

219. Basil Cod Mix

Preparation time: 10 minutes
Cooking time: 20 minutes
Servings: 2

Ingredients:

- 2 medium cod fillets, boneless
- 1 tablespoon basil, chopped

- 2 medium tomatoes, cored and sliced
- 1 tablespoon avocado oil
- A pinch of salt and black pepper

Directions:

1. Put the cod in a baking dish, drizzle the oil all over, add basil, tomatoes, salt and pepper, place in the oven and bake at 375°F for 20 minutes. Divide between plates and serve.

Nutrition Value: Calories - 360, Fat - 4, Fiber - 7, Carbs - 9, Protein - 11

220. Orange and Ginger Salmon

Preparation time: 10 minutes
Cooking time: 10 minutes
Servings: 4

Ingredients:

- Juice of 1 orange
- 2 tablespoons coconut aminos
- 1 tablespoon olive oil
- 2 garlic cloves, peeled and minced
- 4 salmon fillets, boneless
- 1 teaspoon fresh ginger, grated
- A pinch of salt and black pepper
- 1 tablespoon parsley, chopped

Directions:

1. In a bowl, mix the orange juice with the ginger, aminos, oil, garlic, salt and pepper and whisk well. Add the salmon, toss, place the fish on preheated kitchen grill and cook over medium heat for 5 minutes on each side. Divide between plates and serve with a side salad.

Nutrition Value: Calories - 230, Fat - 4, Fiber - 2, Carbs - 6, Protein - 8

221. Salmon Curry

Preparation time: 10 minutes
Cooking time: 15 minutes
Servings: 2

Ingredients:

- 2 medium salmon fillets, skinless, boneless and cubed
- A drizzle of olive oil

- 1 tablespoon fresh basil, chopped
- 1 tablespoon lemon juice
- A pinch of sea salt and black pepper
- 1 cup coconut cream
- 2 teaspoons curry powder
- 1 garlic clove, peeled and minced
- ½ teaspoon fresh parsley, chopped
- ½ teaspoon mint leaves, chopped

Directions:

1. Heat a pan with the oil over medium high heat, add the salmon cubes and cook for 2 minutes on each side. Add the basil, lemon juice, salt, pepper, curry powder, garlic, cream, parsley and mint, toss, cook for 10 minutes more, divide into bowls and serve.

Nutrition Value: Calories - 130, Fat - 3, Fiber - 3, Carbs - 7, Protein - 9

222. Cod and Cucumber Salad

Preparation time: 10 minutes
Cooking time: 8 minutes
Servings: 4

Ingredients:

- 4 medium cod fillets, skinless and boneless
- 1 tablespoon fresh tarragon, chopped
- 3 tablespoons olive oil
- A pinch of salt and black pepper
- 1 small onion, sliced
- 5 cucumbers, sliced
- 2 tablespoons lemon juice

Directions:

1. Heat a pan with 2 tablespoon olive oil over medium high heat, add the cod, season with salt and pepper, cook for 4 minutes on each side and divide between plates. Meanwhile, in a bowl, mix the cucumbers with the rest of the oil, tarragon, salt, pepper, onion and lemon juice, toss, divide next to the cod and serve.

Nutrition Value: Calories - 278, Fat - 10, Fiber - 1, Carbs - 5, Protein - 13

223. Greek Shrimp Mix

Preparation time: 10 minutes
Cooking time: 6 minutes

Servings: 4

Ingredients:

- 1 pound shrimp, deveined and peeled
- 2 teaspoons olive oil
- 6 tablespoons lemon juice
- 3 tablespoons fresh dill, chopped
- 1 tablespoon fresh oregano, chopped
- 2 garlic cloves, peeled and minced
- Ground black pepper, to taste
- ¾ cup coconut cream
- ½ pounds cherry tomatoes

Directions:

1. Heat a pan with the oil over medium high heat, add the shrimp, season with some black pepper and cook for 2 minutes. Add the lemon juice, dill, oregano, garlic, cream and cherry tomatoes, toss, cook for 4 minutes more, divide between plates and serve.

Nutrition Value: Calories - 253, Fat - 6, Fiber - 6, Carbs - 10, Protein - 11

224. Cod Soup

Preparation time: 10 minutes
Cooking time: 16 minutes
Servings: 4

Ingredients:

- 1 carrot, peeled and grated
- 2 sweet potatoes, peeled and cut in half
- 3½ cups vegetable stock
- A pinch of salt and black pepper
- 1 onion, peeled and chopped
- 10 ounces cod fillets, cubed
- 1 tablespoon coconut cream
- 3 tablespoons fresh dill, chopped

Directions:

1. Put the stock in a pot, heat over medium high heat, add the carrot, sweet potatoes, salt, pepper and the onion, stir and cook for 10 minutes. Add the cod, the cream and the dill, cook for 5-6 minutes, ladle into bowls and serve.

225. Salmon Stew

Preparation time: 10 minutes
Cooking time: 30 minutes
Servings: 4

Ingredients:

- 2 tablespoons fresh parsley, chopped
- 2 tomatoes, peeled and grated
- 1 tablespoon lemon juice
- 2 tablespoons fresh cilantro, chopped
- 2 garlic cloves, peeled and minced
- ½ teaspoon sweet paprika
- ½ cup vegetable stock
- A pinch of salt and black pepper
- 4 salmon fillets, boneless, skinless and cubed
- ¼ cup olive oil
- 3 carrots, peeled and sliced
- 1 red bell pepper, seeded and cut into thin strips
- 3 sweet potatoes, peeled and cubed
- ½ cup black olives, pitted and sliced
- 1 onion, sliced

Directions:

1. Heat a pot with the oil over medium high heat, add the garlic and the onion, stir and cook for 2 minutes. Add the tomatoes, paprika, stock, carrots, bell pepper, olives and sweet potatoes, stir and cook for 7-8 minutes more. Add the lemon juice, salmon, salt and pepper, stir and cook for 10 minutes. Add parsley and cilantro, toss, divide into bowls and serve.

Nutrition Value: Calories - 340, Fat - 10, Fiber - 8, Carbs - 23, Protein - 14

226. Tomato and Shrimp Soup

Preparation time: 10 minutes
Cooking time: 12 minutes
Servings: 4

Ingredients:

- 3 cups tomato juice
- 3 jarred roasted red bell peppers, chopped
- 2 tablespoons olive oil
- 2 tablespoons vinegar
- 1 garlic clove, peeled and minced

- A pinch of salt and ground black pepper
- ½ teaspoon cumin
- ¾ pounds shrimp, peeled and deveined
- 1 teaspoon fresh parsley, chopped

Directions:

1. Heat a pot with the oil over high heat, add the shrimp, stir, and cook for 2 minutes. Add the tomato juice, bell peppers, vinegar, garlic, salt, pepper and cumin, stir and simmer over medium heat for 10 minutes. Add the parsley, toss, ladle into bowls and serve.

Nutrition Value: Calories - 200, Fat - 4, Fiber - 10, Carbs - 20, Protein - 14

227. Coconut and Tomato Shrimp Soup

Preparation time: 10 minutes
Cooking time: 20 minutes
Servings: 4

Ingredients:

- 2 pounds tomatoes, cored, seeded, and cut in half
- 3 tablespoons olive oil
- ½ cup onion, diced
- 2 tablespoons tomato paste
- A pinch of salt and black pepper
- ¼ cup coconut cream
- 3 cups vegetable stock
- 1 pound shrimp, peeled, deveined and chopped

Directions:

1. Heat a pot with the oil over medium-high heat, add the onion and tomatoes, stir, and cook for 7 minutes. Add the tomato paste, stock, and salt, and pepper, stir, bring to a boil, reduce heat to medium, and simmer for 10 minutes. Add the cream, blend the soup with an immersion blender, heat everything up over medium low heat, add the shrimp, cook for 3 minutes, ladle into bowls and serve.

Nutrition Value: Calories - 240, Fat - 4, Fiber - 5, Carbs - 8, Protein - 9

228. Shrimp and Bacon Cold Mix

Preparation time: 1 hour
Cooking time: 0 minutes
Servings: 4

Ingredients:

- 4 tomatoes, cored and cut in wedges
- ½ pound shrimp, peeled, deveined, and cooked
- A pinch of salt and black pepper
- 2 spring onions, chopped
- 1 jalapeño, chopped
- 2 garlic cloves, peeled and minced
- ¼ cup lemon juice
- 1 teaspoon lemon zest
- ¼ cup fresh parsley, chopped
- ⅓ cup olive oil
- 5 bacon slices, cooked and crumbled

Directions:

1. In a bowl, mix the shrimp with the tomatoes, spring onions, garlic, jalapeno, salt, pepper, lemon juice, lemon zest, bacon, parsley and oil toss and keep in the fridge for 1 hour before serving.

Nutrition Value: Calories - 200, Fat - 3, Fiber - 4, Carbs - 8, Protein - 10

229. Fish and Veggie Soup

Preparation time: 10 minutes
Cooking time: 30 minutes
Servings: 6

Ingredients:

- 6 tomatoes, peeled and chopped
- 2 tablespoons olive oil
- 1 onion, peeled and chopped
- 2 celery stalks, chopped
- 1 carrot, peeled and chopped
- 1 jalapeño, chopped
- 1 red bell pepper, seeded and chopped
- 2 garlic cloves, peeled and minced
- 3 white fish fillets, skinless, boneless, and cubed
- 4 cups vegetable stock
- A pinch of salt and black pepper
- A drizzle of balsamic vinegar
- ½ cup fresh parsley, chopped

Directions:

1. Heat a pot with the oil over medium-high heat, add the onion, jalapeno and the garlic, stir and cook for 5 minutes. Add the celery, the bell pepper and the carrot, stir and cook for 5 minutes more. Add the tomatoes, the stock, salt and pepper, bring to a simmer, reduce heat to medium and cook everything for 10 minutes. Add the fish, simmer the soup for 8 more minutes. Ladle into bowls, drizzle some vinegar all over and serve with the parsley sprinkled on top.

Nutrition Value: Calories - 240, Fat - 4, Fiber - 4, Carbs - 8, Protein - 12

230. Shrimp and Crab Salad

Preparation time: 10 minutes
Cooking time: 0 minutes
Servings: 6

Ingredients:

- 6 sweet potatoes, peeled, cut into medium-sized chunks and boiled
- 15 ounces shrimp, peeled, deveined, cooked, and chopped
- 4 eggs, hard boiled, peeled and chopped
- 2 shallots, peeled and chopped
- 15 ounces canned crab meat, drained
- 1 tablespoon fresh cilantro, chopped
- 1 tablespoon green onions, chopped
- ½ cup lime juice
- 2 tablespoons coconut cream
- A pinch of salt and black pepper

Directions:

1. In a salad bowl, mix the potatoes with the shrimp, eggs, shallots, crabmeat, cilantro, green onions, lime juice, cream, salt and pepper, toss and serve cold.

Nutrition Value: Calories - 200, Fat - 5, Fiber - 8, Carbs - 10, Protein - 12

231. Salmon Carpaccio and Sauce

Preparation time: 1 day and 10 minutes
Cooking time: 0 minutes
Servings: 4

Ingredients:

For the Carpaccio:

- 1 teaspoon black peppercorns, toasted
- 1 teaspoon white peppercorns, toasted
- A pinch of sea salt
- A drizzle of olive oil
- 1 teaspoon coriander seeds
- 1 pound salmon fillet, thinly sliced
- 1 cup fresh dill, chopped

For the sauce:

2. 1 tablespoon white vinegar
3. 2 tablespoons mustard
4. 3 tablespoons avocado oil
5. A pinch of salt
6. 2 tablespoons fresh dill, chopped

Directions:

1. In a bowl, mix the peppercorns with salt, coriander, oil and 1 cup dill and toss. Rub the salmon with this mix, put in a bowl, cover and keep in the fridge for 24 hours. In a bowl, mix the vinegar with the mustard, oil, salt and 2 tablespoons dill and whisk well. Arrange the salmon slices on a platter, drizzle the sauce all over and serve.

Nutrition Value: Calories - 245, Fat - 7, Fiber - 8, Carbs - 10, Protein - 7

232. Mackerel and Chicory Salad

Preparation time: 15 minutes
Cooking time: 0 minutes
Servings: 8

Ingredients:

- 7 ounces smoked mackerel fillets, skinless, boneless, and flaked
- Juice and zest of ½ lemon
- 4 tablespoons coconut cream
- Ground black pepper, to taste
- A small bunch of chives diced
- 1 radicchio, chopped
- ½ cup fresh dill, chopped
- 2 chicory heads, chopped

Directions:

1. In a bowl, mix the mackerel with lemon juice, lemon zest, chives, radicchio, chicory, dill, black pepper and the cream, toss and serve cold.

Nutrition Value: Calories - 190, Fat - 5, Fiber - 4, Carbs - 8, Protein - 10

233. Spicy Clam Soup

Preparation time: 1 hour
Cooking time: 10 minutes
Servings: 4

Ingredients:

- 2 pounds clams, scrubbed
- 3 cups vegetable stock
- 1 jalapeño pepper, sliced
- 1 garlic clove, peeled and sliced
- 1 red chili pepper, sliced
- ½ scallion sliced thin

Directions:

1. Put the clams in a large bowl, add enough water to cover, set them aside for 1 hour, and then drain. Heat a pot with the stock over medium heat, add the clams, jalapeno, chili, scallion and garlic, toss, cook for 10 minutes, discard unopened clams, ladle the soup into bowls and serve.

Nutrition Value: Calories - 200, Fat - 3, Fiber - 3, Carbs - 7, Protein - 9

234. Shrimp and Bell Pepper Salsa

Preparation time: 10 minutes
Cooking time: 4 minutes
Servings: 4

Ingredients:

- 1 pound shrimp, peeled and deveined
- 2 tablespoons lime juice
- 4 teaspoons coconut aminos
- 1 jalapeño pepper, chopped
- 1 teaspoon fresh ginger, grated
- 1 garlic clove, peeled and minced
- 1 tablespoon olive oil+ a drizzle
- 3 red bell peppers, seeded and cut into strips
- A pinch of salt and black pepper
- 1 tablespoon parsley, chopped

Directions:

1. Heat a pan with 1 tablespoon oil over medium high heat, add the shrimp, season with salt and black pepper, also add the aminos, cook for 2 minutes on each side and divide between plates. In a bowl, mix the bell peppers with lime juice, jalapeno, ginger, garlic, a drizzle of oil and parsley, toss, add next to the shrimp and serve.

Nutrition Value: Calories - 281, Fat - 6, Fiber - 8, Carbs - 10, Protein - 18

235. Rosemary Shrimp Mix

Preparation time: 10 minutes
Cooking time: 10 minutes
Servings: 2

Ingredients:

- 17 ounces shrimp, peeled and deveined
- 4 garlic cloves, peeled and minced
- 2 tablespoons olive oil
- 1 tablespoon rosemary, chopped
- A pinch of salt and black pepper
- 1 tablespoon lime juice
- 2 tomatoes, cored and chopped
- 1 tablespoon parsley, chopped

Directions:

1. Heat a pan with the oil over medium high heat, add the shrimp and cook for 2 minutes on each side. Add the garlic, rosemary, salt, pepper, lime juice, tomatoes and parsley, toss, cook for 5 minutes more, divide into bowls and serve.

Nutrition Value: Calories - 243, Fat - 4, Fiber - 7, Carbs - 12, Protein - 6

236. Fish Soup

Preparation time: 10 minutes
Cooking time: 30 minutes
Servings: 4

Ingredients:

- 9 ounces small fish, without heads
- ½ teaspoon lemon zest
- Juice of ½ lemon
- 3 tablespoons olive oil
- A pinch of salt and black pepper
- 3 cups hot water
- 1 celery stalk, chopped

- 3 tomatoes, cored and chopped
- 2 onions, peeled and chopped
- 2 tablespoons fresh parsley, chopped
- 2 tablespoons fresh cilantro, chopped

Directions:

1. Heat a pot with the water over medium high heat, add lemon zest, lemon juice, salt, pepper and the oil and whisk really well. Add the fish and cook for 15 minutes. Add celery, tomatoes and onions, toss, and cook for 15 minute more, ladle into bowls and serve with parsley and cilantro sprinkled on top.

Nutrition Value: Calories - 200, Fat - 3, Fiber - 5, Carbs - 9, Protein - 10

237. Halibut and Parsley Sauce

Preparation time: 10 minutes
Cooking time: 15 minutes
Servings: 4

Ingredients:

- 1½ pounds halibut boneless, cubed
- ½ teaspoon cumin seeds, ground
- A pinch of salt and black pepper
- ½ teaspoon sweet paprika
- ½ teaspoon coriander seeds
- Juice of ½ lime
- 2 garlic cloves, peeled and minced
- 1 onion, sliced
- 2 tablespoons olive oil
- 1 cup coconut cream
- 1 tablespoon fresh parsley, chopped
- 1 tablespoon fresh dill, chopped
- 1 tablespoon mint leaves, chopped

Directions:

1. Heat a pan with the oil over medium high heat, add coriander seeds, cumin seeds, garlic, onion, salt and pepper, stir and cook for 5 minutes. Add the halibut and the lime juice and cook for 5 minutes more. Add the cream, mint, dill and parsley, toss, cook for another 5 minutes, divide between plates and serve.

Nutrition Value: Calories - 240, Fat - 4, Fiber - 4, Carbs - 8, Protein - 10

238. Cod and Endives Mix

Preparation time: 10 minutes
Cooking time: 20 minutes
Servings: 4

Ingredients:

- 4 cod fillets, skinless and boneless
- A pinch of salt and black pepper
- Juice of 1 small lemon
- 2 endives, shredded
- 1 tablespoon coconut oil, melted
- 1 tablespoon olive oil

Directions:

1. Heat a pan with the coconut oil over medium-high heat, add the endives, salt, pepper and half of the lemon juice, toss, cook them for 10 minutes and divide between plates. Heat another pan with the olive oil over medium high heat, add the cod, salt and pepper, cook for 4 minutes on each side, add next to the endives, drizzle the rest of the lemon juice all over and serve.

Nutrition Value: Calories - 200, Fat - 2, Fiber - 4, Carbs - 7, Protein - 8

239. Shrimp, Tomato and Avocado Mix

Preparation time: 10 minutes
Cooking time: 6 minutes
Servings: 6

Ingredients:

- 1 pound shrimp, deveined and peeled
- A drizzle of olive oil
- 2 cups cherry tomatoes, cut in half
- 1 cucumber, chopped
- 1 avocado, pitted, peeled, and chopped
- ½ cup fresh cilantro, chopped
- A pinch of salt and black pepper
- 2 tablespoon vegetable stock
- 2 tablespoons lime juice
- ½ teaspoon lime zest, grated

Directions:

1. Heat a pan with the oil over medium high heat, add the shrimp, some salt and pepper

and cook for 2 minutes. Add the tomatoes, the cucumber, the avocado, cilantro, stock, lime juice and lime zest, toss, cook for 4 minutes more, divide into bowls and serve.

Nutrition Value: Calories - 156, Fat - 3, Fiber - 5, Carbs - 8, Protein - 12

240. Veggie and Snapper Warm Salad

Preparation time: 10 minutes
Cooking time: 25 minutes
Servings: 2

Ingredients:

- 1 red bell pepper, chopped
- 3 summer squash, peeled and chopped
- 1 baby eggplant, chopped
- ½ sweet potato, chopped
- 1 tablespoon olive oil
- 1 onion, cut into wedges
- 1 teaspoon hot paprika
- 2 teaspoons cumin
- A pinch of salt and ground black pepper
- 2 snapper fillets, boneless and skinless
- 4 cups baby spinach leaves

For the salad dressing:

- 2 tablespoons fresh cilantro, chopped
- ¼ cup lime juice
- ¼ cup coconut oil, melted

Directions:

1. Put the bell peppers in a baking dish, add the squash, eggplant, sweet potato, onion and the olive oil, toss to coat, place in the oven at 400°F, bake for 15 minutes, transfer to a salad bowl, add the spinach and leave aside. Put the snapper in another baking dish, season with salt, pepper, paprika and cumin, bake in the oven at 400°F for 10 minutes, take out of the oven, flake and add it over the veggies. In a bowl, mix the cilantro with salt, pepper, coconut oil, and lime juice, whisk well, add over the salad, toss and serve.

Nutrition Value: Calories - 250, Fat - 4, Fiber - 4, Carbs - 7, Protein - 12

241. Simple Sea Bass Mix

Preparation time: 10 minutes
Cooking time: 12 minutes
Servings: 4

Ingredients:

- 3 garlic cloves, peeled and minced
- 1 pound fresh sea bass, diced
- A pinch of salt and black pepper
- ¼ cup fresh cilantro, chopped
- ¾ cup lime juice
- 1 jalapeño pepper, chopped
- 1 onion, peeled and sliced
- 1 cup cherry tomatoes, cut in half
- 1 tablespoon olive oil
- 1 avocado, pitted, peeled, and chopped

Directions:

1. Heat a pan with the oil over medium high heat, add the sea bass and cook for 4 minutes on each side. Add garlic, salt, pepper, cilantro, lime juice, jalapeno, onion, cherry tomatoes and avocado, toss, cook for 5 minutes more, divide between plates and serve.

Nutrition Value: Calories - 200, Fat - 3, Fiber - 3, Carbs - 7, Protein - 10

242. Sardines with Tapenade

Preparation time: 10 minutes
Cooking time: 10 minutes
Servings: 4

Ingredients:

For the olive tapenade:

- 1 tablespoon lemon, chopped
- 3 garlic cloves, peeled and minced
- 1 cup green olives, pitted and chopped
- 1 shallot, peeled and chopped
- 2 teaspoons lemon juice
- 1 teaspoon red pepper flakes
- 3 tablespoons fresh parsley, chopped
- 1 cup olive oil
- 3 tablespoons fresh chives, minced
- 3 tablespoons fresh thyme, chopped

For the sardines:

- 12 fresh sardines
- 2 tablespoons olive oil

- ½ bunch fresh parsley, chopped
- 2 garlic cloves, peeled and minced
- 1 cup frisee
- 2 radishes, shaved

Directions:

1. In a bowl, mix the olives with the lemon, garlic, shallot, lemon juice, pepper flakes, parsley, 1 cup oil, chives and thyme and whisk well. Spread this over the sardines, toss well, put them on your preheated kitchen grill and cook for 5 minutes on each side over medium high heat. In a bowl, mix the radishes with the frisee, 2 garlic cloves, ½ bunch parsley and 2 tablespoons oil and toss well. Divide this between plates, top with the sardines and serve.

Nutrition Value: Calories - 300, Fat - 5, Fiber - 9, Carbs - 8, Protein - 12

243. Shrimp and Veggie Salad

Preparation time: 10 minutes
Cooking time: 6 minutes
Servings: 4

Ingredients:

- 1 pound shrimp, peeled and deveined
- 8 Kalamata olives, pitted and chopped
- 1 tablespoon capers, chopped
- 3 tablespoons balsamic vinegar
- A pinch of salt and black pepper
- 3 tablespoons olive oil
- 3 tomatoes, cored and chopped
- ¼ cup onion, chopped
- ¼ cup fresh basil, chopped

Directions:

1. Heat a pan with the oil over medium high heat, add the shrimp, salt and pepper and cook for 2 minutes. Add the olives, capers, vinegar, tomatoes, onion and basil, toss a bit, cook for 3-4 minutes more, divide between plates and serve warm.

Nutrition Value: Calories - 190, Fat - 4, Fiber - 7, Carbs - 8, Protein - 9

244. Greek Sardine Salad

Preparation time: 10 minutes
Cooking time: 0 minutes
Servings: 4

Ingredients:

- 3 tablespoons lime juice
- 2 tablespoons olive oil
- 2 teaspoons dried basil
- 1 garlic clove, peeled and minced
- A pinch of ground black pepper
- 3 tomatoes, cored and cut into chunks
- ¼ cup onion, sliced
- 2 tablespoons Kalamata olives, pitted, peeled, and sliced
- 8 ounces canned sardines, drained

Directions:

1. In a bowl, mix the sardines with black pepper, oil, lime juice, basil, garlic, tomatoes, onion and olives, toss and serve cold.

Nutrition Value: Calories - 140, Fat - 1, Fiber - 3, Carbs - 7, Protein - 9

245. Fish, Shrimp and Veggie Soup

Preparation time: 10 minutes
Cooking time: 4 hours
Servings: 4

Ingredients:

- 1 onion, peeled and chopped
- 2 garlic cloves, peeled and minced
- 14 ounces canned diced tomatoes
- 28 ounces vegetable stock
- 8 ounces canned tomato sauce
- 2½ ounces mushrooms, sliced
- ¼ cup black olives, pitted and sliced
- ½ cup orange juice
- 1 teaspoon dried basil
- ¼ teaspoon fennel seeds, crushed
- A pinch of ground black pepper
- 1 pound shrimp, deveined and peeled
- 1 pound cod fillets, skinless, boneless, and cubed

Directions:

1. In your Crockpot, mix the onion with the garlic, tomatoes, stock, tomato sauce, mushrooms, olives, orange juice, basil, fennel and black pepper, cover and cook on Low for 3 hours and 30 minutes. Add the shrimp and the cod, cover, cook on Low for 30 minutes more, ladle into bowls and serve.

Nutrition Value: Calories - 230, Fat - 4, Fiber - 5, Carbs - 7, Protein - 10

246. Herbed Shrimp Mix

Preparation time: 10 minutes
Cooking time: 6 minutes
Servings: 4

Ingredients:

- ⅓ cup lemon juice
- 1 teaspoon lemon zest
- 3 tablespoons olive oil
- 2 tablespoons fresh oregano, chopped
- 2 tablespoons fresh sage, chopped
- 2 tablespoons fresh chives, minced
- A pinch of salt and black pepper
- 12 cherry tomatoes, cut in half
- 1 cup celery, chopped
- 1 pound shrimp, peeled and deveined

Directions:

2. Heat a pan with the oil over medium high heat, add the shrimp, salt and pepper, toss and cook for 2 minutes. Add the lemon juice, lemon zest, sage, oregano, chives, tomatoes and celery, toss, cook for 4 minutes more, divide into bowls and serve.

Nutrition Value: Calories - 150, Fat - 3, Fiber - 4, Carbs - 7, Protein - 8

247. Asian Shrimp Salad

Preparation time: 10 minutes
Cooking time: 20 minutes
Servings: 4

Ingredients:

- 2 pounds Asian eggplants
- ¼ pound shrimp, peeled, deveined, and poached
- 4 eggs, hard boiled, peeled and cut into

quarters
- 2 shallots, peeled and sliced
- 2 tablespoons coconut aminos
- 3 tablespoons lime juice
- 1 tablespoon parsley, chopped
- 3 Serrano chilies, sliced

Directions:

1. Arrange the eggplants on a lined baking dish, place in the oven, and bake at 450 ° F for about 20 minutes. Allow to cool, peel, cut into medium chunks, and transfer to a bowl. Add shrimp, eggs, shallots, aminos, lime juice, chilies and the parsley, toss and serve.

Nutrition Value: Calories - 200, Fat - 5, Fiber - 7, Carbs - 10, Protein - 12

248. Cod and Mustard Sauce

Preparation time: 10 minutes
Cooking time: 20 minutes
Servings: 4

Ingredients:

- ¼ cup olive oil+ 2 tablespoons
- 4 medium cod fillets, skinless and boneless
- 2 garlic cloves, peeled and minced
- A pinch of salt and black pepper
- 1 tablespoon fresh cilantro, minced
- 1 teaspoon Dijon mustard
- 1 shallot, peeled and chopped
- 2 tablespoons lemon juice

Directions:

1. Heat a pan with 2 tablespoons oil over medium-high heat, add the fish, season with salt and pepper, cook for 4 minutes on each side and transfer to a baking dish. In a bowl, mix the rest of the oil with the garlic, salt, pepper, cilantro, mustard, shallot and lime juice, whisk well, pour over the fish, bake in the oven at 425°F for 10 minutes, divide between plates, and serve.

Nutrition Value: Calories - 145, Fat - 2, Fiber - 1, Carbs - 10, Protein - 16

249. Salmon and Quinoa Salad

Preparation time: ten mins

Cooking time: 10 minutes

Servings: 1

Ingredients:

- 1 medium salmon fillet, boneless
- 1 teaspoon essential olive oil
- A pinch of black pepper
- Cooking spray
- 1 and ½ cups kale, chopped
- ½ cup quinoa, already cooked
- 1 tablespoon freshly squeezed freshly squeezed lemon juice
- 5 red grapes, halved

Directions:

1. 1.Put the salmon inside a very baking dish greased with cooking spray, drizzle the oil within the fish, season with black pepper and bake inside oven at 425 degrees F for ten mins.
2. 2.Meanwhile, in a very bowl, combine the quinoa with all the grapes, kale and lemon juice and toss well.
3. 3.Arrange the salmon on the plate, add the quinoa salad all-around it and serve.
4. Enjoy!

Nutrition Value: calories 261, fat 5, fiber 7, carbs 10, protein 15

250. Salmon and Horseradish Sauce

Preparation time: ten mins

Cooking time: 10 mins

Servings: 4

Ingredients:

- 1 and ½ tablespoons organic olive oil
- 4 medium salmon fillets, boneless and skin-on
- ½ cup coconut cream
- A pinch of black pepper
- 2 tablespoons dill, chopped
- 1 tablespoon prepared horseradish

Directions:

1. 1.Heat up a pan while using the oil over medium-high heat, add salmon fillets, season with black pepper and cook for 5

minutes one each side.

2. 2.In a bowl, combine the cream with the dill and horseradish and whisk well.
3. 3.Divide the salmon between plates and serve with all the horseradish cream for the top.
4. Enjoy!

Nutrition Value: calories 275, fat 12, fiber 4, carbs 14, protein 27

251. Tuna Salad

Preparation time: ten mins

Cooking time: 0 minutes

Servings: 2

Ingredients:

- 2 teaspoons extra virgin essential olive oil
- 1 teaspoon red vinegar
- ½ teaspoon fresh lemon juice
- ½ teaspoon mustard
- A pinch of black pepper
- ½ cup already cooked quinoa
- ¼ cup canned chickpeas, no-salt-added, drained and rinsed
- ¼ cup cucumber, chopped
- 5 cherry tomatoes, halved
- 5 ounces white tuna canned in water, drained
- 1 tablespoon low-fat cheese, crumbled

Directions:

1. 1.In a salad bowl, combine the quinoa with chickpeas, cucumber, tomatoes, tuna and cheese and toss.
2. 2.Add black pepper, oil, vinegar, fresh freshly squeezed lemon juice and mustard, toss well and serve.
3. Enjoy!

Nutrition Value: calories 241, fat 4, fiber 5, carbs 12, protein 14

252. Cod and Tasty Relish

Preparation time: 10 mins

Cooking time: ten mins

Servings: 4

Ingredients:

- 1 and ½ tablespoons oregano, chopped

- 1 cup peas
- 2 tablespoons shallots, chopped
- 2 tablespoons lime juice
- 2 tablespoons capers
- 3 tablespoons essential olive oil
- A pinch of black pepper
- 4 medium cod fillets, boneless

Directions:

1. 1.Heat up a pan with 1 tablespoon oil over medium-high heat, add the cod fillets, cook for 5 minutes on them and divide between plates.
2. 2.In a bowl, combine the oregano while using peas, shallots, lime juice, capers, black pepper along with a couple of tablespoons oil and toss well.
3. 3.Divide this next for the cod and serve.
4. Enjoy!

Nutrition Value: calories 221, fat 11, fiber 3, carbs 8, protein 20

253. Smoked Salmon Mix

Preparation time: ten mins
Cooking time: 0 minutes
Servings: 4

Ingredients:

- 2 tablespoons dill, chopped
- 1 teaspoons lemon zest, grated
- 8 ounces low-fat cream cheese
- A pinch of black pepper
- 1 pound smoked salmon, flaked
- 7 ounces cucumber, sliced
- ¼ cup shallot, chopped
- 2 tablespoons mint, chopped

Directions:

1. 1.In a bowl, combine the dill with lemon zest, cream cheese, black pepper, salmon, cucumber, shallot and mint and toss well.
2. 2.Serve cold with whole wheat grains bread slices.
3. Enjoy!

Nutrition Value: calories 277, fat 4, fiber 6, carbs 15, protein 15

254. Halibut and Kale Pesto

Preparation time: ten mins
Cooking time: 6 minutes
Servings: 4

Ingredients:

- 2 tablespoons almonds, chopped
- 2 garlic cloves
- 4 cups kale, torn
- ½ cup organic essential olive oil+1 tablespoon
- ¼ cup low-fat parmesan, grated
- 2 tablespoons fresh lemon juice
- A pinch of black pepper
- 4 halibut fillets
- 1 pound cherry tomatoes, halved

Directions:

1. 1.In a blender, combine the almonds using the garlic, kale, ½ cup oil, freshly squeezed fresh lemon juice and parmesan and pulse well.
2. 2.Heat up a pan with 1 tablespoon oil over medium-high heat, add the fish, season with black pepper, cook for 3 minutes on each side and divide between plates
3. 3.Serve with all the cherry tomatoes quietly and using the kale pesto on the top.
4. Enjoy!

Nutrition Value: calories 261, fat 4, fiber 7, carbs 14, protein 14

255. Simple Grilled Tilapia

Preparation time: ten mins
Cooking time: 8 minutes
Servings: 4

Ingredients:

- 1 and ½ tablespoons extra virgin extra virgin olive oil
- 1 teaspoon smoked paprika
- ½ teaspoon garlic powder
- A pinch of black pepper
- 4 medium tilapia fillets

Directions:

1. 1.Heat up a pan while using oil over medium-high heat, season the fish with paprika, garlic powder and black pepper, add it for the pan, cook for 4 minutes on

them, divide between plates and serve employing a side salad.
2. Enjoy!

Nutrition Value: calories 222, fat 4, fiber 4, carbs 14, protein 25

256. Delicious Arctic Char

Preparation time: ten mins
Cooking time: 8 minutes
Servings: 4

Ingredients:

- 1 cup orange segments
- 1 tablespoon parsley, chopped
- 2 tablespoons red onions, chopped
- 1 tablespoon capers, chopped
- 1 teaspoon orange zest, grated
- 1 tablespoon orange juice
- 1 tablespoon organic olive oil
- 1 teaspoon balsamic vinegar
- A pinch of black pepper
- Cooking spray
- 4 arctic char fillets

Directions:

1. 1.Grease a pan with cooking spray, add fish fillets, season with black pepper, cook for 4 minutes on both sides and divide between plates.
2. 2.In a bowl, combine the orange with parsley, onions, capers, orange zest, orange juice, oil and vinegar and toss well.
3. 3.Divide this ahead from your fish fillets and serve.
4. Enjoy!

Nutrition Value: calories 231, fat 12, fiber 3, carbs 8, protein 14

257. Tasty Halibut and Cherry Tomatoes

Preparation time: ten mins
Cooking time: 13 minutes
Servings: 4

Ingredients:

- 1 and ½ tablespoon organic olive oil
- 4 halibut fillets, skinless
- 2 cups cherry tomatoes

- A pinch of black pepper
- 3 garlic cloves, minced
- 2 tablespoons balsamic vinegar
- 2 tablespoons basil, chopped

Directions:

1. 1.Heat up a pan with 1 tablespoon organic essential olive oil, add halibut fillets, cook them for 5 minutes on both sides and divide between plates.
2. 2.Heat up another pan because of the rest within the oil over medium-high heat, add the tomatoes, garlic, vinegar and basil, toss, cook for 3 minutes, add next on the fish and serve.
3. Enjoy!

Nutrition Value: calories 221, fat 4 fiber 1, carbs 6, protein 21

258. Salmon and Sauce

Preparation time: ten mins
Cooking time: 10 mins
Servings: 4

Ingredients:

- 1 and ½ tablespoons avocado mayonnaise
- 3 tablespoons non-fat yogurt
- 1 and ½ tablespoons mustard
- 2 tablespoons dill, chopped
- 2 tablespoons fresh lemon juice
- A pinch of black pepper
- 1 garlic herb minced
- 4 salmon fillets, boneless
- Cooking spray

Directions:

1. 1.Grease a baking dish with cooking spray, arrange the salmon fillets inside dish and season all of them black pepper.
2. 2.In a bowl, combine the mayo with the yogurt, mustard, dill, freshly squeezed lemon juice, black pepper, whisk, pour around the fish, introduce within the oven and cook at 425 degrees F for ten mins.
3. 3.Divide everything between plates and serve.
4. Enjoy!

Nutrition Value: calories 261, fat 12, fiber 3, carbs

8, protein 16

259. Arctic Char and Cucumber Relish

Preparation time: 10 mins
Cooking time: 6 minutes
Servings: 2

Ingredients:

- ¾ cup cucumber, chopped
- ¼ cup shallots, chopped
- 1 tablespoon cilantro, chopped
- 2 teaspoons mint, chopped
- 2 teaspoons fresh lemon juice
- ½ teaspoon mustard
- A pinch of black pepper
- 1 tablespoon extra virgin extra virgin olive oil
- 2 arctic char fillets

Directions:

1. 1.Season the fish with black pepper, drizzle the oil, position them in a very baking dish, introduce inside the oven and bake at 425 degrees F for 6 minutes.
2. 2.In a bowl, combine the cucumber with all the shallots, cilantro, mint, lemon juice and mustard, toss well, add next for the fish and serve.
3. Enjoy!

Nutrition Value: calories 231, fat 3, fiber 6, carbs 9, protein 22

260. Soft Parsley Salmon

Preparation time: 10 mins
Cooking time: quarter-hour
Servings: 6

Ingredients:

- 3 tablespoons organic olive oil
- 3 tablespoons mustard
- 5 teaspoons stevia
- ½ cup whole wheat grains breadcrumbs
- ½ cup pecans, chopped
- 6 salmon fillets, boneless
- 2 tablespoons parsley, chopped
- Black pepper towards the taste

Directions:

1. 1.In a bowl, mix mustard with oil and stevia and whisk.
2. 2.In another bowl, mix pecans with parsley and breadcrumbs.
3. 3.Season salmon fillets with black pepper for your taste, put in the baking dish brush with mustard mixture, top with breadcrumbs mix, introduce inside the oven and bake at 400 degrees F for quarter-hour.
4. 4.Divide between plates and serve by using a side salad.
5. Enjoy!

Nutrition Value: calories 230, fat 4, fiber 2, carbs 14, protein 12
Salmon and Cauliflower Mix

261. Preparation time: ten mins

Cooking time: twenty minutes
Servings: 4

- Ingredients:
- ¼ cup coconut sugar
- 2 tablespoons coconut aminos
- 1 cauliflower head, florets separated
- 4 salmon fillets, boneless
- 1 big red onion, cut into wedges
- 2 tablespoons olive oil
- Black pepper to the taste

Directions:

1.In a smaller bowl, mix sugar with coconut aminos and whisk.

2.Heat up a pan with half the oil over medium-high heat, add cauliflower and onion, stir and cook for 10 mins.

3.Put the salmon inside baking dish, drizzle the remainder inside oil, add coconut aminos, toss somewhat, season with black pepper, introduce within the oven and bake at 400 degrees F for 10 minutes.

4.Divide the salmon along using the cauliflower mix between plates and serve.

Enjoy!

Nutrition Value: calories 220, fat 3, fiber 3, carbs 12, protein 9

262. Salmon and Peaches Mix

Preparation time: ten mins

Cooking time: 10 minutes

Servings: 4

Ingredients:

- 1 tablespoon balsamic vinegar
- 1 teaspoon thyme, chopped
- 1 tablespoon ginger, grated
- 4 tablespoons extra virgin olive oil
- Black pepper about the taste
- 2 red onions, cut into wedges
- 3 peaches cut into wedges
- 4 salmon steaks

Directions:

1. 1.In a small bowl, combine vinegar with ginger, thyme, 3 tablespoons essential olive oil and black pepper and whisk
2. 2.In another bowl, mix onion with peaches, 1 tablespoon oil and pepper and toss.
3. 3.Season salmon with black pepper, place on preheated grill over medium heat, cook for 5 minutes on either side and divide between plates.
4. 4.Put the peaches and onions about the same grill, cook for 4 minutes on either side, divide next on the salmon, drizzle the vinegar mix and serve.
5. Enjoy!

Nutrition Value: calories 200, fat 2, fiber 2, carbs 3, protein 2

263. Salmon and Beans Mix

Preparation time: 10 mins

Cooking time: 20 min

Servings: 4

Ingredients:

- 2 tablespoons coconut aminos
- ½ cup essential olive oil
- 1 and ½ cup low-sodium chicken stock
- 6 ounces salmon fillets
- 2 garlic cloves, minced
- 1 tablespoon ginger, grated
- 1 cup canned black beans, no-salt-added, drained and rinsed
- 2 teaspoons balsamic vinegar
- ¼ cup radishes, grated

- ¼ cup carrots, grated
- ¼ cup scallions, chopped

Directions:

1. 1.In a bowl, combine the aminos with 50 % of the oil and whisk.
2. 2.Put the salmon in a very baking dish, pour add coconut aminos and the stock, toss a lttle bit, leave aside inside fridge for ten mins, introduce in preheated broiler and cook over medium-high heat for 4 minutes on either side.
3. 3.Heat up a pan using the rest inside the oil over medium heat, add garlic, ginger and black beans, stir and cook for 3 minutes.
4. 4.Add vinegar, radishes, carrots and scallions, toss and cook for 5 minutes more.
5. 5.Divide fish also as the black beans mix between plates and serve.
6. Enjoy!

Nutrition Value: calories 220, fat 4, fiber 2, carbs 12, protein 7

264. Salmon and Pomegranate Mix

Preparation time: twenty minutes

Cooking time: ten mins

Servings: 4

Ingredients:

- 1 tablespoon organic essential olive oil
- 4 salmon fillets, skinless and boneless
- 4 tablespoons sesame paste
- Juice of a single lemon
- 1 lemon, cut into wedges
- ½ cucumber, chopped
- Seeds from 1 pomegranate
- A few parsley, chopped

Directions:

1. 1.Heat up a pan with all the oil over medium heat, add salmon, cook for 5 minutes on them and divide between plates
2. 2.In a bowl, mix sesame paste and freshly squeezed freshly squeezed lemon juice and whisk.
3. 3.Add cucumber, parsley and pomegranate seeds and toss

4. 4.Divide this around the salmon and serve..
5. Enjoy!

Nutrition Value: calories 254, fat 3, fiber 6, carbs 9, protein 14

265. Salmon and Veggie Mix

Preparation time: 10 mins
Cooking time: thirty minutes
Servings: 6

Ingredients:

- 3 red onions, cut into wedges
- ¾ cup green olives, pitted
- 3 red sweet peppers, cut into strips
- ½ teaspoon smoked paprika
- Black pepper on the taste
- 5 tablespoons extra virgin essential olive oil
- 6 salmon fillets, skinless and boneless
- 2 tablespoons parsley, chopped

Directions:

1. 1.Spread sweet peppers, onions and olives on a lined baking sheet, add smoked paprika, black pepper and 3 tablespoons organic organic olive oil, toss to coat, bake inside oven at 375 degrees F for fifteen minutes and divide between plates.
2. 2.Heat up a pan using the rest within the oil over medium-high heat, add the salmon, season with black pepper, cook for 5 minutes on either sides, divide next towards the peppers and olives mix, sprinkle parsley around the top and serve.
3. Enjoy!

Nutrition Value: calories 221, fat 2, fiber 3, carbs 8, protein 10

266. Greek Salmon

Preparation time: ten mins
Cooking time: quarter-hour
Servings: 4

Ingredients:

- 4 medium salmon fillets, skinless and boneless
- 1 fennel bulb, chopped
- Black pepper to the taste
- ¼ cup low-sodium veggie stock

- 1 cup non-fat yogurt
- ¼ cup green olives pitted and chopped
- ¼ cup chives, chopped
- 1 tablespoon extra virgin olive oil
- 1 tablespoon lemon juice

Directions:

1. 1.Arrange the fennel in the baking dish, add salmon fillets, season with black pepper, add stock, bake inside oven at 390 degrees F for 10 minutes and divide everything between plates.
2. 2.In a bowl, mix yogurt with chives, olives, freshly squeezed lemon juice, olive oil and black pepper and whisk well.
3. 3.Top the salmon with this particular mix and serve.
4. Enjoy!

Nutrition Value: calories 252, fat 2, fiber 4, carbs 12, protein 9

267. Creamy Salmon and Asparagus Mix

Preparation time: ten mins
Cooking time: ten mins
Servings: 6

Ingredients:

- 1 tablespoon lemon zest, grated
- 1 tablespoon fresh fresh lemon juice
- Black pepper for the taste
- 1 cup coconut cream
- 1 pound asparagus, trimmed
- 20 ounces salmon, skinless and boneless
- 1-ounce mozzarella, grated

Directions:

1. 1.Put some water in the pot, put in a very pinch of salt, bring to your boil over medium heat, add asparagus, cook for 1 minute, transfer for a bowl filled up with ice water, drain and hang up in the bowl.
2. 2.Heat inside pot with the water again over medium heat, add salmon, cook for 5 minutes and in addition drain.
3. 3.In a bowl, mix lemon peel with cream and lemon juice and whisk
4. 4.Heat up a pan over medium-high heat, asparagus, cream and pepper, cook for 1

more minute, divide between plates, add salmon and serve with grated parmesan.

5. Enjoy!

Nutrition Value: calories 354, fat 2, fiber 2, carbs 2, protein 4

268. Easy Salmon and Brussels sprouts

Preparation time: 10 minutes
Cooking time: 20 mins
Servings: 6

Ingredients:

- 2 tablespoons brown sugar
- 1 teaspoon onion powder
- 1 teaspoon garlic powder
- 1 teaspoon smoked paprika
- 3 tablespoons extra virgin extra virgin olive oil
- 1 and ¼ pounds Brussels sprouts, halved
- 6 medium salmon fillets, boneless

Directions:

1. 1.In a bowl, mix sugar with onion powder, garlic powder, smoked paprika as well as a number of tablespoon olive oil and whisk well.
2. 2.Spread Brussels sprouts about the lined baking sheet, drizzle the rest in the essential extra virgin olive oil, toss to coat, introduce in the oven at 450 degrees F and bake for 5 minutes.
3. 3.Add salmon fillets brush with sugar mix you've prepared, introduce inside the oven and bake for 15 minutes more.
4. 4.Divide everything between plates and serve.
5. Enjoy!

Nutrition Value: calories 212, fat 5, fiber 3, carbs 12, protein 8

269. Salmon and Beets Mix

Preparation time: 10 mins
Cooking time: 35 minutes
Servings: 4

Ingredients:

- 1 pound medium beets, sliced
- 6 tablespoons essential extra virgin olive oil

- 1 and ½ pounds salmon fillets, skinless and boneless
- Black pepper for the taste
- 1 tablespoon chives, chopped
- 1 tablespoon parsley, chopped
- 3 tablespoon shallots, chopped
- 1 tablespoon lemon zest, grated
- ¼ cup freshly squeezed fresh lemon juice

Directions:

1. 1.In a bowl, mix beets with ½ tablespoon oil and toss to coat, season with black pepper, spread on the lined baking sheet and bake inside oven at 450 degrees F for twenty or so minutes.
2. 2.Add salmon, brush it with the rest in the oil, introduce inside the oven and bake for quarter-hour more.
3. 3.In a bowl, combine the chives with all the parsley, shallots, lemon zest and lemon juice and toss.
4. 4.Divide the salmon as well as the beets between plates, drizzle the chives mix around the top and serve.
5. Enjoy!

Nutrition Value: calories 272, fat 6, fiber 2, carbs 12, protein 9

270. Fresh Shrimp Mix

Preparation time: 10 mins
Cooking time: 10 minutes
Servings: 4
Ingredients:

- 1 pound shrimp, deveined and peeled
- 2 teaspoons organic essential olive oil
- 6 tablespoons lemon juice
- 3 tablespoons dill, chopped
- 1 tablespoon oregano, chopped
- 2 garlic cloves, chopped
- Black pepper towards the taste
- ¾ cup non-fat yogurt
- ½ pounds cherry tomatoes, halved

Directions:

1. 1.Heat up a pan with all the oil over medium-high heat, add the shrimp and cook for 3 minutes.
2. 2.Add fresh fresh lemon juice, dill,

oregano, garlic, black pepper, yogurt and
tomatoes, toss, cook for 5 minutes more,
divide into bowls and serve.

3. Enjoy!

**Nutrition Value: calories 253, fat 6, fiber 6, carbs
10, protein 17**

271. Salmon and Potatoes Mix

Preparation time: 10 minutes
Cooking time: 10 mins
Servings: 4

Ingredients:

- 1 and ½ pounds potatoes, chopped
- 1 tablespoon essential essential olive oil
- 4 ounces smoked salmon, chopped
- 1 tablespoon chives, chopped
- 2 teaspoons prepared horseradish
- ¼ cup coconut cream
- Black pepper for the taste

Directions:

1. 4   Heat up a pan using the oil over
medium heat, add potatoes and cook for 10
mins.
2. 5   Add salmon, chives, horseradish,
cream and black pepper, toss, cook for 1
minute more, divide between plates and
serve.
3. Enjoy!

**Nutrition Value: calories 233, fat 6, fiber 5, carbs
9, protein 11**

272. Cod Salad

Preparation time: 12 minutes
Cooking time: 12 minutes
Servings: 4

Ingredients:

- 4 medium cod fillets, skinless and boneless
- 2 tablespoons mustard
- 1 tablespoon tarragon, chopped
- 1 tablespoon capers, drained
- 4 tablespoons extra virgin olive oil+ 1
teaspoon
- Black pepper to the taste
- 2 cups baby arugula
- 1 small red onion, sliced

- 1 small cucumber, sliced
- 2 tablespoons freshly squeezed freshly
squeezed lemon juice

Directions:

1. 4   In a bowl, mix mustard with 2
tablespoons extra virgin olive oil, tarragon
and capers and whisk.
2. 5   Heat up a pan with 1 teaspoon oil
over medium-high heat, add fish, season
with black pepper towards taste, cook for 6
minutes on both sides and cut into medium
cubes.
3. 6   In a salad bowl, combine the arugula
with onion, cucumber, fresh lemon juice,
cod and mustard mix, toss and serve.
4. Enjoy!

**Nutrition Value: calories 258, fat 12, fiber 6, carbs
12, protein 18**

273. Cheesy Shrimp Mix

Preparation time: 10 minutes
Cooking time: half an hour
Servings: 10

Ingredients:

- ½ pound shrimp, already peeled and
deveined
- 1 cup avocado mayonnaise
- ½ cup low-fat mozzarella cheese, shredded
- 3 garlic cloves, minced
- ¼ teaspoon hot sauce
- 1 tablespoon freshly squeezed lemon juice
- A drizzle of essential organic olive oil
- ½ cup scallions, sliced

Directions:

1. 1.In a bowl, mix mozzarella with mayo, hot
sauce, garlic and freshly squeezed lemon
juice and whisk well.
2. 2.Add scallions and shrimp, toss, pour into
a baking dish greased with all the olive oil,
introduce inside oven at 350 degrees F and
bake for thirty minutes.
3. 3.Divide into bowls and serve.
4. Enjoy!

**Nutrition Value: calories 275, fat 3, fiber 5, carbs
10, protein 12**

274. Smoked Salmon and Radishes

Preparation time: ten mins
Cooking time: 0 minutes
Servings: 8

Ingredients:

- 3 tablespoons beet horseradish, prepared
- 1 pound smoked salmon, skinless, boneless and flaked
- 2 teaspoons lemon zest, grated
- 4 radishes, chopped
- ½ cup capers, drained and chopped
- 1/3 cup red onion, roughly chopped
- 3 tablespoons chives, chopped

Directions:

1. 1.In a bowl, combine the salmon while using the beet horseradish, lemon zest, radish, capers, onions and chives, toss and serve cold.
2. Enjoy!

Nutrition Value: calories 254, fat 2, fiber 1, carbs 7, protein 7

275. Trout Spread

Preparation time: ten mins
Cooking time: 0 minutes
Servings: 8

Ingredients:

- 4 ounces smoked trout, skinless, boneless and flaked
- ¼ cup coconut cream
- 1 tablespoon freshly squeezed lemon juice
- 1/3 cup non-fat yogurt
- 1 and ½ tablespoon parsley, chopped
- 3 tablespoons chives, chopped
- Black pepper for your taste
- A drizzle of organic essential olive oil

Directions:

1. 1.In a bowl mix trout with yogurt, cream, black pepper, chives, fresh freshly squeezed lemon juice along with the dill and stir.
2. 2.Drizzle the organic essential olive oil at the conclusion and serve.
3. Enjoy!

Nutrition Value: calories 204, fat 2, fiber 2, carbs 8, protein 15

276. Shrimp and Mango Mix

Preparation time: ten mins
Cooking time: 0 minutes
Servings: 4

Ingredients:

- 3 tablespoons balsamic vinegar
- 3 tablespoons coconut sugar
- 6 tablespoons avocado mayonnaise
- 3 mangos, peeled and cubed
- 3 tablespoons parsley, finely chopped
- 1 pound shrimp, peeled, deveined and cooked

Directions:

1. 1.In a bowl, mix vinegar with sugar and mayo and whisk.
2. 2.In another bowl, combine the mango with the parsley and shrimp, add the mayo mix, toss and serve.
3. Enjoy!

Nutrition Value: calories 204, fat 3, fiber 2, carbs 8, protein 8

277. Spring Salmon Mix

Preparation time: ten mins
Cooking time: 0 minutes
Servings: 4

Ingredients:

- 2 tablespoons scallions, chopped
- 2 tablespoons sweet onion, chopped
- 1 and ½ teaspoons lime juice
- 1 tablespoon chives, minced
- 1 tablespoon essential extra virgin olive oil
- 1 pound smoked salmon, flaked
- 1 cup cherry tomatoes, halved
- Black pepper for the taste
- 1 tablespoon parsley, chopped

Directions:

1. 1.In a bowl, mix the scallions with sweet onion, lime juice, chives, oil, salmon, tomatoes, black pepper and parsley, toss and serve.

2. Enjoy!

Nutrition Value: calories 200, fat 8, fiber 3, carbs 8, protein 6

278. Salmon and Green Beans Mix

Preparation time: ten mins
Cooking time: 0 minutes
Servings: 4

Ingredients:

- 3 tablespoons balsamic vinegar
- 2 tablespoons organic extra virgin olive oil
- 1/3 cup kalamata olives, pitted and minced
- 1 garlic oil, minced
- Black pepper towards the taste
- ½ teaspoon lemon zest, grated
- 1 pound green beans, blanched and halved
- ½ pound cherry tomatoes, halved
- ½ fennel bulb, sliced
- ½ red onion, sliced
- 2 cups baby arugula
- ¾ pound smoked salmon, flaked

Directions:

1. 1.In a bowl, combine the green beans with cherry tomatoes, fennel, onion, arugula and salmon and toss.
2. 2.Add vinegar, oil, olives, garlic, black pepper and lemon zest, toss and serve.
3. Enjoy!

Nutrition Value: calories 212, fat 3, fiber 3, carbs 6, protein 4

279. Saffron Shrimp

Preparation time: 10 minutes
Cooking time: 30 mins
Servings: 4

Ingredients:

- 1 teaspoon fresh lemon juice
- Black pepper for the taste
- ½ cup avocado mayo
- ½ teaspoon sweet paprika
- 3 tablespoons organic essential olive oil
- 1 fennel bulb, chopped
- 1 yellow onion, chopped
- 2 garlic cloves, minced

- 1 cup canned tomatoes, no-salt-added and chopped
- 1 and ½ pounds big shrimp, peeled and deveined
- ¼ teaspoon saffron powder

Directions:

1. 1.In a bowl, combine the garlic with freshly squeezed lemon juice, black pepper, mayo and paprika and whisk.
2. 2.Add the shrimp and toss.
3. 3.Heat up a pan while using the oil over medium-high heat, add the shrimp, fennel, onion and garlic mix, toss and cook for 4 minutes.
4. 4.Add tomatoes and saffron, toss, divide into bowls and serve.
5. Enjoy!

Nutrition Value: calories 210, fat 2, fiber 5, carbs 8, protein 4

280. Chicken and Radish Mix

Preparation time: 10 minutes
Cooking time: 30 minutes
Servings: 4

Ingredients:

- 8 chicken thighs
- A pinch of salt and black pepper
- 1 tablespoon olive oil
- 1 cup vegetable stock
- 12 radishes, cut in half
- 1 tablespoon parsley, chopped
- 2 tablespoon fresh chives, minced

Directions:

1. Heat a pot with the oil over medium-high heat, add the chicken, salt, and pepper, stir, and brown for 5 minutes on each side. Add the stock, radishes and chives, stir, reduce heat to medium, cover, and simmer for 20 minutes. Divide between plates and serve with the parsley sprinkled on top.

Nutrition Value: Calories - 187, Fat - 10, Fiber - 3, Carbs - 9, Protein - 29

281. Turkey and Peach Mix

Preparation time: 10 minutes
Cooking time: 12 minutes
Servings: 4

Ingredients:

- 1 pound turkey breast, skinless, boneless, and cut into thin strips
- 3 tablespoon olive oil
- A pinch of salt and black pepper
- 2 tablespoon vinegar
- 3 cups peaches, pitted and sliced
- 1 tablespoon fresh chives, minced
- ¼ cup tomato sauce, unsweetened
- 2 bacon slices, cooked and crumbled

Directions:

1. In a bowl, mix 1 tablespoon oil with the vinegar, salt, and pepper and whisk. Add the peaches and toss to coat. Heat a pan with the rest of the oil over medium-high heat, add the turkey strips season with salt and black pepper, cook for 10 minutes. Add tomato sauce, toss, cook for 1-2 minutes more, divide between plates and serve with the peaches salad on the side and with crumbled bacon on top.

Nutrition Value: Calories - 200, Fat - 15, Fiber - 3, Carbs - 10, Protein - 33

282. Chicken Ramekins

Preparation time: 20 minutes
Cooking time: 20 minutes
Servings: 4

Ingredients:

- 1 onion, peeled and chopped
- 28 ounces canned diced tomatoes
- 2 chipotle chilies, chopped
- 4 garlic cloves, peeled
- A pinch of sweet paprika
- ½ cup fresh cilantro, chopped
- 2 tablespoons olive oil
- A pinch of salt and black pepper
- 2 cups chicken meat, cooked and shredded
- 6 eggs, scrambled
- 2 avocados, pitted, peeled, and sliced
- 1 tablespoon parsley, chopped

Directions:

1. In a blender, mix the onion with tomatoes, chilies, garlic, paprika, cilantro, oil, salt and pepper, pulse well. Pour into a pan, heat over medium heat, boil for 20 minutes and take off heat. Spoon sauce into 6 ramekins, divide the chicken, scrambled eggs, avocado and top with the parsley and serve.

Nutrition Value: Calories - 190, Fat - 5, Fiber - 5, Carbs - 8, Protein - 12

283. Chicken, Radish and Jicama Salad

Preparation time: 10 minutes

Cooking time: 0 minutes

Servings: 4

Ingredients:

- 3 cups rotisserie chicken breast, cooked and shredded
- A pinch of salt and black pepper
- 1 onion, peeled and chopped
- 1 bunch fresh parsley, chopped
- 1 cup coconut cream
- Juice of 1 lime
- 2 jalapeño chilies, chopped
- 12 cups mixed salad greens
- 2 cups Jicama, peeled and chopped
- 1 cup radishes, sliced

Directions:

1. In a bowl, mix the chicken with salt, pepper, onion, parsley, cream, lime juice, salad greens, jalapenos, Jicama and radishes, toss and serve cold.

Nutrition Value: Calories - 230, Fat - 4, Fiber - 2, Carbs - 7, Protein - 12

284. Simple Chicken Soup

Preparation time: 10 minutes

Cooking time: 40 minutes

Servings: 4

Ingredients:

- 1½ pounds chicken breasts, skinless, boneless and cubed
- 15 ounces canned diced tomatoes
- 1 chili pepper, chopped
- 2 tablespoons olive oil
- 3 garlic cloves, peeled and minced
- 8 cups vegetable stock
- 1 onion, peeled and chopped
- 1 avocado, pitted, peeled, and chopped
- A pinch of salt and black pepper

Directions:

1. Heat a pot with the oil over medium heat, add the onion and garlic, stir, and cook for 10 minutes. Add tomatoes, chili and the chicken, stir and cook for 6 minutes more. Add the stock, salt and pepper, bring to a simmer, cook for 25 minutes, ladle into

bowls, top with avocado and serve.

Nutrition Value: Calories - 250, Fat - 2, Fiber - 8, Carbs - 10, Protein - 15

285. Chicken and Potato Stew

Preparation time: 10 minutes

Cooking time: 1 hour

Servings: 6

Ingredients:

- 1½ pounds chicken thighs, boneless and skinless
- ¼ cup olive oil
- 1 onion, peeled and chopped
- A pinch of salt and black pepper
- 1 red bell pepper, seeded and chopped
- 1 carrot, peeled and chopped
- 1 teaspoon cumin
- 1 cup pineapple, peeled and chopped
- 2 canned chipotle peppers, chopped
- 6 garlic cloves, peeled and minced
- 4 cups vegetable stock
- 1 pound potatoes, peeled and cubed,
- 3 cilantro sprigs, chopped
- 14 ounces canned tomatoes in juice, chopped
- Juice of 1 lime

Directions:

1. Heat a pot with the oil over medium-high heat, add the chicken, salt, and pepper, stir, cook for 15 minutes, transfer to a plate and shred. Heat the same pot over medium heat, add the carrot, bell pepper, and onion, stir, and cook for 8 minutes. Add the cumin, pineapple, chipotle, garlic, return the chicken to the pot. Add the stock, potatoes, tomatoes, and cilantro, bring to a boil, reduce heat to low, and cook for 30 minutes, stirring occasionally. Add the lime juice, stir, ladle into bowls, and serve.

Nutrition Value: Calories - 250, Fat - 3, Fiber - 4, Carbs - 7, Protein - 10

286. Chicken and Zucchini Stew

Preparation time: 10 minutes

Cooking time: 1 hour

Servings: 6

Ingredients:

- 1 medium chicken, cut into medium pieces
- 3½ pounds small tomatoes, cored and cut in half
- 3 zucchinis, chopped
- 2 tablespoons olive oil
- 2 onions, peeled and cut into wedges
- 3 garlic cloves, peeled and minced
- 3 red chili peppers, chopped
- 1 tablespoon ground coriander seeds
- 4 tablespoons chipotle chili peppers paste
- Zest of 1 lime
- Juice of 1 lime
- A pinch of salt and black pepper
- ½ cup cilantro leaves, chopped

Directions:

1. Heat a pot with the oil over medium high heat, add the chicken and brown for 5 minutes. Add the tomatoes, onions, garlic, chili peppers, coriander, chili paste, salt and pepper, toss, cover the pot, reduce heat to medium and simmer the stew for 45 minutes. Add the zucchinis, lime zest, juice, and cilantro, toss, cook for 15 minutes more, divide into bowls and serve.

Nutrition Value: Calories - 250, Fat - 5, Fiber - 3, Carbs - 7, Protein - 12

287. Creamy Coconut Chicken

Preparation time: 10 minutes
Cooking time: 30 minutes
Servings: 4

Ingredients:

- 5 chicken thighs
- 1 tablespoon olive oil
- 1 tablespoon fresh thyme, chopped
- 2 garlic cloves, peeled and minced
- 1 teaspoon red pepper flakes
- ½ cup coconut cream
- ¾ cup vegetable stock
- ½ cup sun-dried tomatoes, chopped
- A pinch of salt and black pepper

Directions:

1. Heat a pan with the oil over medium heat; add the chicken, season with salt and black pepper, brown for 3 minutes on each side and transfer to a plate. Heat the pan over medium heat, add thyme, garlic, chili flakes and the tomatoes, toss and cook for 5 minutes more. Add the stock, the cream and return the chicken, toss, place in the oven and bake at 350°F for 15 minutes. Divide between plates and serve.

Nutrition Value: Calories - 237, Fat - 5, Fiber - 8, Carbs - 10, Protein - 12

288. Turkey with Veggies

Preparation time: 10 minutes
Cooking time: 40 minutes
Servings: 4

Ingredients:

- 14 ounces canned diced tomatoes
- 1 pound turkey breast, boneless, skinless and cubed
- 2 tablespoons olive oil
- 1 cup vegetable stock
- A pinch of salt and black pepper
- 2 zucchinis, chopped
- 2 red bell peppers, chopped
- 1 onion, peeled and chopped
- 2 garlic cloves, peeled and minced
- ¼ cup basil leaves, chopped

Directions:

1. Heat a pan with the oil over medium heat; add the turkey, season with salt and pepper, brown for 6 minutes on each side and transfer to a plate. Heat the same pan over medium heat, add the onion and the garlic, stir and cook for 3 minutes more. Return the turkey, also add the tomatoes, stock, zucchinis and bell peppers, toss, cover the pan and simmer everything for 15 minutes. Add the basil, toss, divide into bowls and serve.

Nutrition Value: Calories - 250, Fat - 4, Fiber - 6, Carbs - 8, Protein - 10

289. Fruity Chicken Salad

Preparation time: 10 minutes
Cooking time: 0 minutes

Servings: 6

Ingredients:

- 20 ounces chicken, cooked and chopped
- ½ cup walnuts, chopped
- 1 cup green grapes, cut in half
- 11 ounces canned oranges, drained and chopped
- 1 cup homemade mayonnaise
- 1 cucumber, chopped
- 1 garlic clove, peeled and chopped
- A pinch of salt and white pepper
- 1 teaspoon lemon juice

Directions:

1. In a bowl, mix the chicken with the walnuts, grapes, oranges, cucumber, garlic, salt, pepper, lemon juice and mayonnaise. Toss and serve.

Nutrition Value: Calories - 250, Fat - 3, Fiber - 4, Carbs - 10, Protein - 12

290. Chicken and Chilli Paste

Preparation time: 10 minutes
Cooking time: 15 minutes
Servings: 4

Ingredients:

- 4 chicken breasts, boneless and skinless
- A pinch of salt and black pepper
- 1 tablespoon fresh ginger, grated
- 1 tablespoon garlic, minced
- 2 tablespoons coconut aminos
- 3 tablespoons olive oil
- 1 teaspoon chili paste

Directions:

1. Heat a pan with the oil over medium high heat, add the chicken and brown for 3 minutes on each side. Add salt, pepper, ginger, garlic, chili paste and aminos, toss well, cook for 10 minutes more, divide between plates and serve with a side salad.

Nutrition Value: Calories - 240, Fat - 5, Fiber - 8, Carbs - 10, Protein - 10

291. Moroccan Chicken Soup

Preparation time: 10 minutes

Cooking time: 45 minutes
Servings: 8

Ingredients:

- 6 cups eggplant, diced
- A pinch of salt and black pepper
- ¼ cup olive oil
- 1 cup onion, chopped
- 2 tablespoons garlic, minced
- 1 red bell pepper, seeded and chopped
- 2 tablespoons sweet paprika
- ¼ cup fresh parsley, chopped
- 1 teaspoon turmeric powder
- 1½ tablespoons fresh oregano, chopped
- 7 cups vegetable stock
- 1 pound chicken breast, skinless, boneless, and cubed
- 1 cup coconut cream
- 1 tablespoon lemon juice

Directions:

1. Heat a pot with the oil over medium high heat, add the chicken, salt and pepper. Stir, brown for 5 minutes and transfer to a bowl. Heat the same pot over medium high heat, add the eggplants, toss, cook for 5 minutes, drain excess grease on paper towels and put in a bowl. Heat the pot again over medium heat, add the onion, garlic, bell pepper, paprika, turmeric, salt and pepper, stir and cook for 5 minutes. Return the chicken and the eggplant, also add the stock and the cream, stir and cook for 25 minutes. Add the oregano and the parsley, toss, divide into bowls and serve.

Nutrition Value: Calories - 240, Fat - 3, Fiber - 2, Carbs - 7, Protein - 10

292. Oregano Chicken Stew

Preparation time: 10 minutes
Cooking time: 1 hour
Servings: 4

Ingredients:

1. 3½ pounds chicken, cut into medium pieces
2. 2 onions, peeled and chopped
3. 2 tablespoons olive oil
4. 1 garlic clove, peeled and minced

5. ¼ pint chicken stock
6. 1 tablespoon tapioca flour
7. 2 teaspoons oregano, dried
8. 14 ounces canned diced tomatoes
9. Salt and ground black pepper, to taste

Directions:

1. Heat a pot with the oil over medium heat; add the chicken, stir, and brown for 5 minutes and transfer to a plate. Heat the pot again over medium heat, add the garlic and the onions, stir and cook for 3 minutes. Add the stock, the tomatoes, the oregano, return the chicken, salt and pepper, stir, bring to a simmer and cook for 45 minutes. Add the tapioca, stir, cook for 10 minutes more, divide into bowls and serve.

Nutrition Value: Calories - 260, Fat - 5, Fiber - 5, Carbs - 6, Protein - 9

293. Chicken and Garlic Sauce

Preparation time: 10 minutes
Cooking time: 30 minutes
Servings: 4

Ingredients:

- 10 chicken pieces
- 3 tablespoons olive oil
- Salt and ground black pepper, to taste
- 12 garlic cloves
- 1 bay leaf
- 1 cup red vinegar
- 2 cups chicken stock
- ¼ cup coconut cream

Directions:

1. Heat a pan with the oil over medium heat, add the chicken and brown it for 5 minutes on each side. Add salt, pepper, garlic, bay leaf, stock and vinegar, toss and bake in the oven at 450°F for 10 minutes. Discard bay leaf, add the cream, toss, bake for 10 minutes more, divide everything between plates and serve.

Nutrition Value: Calories - 240, Fat - 4, Fiber - 5, Carbs - 9, Protein - 10

294. French Chicken Soup

Preparation time: 10 minutes
Cooking time: 3 hours
Servings: 8

Ingredients:

- 1 whole chicken, skinless and cut into medium pieces
- 12 cups chicken stock
- 1 tablespoon Dijon mustard
- ½ teaspoon ground nutmeg
- A pinch of salt and white pepper
- 4 carrots, peeled and sliced
- 6 baby carrots, chopped
- 3 leeks, chopped
- 2 celery stalks, chopped

Directions:

1. Put the chicken pieces in a big pot, add the stock, stir, bring to a boil over medium-high heat, skim the foam, and reduce heat to medium. Add the mustard, potatoes, celery, carrots, leeks, nutmeg, salt, and pepper, stir well, cover the pot, cook for 3 hours, ladle into bowls and serve.

Nutrition Value: Calories - 102, Fat - 3, Fiber - 4, Carbs - 10, Protein - 9

295. Chicken and Asparagus Soup

Preparation time: 15 minutes
Cooking time: 1 hour
Servings: 4

Ingredients:

- 3 carrots, peeled and cut in half
- 1 chicken, cut into medium pieces
- 1 onion, peeled and cut into quarters
- 2 celery stalks, cut in half
- A pinch of salt and black pepper
- 12 ounces asparagus, chopped
- 2 tomatoes, cored and chopped
- 8 cups water

Directions:

1. Put the chicken in a pot, add the water, also add the onion, celery and carrots, stir, bring to a boil over medium heat, and simmer for 45 minutes skimming foam and discard the veggies. Transfer chicken to a

cutting board, discard bones, shred the meat and return it to the soup. Also, add the asparagus, tomatoes, salt and pepper, toss, cook for 10 minutes over medium heat, ladle into bowls and serve.

Nutrition Value: Calories - 194, Fat - 6, Fiber - 5, Carbs - 13, Protein - 13

296. Chicken and Mixed Pepper Stew

Preparation time: 10 minutes
Cooking time: 1 hour and 20 minutes
Servings: 6

Ingredients:

- 4 chicken breasts, boneless, skinless and cubed
- 2 tablespoons olive oil
- 3 onions, peeled and chopped
- 2 tablespoons garlic, minced
- 2 yellow bell peppers, seeded and chopped
- 2 red bell peppers, seeded and chopped
- 1 teaspoon chili powder
- A pinch of red pepper flakes
- 1 teaspoon cumin, ground
- A pinch of salt and black pepper
- 4 cups plum tomatoes, pureed
- 4 tablespoons fresh basil, chopped

Directions:

1. Heat a pot with the oil over medium high heat, add the chicken, stir, cook for 5 minutes and transfer to a bowl. Heat the pot over medium heat again, add the onions and the garlic, stir and cook for 5 minutes more. Return the chicken to the pot, also add the yellow bell peppers, the red bell peppers, chili powder, pepper flakes, cumin, salt, pepper and tomatoes, stir, cover the pot, reduce the heat to medium low and cook for 1 hour. Add the basil, stir, cook for 10 minutes more, divide everything between plates and serve.

Nutrition Value: Calories - 250, Fat - 4, Fiber - 4, Carbs - 7, Protein - 10

297. Chicken and Pearl Onion Stew

Preparation time: 10 minutes
Cooking time: 1 hour and 10 minutes
Servings: 12

Ingredients:

- 1½ pounds chicken breast, boneless, skinless, and cubed
- 3 cups pearl onions, peeled
- 2 tablespoons olive oil
- 4 garlic cloves, peeled and chopped
- 1 cup green bell peppers, chopped
- 3 tablespoons chili powder
- 2 teaspoons parsley, chopped
- A pinch of salt and black pepper
- 4 cups chicken stock
- 4 cups tomatoes, chopped
- 1½ cups tomato paste

Directions:

1. Heat a large pot with the oil over medium-high heat, add the onions, garlic, salt and pepper, stir and cook for 5 minutes. Add the chicken, bell pepper, chili powder, stock, tomatoes and tomato paste, toss, cover the pot, reduce heat to medium low and cook for 50 minutes. Divide into bowls and serve with parsley sprinkled on top.

Nutrition Value: Calories - 265, Fat - 4, Fiber - 4, Carbs - 7, Protein - 10

298. Chicken, Kale and Purple Potato Mix

Preparation time: 10 minutes
Cooking time: 30 minutes
Servings: 6

Ingredients:

- 1½ pound purple potatoes, peeled and cubed
- A pinch of salt and black pepper
- 1 carrot, peeled and chopped
- ¼ cup olive oil
- 1 pound chicken breasts, boneless, skinless and chopped
- 6 garlic cloves, peeled and minced
- 4 cups kale, chopped
- ¼ cup balsamic vinegar

Directions:

1. Put the potatoes and carrots in a pot, add the water to cover, add salt, bring to a boil over medium-high heat. Cook for 15 minutes, drain and put in a bowl. Heat a pan with the oil over medium heat, add the chicken, season with salt and pepper, and cook for 4 minutes on each side. Add the garlic, the kale, carrots, potatoes, salt, pepper and vinegar, toss, cook for 5 minutes, divide between plates and serve.

Nutrition Value: Calories - 160, Fat - 2, Fiber - 3, Carbs - 6, Protein - 10

299. Baked Chicken

Preparation time: 15 minutes
Cooking time: 30 minutes
Servings: 6

Ingredients:

- 1 and ½ pounds chicken pieces
- Juice of ½ lime
- Zest of ½ lime
- ½ cup celery, chopped
- 1 onion, cut into wedges
- Salt and ground black pepper, to taste
- ½ teaspoon garlic, chopped
- 2 tablespoons olive oil
- 1 cup vegetable stock
- 2 green bell peppers, seeded and chopped
- 4 plum tomatoes, cored and cut into wedges
- 1 cup tomato sauce
- 1 bunch cilantro, chopped

Directions:

1. Put the chicken pieces in a baking dish. Add lime juice, lime zest, oil, salt and pepper, and rub chicken pieces well. Add the onion, the celery, garlic, tomatoes, bell peppers, stock and tomato sauce, toss a bit, cover the dish, bake in the oven at 380°F for 30 minutes. Add the cilantro, toss, divide between plates and serve.

Nutrition Value: Calories - 230, Fat - 3, Fiber - 5, Carbs - 6, Protein - 9

300. Slow Cooked Chicken Stew

Preparation time: 5 minutes
Cooking time: 6 hours
Servings: 6

Ingredients:

- 2 pounds chicken breasts, boneless and skinless
- 28 ounces canned diced tomatoes
- 28 ounces canned artichoke hearts, drained
- 1½ cups chicken stock
- 1 onion, peeled and chopped
- ¼ cup white vinegar
- ½ cup Kalamata olives, pitted and chopped
- 1 tablespoon curry powder
- 2 teaspoons dried thyme
- Salt and ground black pepper, to taste
- ¼ cup fresh cilantro, chopped

Directions:

1. In a slow cooker, mix the chicken with the tomatoes, artichokes, stock, onion, vinegar, olives, curry powder, thyme, salt and pepper. Toss, cover, cook on Low for 6 hours, add cilantro, stir, divide between plates and serve.

Nutrition Value: Calories - 260, Fat - 5, Fiber - 4, Carbs - 6, Protein - 10

301. Herbed Chicken Mix

Preparation time: 10 minutes
Cooking time: 6 hours
Servings: 6

Ingredients:

- 1¾ cups onion, chopped
- 1 teaspoon lemon zest
- 1 tablespoon lemon juice
- 12 Kalamata olives, cut in half
- 2 tablespoons capers, drained
- 15 ounces tomatoes, chopped
- 12 chicken thighs, skinless
- Salt and ground black pepper, to taste
- 1 tablespoon olive oil
- ½ cup fresh rosemary, chopped
- ½ cup fresh parsley, chopped

Directions:

1. In a slow cooker, mix the chicken with salt, pepper, oil, rosemary, parsley, lemon juice, lemon zest, onion, olives, capers and tomatoes. Toss, cover and cook on Low for 6 hours. Divide into bowls and serve.

Nutrition Value: Calories - 300, Fat - 3, Fiber - 4, Carbs - 6, Protein - 12

302. Leftover Chicken Soup

Preparation time: 10 minutes
Cooking time: 25 minutes
Servings: 4

Ingredients:

- Roasted leftover chicken cut into strips
- 6 garlic cloves, peeled and chopped
- 1 onion, peeled and chopped
- 2 zucchinis, chopped
- 2 carrots, peeled and chopped
- 14 ounces canned tomatoes
- 1 bunch fresh parsley, chopped
- 2 pints chicken stock
- 1 tablespoon olive oil
- Salt and ground black pepper, to taste

Directions:

1. Heat a pot with the oil over medium high heat, add the onion and the garlic, stir and cook for 5 minutes. Add the carrots, the zucchini, the tomatoes, stock, salt and pepper, toss, reduce heat to medium and cook for 15 minutes. Add the chicken and the parsley, stir, cook for 5 minutes, ladle into bowls and serve.

Nutrition Value: Calories - 278, Fat - 5, Fiber - 7, Carbs - 8, Protein - 12

303. Chicken Wing Platter

Preparation time: 1 hour
Cooking time: 50 minutes
Servings: 6

Ingredients:

- 12 chicken wings, halved
- 2 garlic cloves, peeled and minced
- Juice of 1 lemon
- Zest of 1 lemon
- 2 tablespoons olive oil

- 1 teaspoon cumin, ground
- Salt and ground black pepper, to taste
- 3 tablespoons black olives, pitted and chopped
- 6 dates, chopped

Directions

1. In a bowl, mix the lemon zest with the lemon juice, garlic, olive oil, cumin, salt, and pepper. Whisk, add the chicken, toss and keep in the fridge for 1 hour. Transfer the mix to a baking dish, bake for 50 minutes at 350°F, transfer to a platter, and serve with olives and dates on top.

Nutrition Value: Calories - 265, Fat - 4, Fiber - 4, Carbs - 7, Protein - 10

304. Coconut Cream Chicken Bites

Preparation time: 10 minutes
Cooking time: 50 minutes
Servings: 4

Ingredients:

- 1 pound chicken breasts, skinless, boneless and cubed
- 2 tablespoons olive oil
- ½ teaspoon paprika
- 1 teaspoon cumin
- 5 ounces chicken stock
- 6 ounces walnuts, chopped
- 1 onion, peeled and chopped
- 2 garlic cloves, peeled and minced
- 1½ tablespoons coconut cream
- ½ cup cilantro, chopped
- Juice of 1 lemon
- Salt and ground black pepper, to taste

Directions:

1. Put the chicken pieces in a baking dish, add the oil, salt, pepper, paprika, cumin, stock, walnuts, onion, garlic, lemon juice, cilantro and cream. Toss, bake at 350°F for 50 minutes, divide into bowls and serve.

Nutrition Value: Calories - 340, Fat - 4, Fiber - 7, Carbs - 9, Protein - 12

305. Lemon Marinated Chicken

Preparation time: 1 hour
Cooking time: 50 minutes
Servings: 4

Ingredients:

- 1 whole chicken without its back bone
- 1 big onion, cut into medium chunks
- 5 lemons, cut in half and juiced
- Salt and ground black pepper, to taste
- 8 garlic cloves, peeled and chopped
- 3 sprigs thyme
- ¼ cup olive oil

Directions:

1. Put the chicken in a bowl, add the onion, lemons, lemon juice, garlic, bay leaf, thyme, oil, salt, and pepper. Toss well, and keep in the refrigerator for 1 hour. Arrange the chicken in a baking dish, place in the oven at 450ºF, and bake for 50 minutes, cut and serve.

Nutrition Value: Calories - 264, Fat - 4, Fiber - 7, Carbs - 12, Protein - 16

306. Chicken and Plum Mix

Preparation time: 30 minutes
Cooking time: 15 minutes
Servings: 2

Ingredients:

- ¾ pound plums, pitted and chopped
- ½ onion, peeled and chopped
- 3 tablespoons fresh cilantro, chopped
- 3 jalapeno peppers, chopped
- Salt and ground black pepper, to taste
- ¾ pound chicken breasts, skinless and boneless
- 2 teaspoons fresh parsley, chopped
- 2 teaspoons olive oil

Directions:

1. In a bowl, mix the plums with the onion, jalapenos, parsley and cilantro, stir, and keep in the refrigerator for 30 minutes. Heat a pan with the oil over medium, add the chicken, season with salt and pepper, cook for 6 minutes on each side, transfer the chicken to plates and serve with the plum salsa on top.

Nutrition Value: Calories - 232, Fat - 3, Fiber - 2, Carbs - 7, Protein - 9

307. Basil Chicken Breasts

Preparation time: 1 hour
Cooking time: 2 hours
Servings: 4

Ingredients:

- 5 medium chicken breasts, boneless with the skin on
- 1 bunch fresh basil, chopped
- ½ cup olive oil
- 6 garlic cloves, peeled and minced
- A pinch of salt and black pepper
- ¼ cup balsamic vinegar

Directions:

1. In a food processor, mix the basil with the salt, pepper, olive oil, and balsamic vinegar and blend well. In a bowl mix chicken breasts with the basil mix, cover, and keep in the refrigerator for 1 hour. Transfer chicken breasts to a slow cooker, add the marinade, cover, cook on high for 2 hours, divide between plates and serve.

Nutrition Value: Calories - 176, Fat - 3, Fiber - 3, Carbs - 6, Protein - 10

308. Indian Chicken Stew

Preparation time: 10 minutes
Cooking time: 50 minutes
Servings: 4

Ingredients:

- 2 lime leaves, chopped
- 6 lemongrass stalks, chopped
- 1 red chili pepper, chopped
- 2 teaspoons ginger, grated
- A small bunch of cilantro, chopped
- 2 tablespoons olive oil
- 14 ounces canned coconut milk
- 8 chicken thighs, skinless, boneless, and cut in half
- A pinch of salt and black pepper
- 6 ounces green beans, trimmed
- Zest of 2 limes
- Juice of 2 limes

Directions:

1. In a blender, mix the lime leaves with the lemongrass, chili pepper, ginger, olive oil and cilantro. Pulse really well, transfer to a pot and heat over medium heat. Add the chicken, toss and cook for 6 minutes. Add the coconut milk, the green beans, salt, pepper, lime zest and juice, toss. Cover the pot, cook for 45 minutes, divide between plates and serve.

Nutrition Value: Calories - 154, Fat - 4, Fiber - 7, Carbs - 8, Protein - 12

309. Easy Chicken Skillet

Preparation time: 10 mins
Cooking time: 20 mins
Servings: 4

Ingredients:

- 2 tablespoons essential essential olive oil
- 4 chicken breasts, skinless and boneless
- A pinch of black pepper
- 2 tablespoons low-fat butter
- ½ teaspoon oregano, dried
- 3 garlic cloves, minced
- 2 cups baby spinach
- 14 ounces canned artichokes, no-salt-added, chopped
- ½ cup roasted red peppers, chopped
- 1 cup coconut cream
- ¾ cup low-fat mozzarella, shredded
- ¼ cup low-fat parmesan, grated

Directions:

1. 1.Heat up a pan while using the oil over medium-high heat, add chicken, season with black pepper and oregano, cook for 6 minutes on them and transfer for your bowl.
2. 2.Heat up the same pan because of the butter over medium-high heat, add garlic, spinach, artichokes and red peppers, stir and cook for 3 minutes more.
3. 3.Return chicken breasts, include mozzarella, parmesan and coconut cream, toss, bring to some simmer, cook for 5 minutes more, divide into bowls and serve.
4. Enjoy!

Nutrition Value: calories 211, fat 4, fiber 5, carbs 14, protein 11

310. Chicken and Onion Mix

Preparation time: ten mins
Cooking time: 45 minutes
Servings: 4

Ingredients:

- 3 tablespoons extra virgin essential olive oil
- 1 yellow onion, roughly chopped
- 2 teaspoons thyme, chopped
- 2 garlic cloves, minced
- A pinch of black pepper
- 4 chicken breasts, skinless, boneless and cubed
- ½ teaspoon oregano, dried
- 1 and ½ cup low-sodium beef stock
- 1 tablespoon parsley, chopped

Directions:

1. 1.Heat up a pan with 2 tablespoons extra virgin organic olive oil over medium-low heat, add the onion, black pepper and thyme, toss and cook for 24 minutes.
2. 2.Add garlic, cook for 1 more minute and transfer to your bowl.
3. 3.Clean the pan, heat it down with all the rest of the oil over medium-high heat, add chicken, black pepper, and oregano, stir and cook for 8 minutes more.
4. 4.Add beef, add the onion mix along with all the parsley, toss, cook for ten mins, divide into bowls and serve.
5. Enjoy!

Nutrition Value: calories 231, fat 4, fiber 7, carbs 14, protein 15

311. Balsamic Chicken Mix

Preparation time: ten mins
Cooking time: 35 minutes
Servings: 4

Ingredients:

- 1 tablespoon essential olive oil
- 1 pound chicken thighs, bone-in, skin-on
- ½ cup cranberries
- 2 garlic cloves, minced

- 1/3 cup balsamic vinegar
- 2 teaspoons thyme, chopped
- 1 teaspoon rosemary, chopped
- Zest of 1 orange, grated

Directions:

1. 1.Heat up a pan using the oil over medium-high heat, add chicken thighs skin side down, cook for 5 minutes and transfer to some plate.
2. 2.Heat inside same pan over medium heat, add cranberries, garlic, vinegar, thyme, rosemary and orange zest, toss and bring to a simmer.
3. 3.Return chicken to the pan as well, cook everything for ten mins, introduce the pan within the oven and bake at 325 degrees F for 25 minutes.
4. 4.Divide between plates and serve.
5. Enjoy!

Nutrition Value: calories 235, fat 5, fiber 6, carbs 14, protein 15

312. Asian Glazed Chicken

Preparation time: 10 mins
Cooking time: a half-hour
Servings: 4

Ingredients:

- 8 chicken thighs, boneless and skinless
- 1/3 cup coconut aminos
- ½ cup balsamic vinegar
- 3 tablespoon garlic, minced
- ¼ cup olive oil
- A pinch of black pepper
- 1 tablespoon green onion, chopped
- 3 tablespoons garlic chili sauce

Directions:

1. 1.Put the oil inside a baking dish, add chicken, aminos, vinegar, garlic, black pepper, onion and chili sauce, toss well, introduce inside oven and bake at 425 degrees F for thirty minutes.
2. 2.Divide the chicken along with the sauce between plates and serve.
3. Enjoy!

Nutrition Value: calories 254, fat 12, fiber 6, carbs

15, protein 20

313. Easy Greek Chicken

Preparation time: ten mins
Cooking time: quarter-hour
Servings: 4

Ingredients:

- 1 pound chicken breasts, skinless and boneless
- A pinch of black pepper
- 1 tablespoon essential olive oil
- 2 garlic cloves, minced
- 1 teaspoon oregano, dried
- 1 cup coconut milk
- 1 tablespoon freshly squeezed lemon juice
- 1 teaspoon lemon zest, grated
- 1 and ½ cups cherry tomatoes, halved
- ½ cup kalamata olives, pitted and sliced
- ¼ cup dill, chopped
- 1 cucumber, sliced

Directions:

1. 1.Heat up a pan when using oil over medium-high heat, add chicken and cook for 4 minutes on both sides.
2. 2.Add black pepper, garlic, oregano, milk, lemon juice, lemon zest, tomatoes, olives, dill and cucumber, toss, cook for ten minutes more, divide between plates and serve.
3. Enjoy!

Nutrition Value: calories 241, fat 4, fiber 8, carbs 15, protein 16

314. Summer Chicken Mix

Preparation time: ten mins
Cooking time: 27 minutes
Servings: 4

Ingredients:

- 1 tablespoon essential olive oil
- 4 chicken breasts, skinless and boneless
- A pinch of black pepper
- 1 shallot, chopped
- 2 garlic cloves, minced
- 4 peaches, sliced
- ¼ cup balsamic vinegar

- ¼ cup basil, chopped

Directions:

1. 1.Heat up a pan because of the oil over medium-high heat, add chicken, season with black pepper, cook for 8 minutes on both sides and transfer for some plate.
2. 2.Heat the identical pan over medium-high heat, add shallot and garlic, stir and cook for just two minutes.
3. 3.Add peaches, stir and cook for 5 minutes more.
4. 4.Add the vinegar, return the chicken, include the basil, toss, cook for 3-4 minutes more, divide everything between plates and serve.
5. Enjoy!

Nutrition Value: calories 241, fat 4, fiber 7, carbs 15, protein 15

315. Cajun Chicken

Preparation time: ten mins
Cooking time: twenty or so minutes
Servings: 4

Ingredients:

- 1 tablespoon extra virgin essential olive oil
- 1 pound chicken, skinless and boneless
- ½ teaspoon oregano, dried
- A pinch of black pepper
- ¼ cup low-sodium veggie stock
- 2 cups cherry tomatoes, halved
- 4 green onions, chopped
- 1 tablespoon Cajun seasoning
- 3 garlic cloves, minced
- ½ teaspoon sweet paprika
- 2/3 cup coconut cream
- 2 tablespoons fresh lemon juice

Directions:

1. 1.Heat up a pan while using oil over medium-high heat, add chicken plus a pinch of black pepper and cook for 5 minutes on either sides.
2. 2.Add oregano, stock, green onions, Cajun seasoning, garlic, paprika, cream and fresh fresh lemon juice, toss, cook for ten mins, divide into bowls and serve.
3. Enjoy!

Nutrition Value: calories 233, fat 4, fiber 6, carbs 15, protein 20

316. Chicken and Veggies

Preparation time: 10 mins
Cooking time: 25 minutes
Servings: 4

Ingredients:

- 4 chicken breasts, skinless, boneless and cubed
- 2 tablespoons organic olive oil
- ½ teaspoon Italian seasoning
- A pinch of black pepper
- ½ cup yellow onion, chopped
- 14 ounces canned tomatoes, no-salt-added, drained and chopped
- 16 ounces cauliflower florets

Directions:

1. 1.Heat up a pan while using the oil over medium-high heat, add chicken, black pepper, onion and Italian seasoning, toss and cook for 5 minutes.
2. 2.Add tomatoes and cauliflower, toss, cover the pan and cook over medium heat for twenty possibly even minutes.
3. 3.Toss again, divide everything between plates and serve.
4. Enjoy!

Nutrition Value: calories 310, fat 6, fiber 4, carbs 14, protein 20

317. Chicken and Broccoli

Preparation time: 10 mins
Cooking time: 25 minutes
Servings: 4

Ingredients:

- 1 tablespoon organic olive oil
- 4 chicken breasts, skinless and boneless
- 1 cup red onions, chopped
- 2 garlic cloves, minced
- 1 tablespoon oregano, chopped
- 2 cups broccoli florets
- ½ cup coconut cream

Directions:

1. 1.Heat up a pan while using the oil over

medium-high heat, add chicken breasts and cook for 5 minutes on each side.

2. 2.Add onions and garlic, stir and cook for 5 minutes more.

3. 3.Add oregano, broccoli and cream, toss everything, cook for ten minutes more, divide between plates and serve.

4. Enjoy!

Nutrition Value: calories 287, fat 10, fiber 2, carbs 14, protein 19

318. Artichoke and Spinach Chicken

Preparation time: 10 mins
Cooking time: twenty or so minutes
Servings: 4

Ingredients:

- 2 tablespoons essential olive oil
- 10 ounces baby spinach
- 14 ounces artichoke hearts, chopped
- 4 chicken breasts, boneless and skinless
- 28 ounces tomato sauce, no-salt-added
- ½ teaspoon red pepper flakes, crushed

Directions:

1. 1.Heat up a pan with the oil over medium-high heat, add chicken and red pepper flakes and cook for 5 minutes on them.

2. 2.Add spinach, artichokes and tomato sauce, toss, cook for ten minutes more, divide between plates and serve.

3. Enjoy!

Nutrition Value: calories 212, fat 3, fiber 7, carbs 16, protein 20

319. Pumpkin and Black Beans Chicken

Preparation time: ten mins
Cooking time: 25 minutes
Servings: 4

Ingredients:

- 1 pound chicken breasts, skinless and boneless
- 2 cups water
- 1 tablespoon essential olive oil
- 1 cup coconut milk

- ½ cup pumpkin flesh
- 15 ounces canned black beans, no-salt-added, drained and rinsed
- 1 tablespoon cilantro, chopped

Directions:

1. 1.Heat up a pan when using oil over medium-high heat, add the chicken and cook for 5 minutes.

2. 2.Add the river, milk, pumpkin and black beans, toss, cover the pan, reduce heat to medium and cook for 20 mins.

3. 3.Add cilantro, toss, divide between plates and serve.

4. Enjoy!

Nutrition Value: calories 254, fat 6, fiber 4, carbs 16, protein 22

320. Chutney Chicken Mix

Preparation time: 10 minutes
Cooking time: 10 mins
Servings: 4

Ingredients:

- 4 chicken white meat halves, skinless and boneless
- 2 tablespoons lime juice
- 2 tablespoons olive oil
- 4 tablespoons mango chutney
- ½ teaspoon ginger, grated
- 1 avocado, peeled, pitted and chopped
- 8 cups micro greens
- A pinch of black pepper

Directions:

1. In a bowl, mix chicken breasts with oil with chutney, lime juice and ginger and toss to coat.

2. 2.Heat the kitchen grill over medium-high heat, add chicken, cook for 5 minutes on both sides, cut into thin strips and put in a salad bowl.

3. 3.Add avocado, black pepper and greens, drizzle the chutney dressing, toss to coat and serve.

4. Enjoy!

Nutrition Value: calories 210, fat 3, fiber 4, carbs 12, protein 9

321. Chicken and Sweet Potato Soup

Preparation time: 10 minutes
Cooking time: twenty approximately minutes
Servings: 6

Ingredients:

- 2 chicken breasts, skinless, boneless and cubed
- 1 yellow onion, chopped
- 2 tablespoons organic olive oil
- 1 garlic cloves, minced
- 4 sweet potatoes, cubed
- 2 carrots, chopped
- ½ teaspoon ginger, grated
- ½ teaspoon cumin, ground
- A pinch of black pepper
- 20 ounces low-sodium veggie stock

Directions:

1. 1.Heat up a pot while using the oil over medium-high heat, add onion and garlic, stir and cook for 5 minutes.
2. 2.Add carrots and potatoes, stir and cook for 5 minutes.
3. 3.Add ginger, cumin, stock, pepper and chicken, stir, give a boil, reduce heat to medium, simmer for ten minutes, ladle into soup bowls and serve.
4. Enjoy!

Nutrition Value: calories 209, fat 5, fiber 5, carbs 13, protein 9

322. Chicken and Dill Soup

Preparation time: ten mins
Cooking time:: an hour and 20 mins
Servings: 6

Ingredients:

- 1 whole chicken
- 1 pound carrots, sliced
- 6 cups low-sodium veggie stock
- 1 cup yellow onion, chopped
- A pinch of salt and black pepper
- 2 teaspoons dill, chopped
- ½ cup red onion, chopped

Directions:

1. 1.Put chicken in a pot, add water to pay for, give your boil over medium heat, cook first hour, transfer to a cutting board, discard bones, shred the meat, strain the soup, get it back on the pot, heat it over medium heat and add the chicken.
2. 2.Also add the carrots, yellow onion, red onion, a pinch of salt, black pepper and also the dill, cook for fifteen minutes, ladle into bowls and serve.
3. Enjoy!

Nutrition Value: calories 202, fat 6, fiber 4, carbs 8, protein 12

323. Cilantro Serrano Chicken Soup

Preparation time: ten minutes
Cooking time: 1 hour
Servings: 4

Ingredients:

- 4 chicken thighs, skin and bone in
- 1 cup cilantro, chopped
- 2 small Serrano peppers, chopped
- 4 and ¼ cups low-sodium veggie stock
- 2 whole garlic cloves+ 2 garlic cloves, minced
- 2 tablespoons extra virgin extra virgin olive oil
- ½ red bell pepper chopped
- ½ yellow onion, chopped
- A pinch of salt and black pepper

Directions:

1. 1.Put cilantro inside meat processor, add Serrano peppers, 2 whole garlic cloves and ¼ cup stock, blend adequately and transfer in your bowl.
2. 2.Heat up a pot while using the essential olive oil over medium-high heat, add chicken thighs, cook for 5 minutes on both sides and transfer to your bowl.
3. 3.Return pot to medium heat, add onion, stir and cook for 5 minutes.
4. 4.Add bell pepper, salt, pepper, minced garlic, cilantro paste, chicken plus the rest within the stock, toss, bring to a simmer over medium heat, cook for 40 minutes, ladle into bowls and serve

5. Enjoy!

Nutrition Value: calories 291, fat 5, fiber 8, carbs 10, protein 12

324. Leek and Chicken Soup

Preparation time: quarter-hour
Cooking time:: 1 hour and 20 mins
Yield: 4

Ingredients:

- 1 whole chicken, cut into medium pieces
- A pinch of salt and black pepper
- 12 cups low-sodium veggie stock
- 3 leek, roughly chopped
- 3 tablespoons organic olive oil
- 2 cups yellow onion, chopped
- ½ cup freshly squeezed freshly squeezed lemon juice

Directions:

1. 1.Put chicken in a very pot, add the stock, a pinch of salt and black pepper, stir, provide a boil over medium heat and skim foam.
2. 2.Add leeks, toss and simmer for an hour or so.
3. 3.Heat up a pan with the oil over medium heat, add onion, stir and cook for 5 minutes.
4. 4.Add this towards pot, also add the freshly squeezed lemon juice, toss, cook for twenty minutes more, ladle into bowls and serve.
5. Enjoy!

Nutrition Value: calories 199, fat 3, fiber 5, carbs 6, protein 11

325. Collard Greens and Chicken Soup

Preparation time: ten mins
Cooking time: 30 mins
Servings: 4

Ingredients:

- 4 cups low-sodium chicken stock
- 1 garlic oil, minced
- 1 yellow onion, chopped
- 8 ounces chicken skinless, boneless and chopped
- 2 cups collard greens, chopped

- A pinch of salt and black pepper
- 2 tablespoons ginger, grated

Directions:

1. 1.Put the stock in a very pot, add garlic, chicken and onion, stir, bring which has a boil over medium heat and simmer for twenty minutes.
2. 2.Add collard greens, salt, pepper and ginger, stir and cook for 10 more minutes, ladle into bowls and serve.
3. Enjoy!

Nutrition Value: calories 199, fat 5, fiber 5, carbs 8, protein 12

326. Chicken, Scallions and Avocado Soup

Preparation time: 10 mins
Cooking time: 25 minutes
Servings: 4

Ingredients:

- 2 cups chicken white meat, skinless, boneless, cooked and shredded
- 2 avocados, peeled, pitted and chopped
- 5 cups low sodium veggie stock
- 1 and ½ cups scallions, chopped
- 2 garlic cloves, minced
- ½ cup cilantro, chopped
- A pinch of salt and black pepper
- 2 teaspoons organic olive oil

Directions:

1. 1.Heat up a pot while using oil over medium heat, add 1 cup scallions and garlic, stir and cook for 5 minutes.
2. 2.Add stock, salt and pepper, bring for some boil, reduce heat to low, cover and simmer for twenty or so minutes.
3. 3.Divide chicken, the remaining while using scallions and avocado in bowls, add soup, top with chopped cilantro and serve.
4. Enjoy!

Nutrition Value: calories 205, fat 5, fiber 6, carbs 14, protein 8

327. Coconut Chicken and Mushrooms

Preparation time: ten mins
Cooking time: 52 minutes
Servings: 8

Ingredients:

- 3 tablespoons extra virgin olive oil
- 8 chicken thighs
- A pinch of salt and black pepper
- 3 garlic cloves, minced
- 8 ounces mushrooms, halved
- 1 cup coconut cream
- ½ teaspoon basil, dried
- ½ teaspoon oregano, dried
- 1 tablespoon mustard

Directions:

1. 1.Heat up a pot with 2 tablespoons oil over medium-high heat, add chicken, salt and pepper, brown for 3 minutes on both sides and transfer with a plate.
2. 2.Heat the same pot while using rest using the oil over medium heat, add mushroom and garlic, stir and cook for 6 minutes.
3. 3.Add salt, pepper, oregano, basil and chicken, stir and bake in the oven at 400 degrees F for a half-hour.
4. 4.Add cream and mustard, stir, simmer for 10 mins more, divide everything between plates and serve.
5. Enjoy!

Nutrition Value: calories 269, fat 5, fiber 6, carbs 13, protein 12

328. Spicy Chicken Gumbo

Preparation Time: 7 hours 10 minutes
Servings: 5

Ingredients:

- Chili powder, 1 tbsp.
- Chopped small yellow onion, 1.
- Chopped canned tomatoes, 28oz.
- Black pepper
- Mustard powder, 2 tbsps.
- Garlic powder, 2 tbsps.
- Dried oregano, 2 tbsps.
- Chopped bell peppers, 2.
- Creole seasoning, 6 tbsps.
- Cubed chicken breasts, 3.

- Sliced sausages, 2.
- Salt
- Cayenne powder, 1tsp.
- Dried thyme, 3 tsp.

Directions:

1. Combine sausages with seasonings, chicken pieces, oregano, bell peppers, garlic powder, onion, thyme, cayenne, mustard powder, tomatoes, chili and Creole seasoning in the slow cooker.
2. Cook for 7 hours on low while covered
3. Gently stir the meal then set into bowls for serving.

Nutrition Values:

Calories: 360, Fat: 23, Fiber: 2, Carbs: 6, Protein: 23

329. Creamy Chicken Pasta

Preparation Time: 40 minutes
Servings: 4

Ingredients:

- Cajun seasoning, 1 tsp.
- Whipping cream, ¼ c.
- Minced garlic, 1 tsp.
- Salt
- Ghee, 2 tbsps.
- Chopped cilantro, ¼ c.
- Chicken cutlets, 1 lb.
- Chicken stock, ½ c.
- Grated cheddar cheese, ½ c.
- Chopped scallions, ¼ c.
- Cream cheese, 1 oz.
- Chopped tomatoes, ½ c.
- Black pepper.

For the pasta:

- Cream cheese, 4 oz.
- Black pepper.
- Eggs, 8.
- Garlic powder.
- Salt.

Directions:

1. Set the pan on fire over medium heat with 1 tablespoon ghee.
2. Season the chicken pieces with Cajun seasoning.

3. Cook the seasoned chicken cutlets for 2 minutes each side then reserve on a plate.
4. Set the same pan on fire with the remaining ghee to cook garlic for 2 minutes over medium heat
5. Stir in tomatoes to cook for 2 more minutes
6. Mix in the remaining Cajun seasoning and stock to cook for 5 minutes
7. Stir in cheddar cheese, whipping cream, pepper, 1 ounce cream cheese, scallions and salt.
8. Allow cooking 2 more minutes then remove from heat.
9. In the meantime, set the food processor in place to combine the egg, 4 ounces cream cheese, salt, garlic powder and pepper to process until done.
10. Set the mixture on a well-lined baking tray and allow to rest for 5 minutes.
11. Set the oven for 10 minutes at 3250F, allow to bake
12. Allow the pasta to cool down before slicing on a chopping board
13. Roll the pasta and serve topped with chicken mix
14. Enjoy.

Nutrition Values:

Calories: 345, Fat: 34, Fiber: 4, Carbs: 4, Protein: 39

330. Chicken Pie

Preparation Time: 55 minutes
Servings: four people.

Ingredients

- Chicken stock – ½ cup
- Dijon Mustard – 2 tablespoon
- Chopped carrots – ½ cup
- Ghee – 3 tablespoon
- Minced garlic cloves – 3
- Salt and black pepper
- Heavy cream – ¾ cup
- Cubed Chicken – 12 ounces
- Chopped yellow onion – ½ cup
- Shredded cheddar cheese = ¾ cup

For the dough

- Onion powder – 1 teaspoon
- Garlic powder - 1 teaspoon

- Cream cheese – 3 tablespoons
- Italian Seasoning – 1 teaspoon
- Salt and black pepper
- Shredded Mozzarella cheese – 1½ cup
- Egg – 1
- Almond flour – ¾ cup

Instructions

1. Put the ghee into a pan and place over medium heat.
2. Add the carrots, onions, garlic, salt and pepper and simmer for 5 minutes
3. Put the chicken and cook for an additional 3 minutes
4. Add the mustard, stock, heavy cream, salt and pepper, cook for further 8 minutes
5. Put the cheddar cheese, stir thoroughly and keep it warm
6. In a separate bowl, mix up the Mozzarella and add the cream cheese, mix evenly and heat up in the microwave
7. Put the Italian Seasoning, onion powder, salt, garlic powder, pepper, egg, flour and stir well
8. Knead the dough very correctly and divide into 4 pieces, ensure each piece is flattened into a circle
9. Share the chicken mix into 4 ramekins, top each with a dough circle
10. Place in 375 degrees heat for 25 minutes
11. Serve your chicken pie warm

Nutrition Values:

Fat: 54, Carbs 10, Protein 45, Calories 600 and Fiber

331. Flavorful Chicken Fajitas

Preparation time: 25 minutes
Servings: four people

Ingredients

- Chili powder- 1 teaspoon
- Cumin – 2 teaspoon
- Sliced red bell pepper – 1
- Chopped Cilantro – 1 tablespoon
- Limes into wedges – 2
- Coconut Oil – 2 tablespoon
- Pitted, peeled and sliced Avocado – 1
- Salt and black pepper

- Sweet Paprika – 1 teaspoon
- Lime Juice - 2 tablespoon
- Ground coriander – 1 teaspoon
- Sliced yellow onion – 1
- Skinless, boneless chicken breast – 2 pounds
- Sliced green bell pepper – 1
- Cumin – 2 teaspoons

Directions:

1. Get a medium size bowl and mix up the pepper, garlic powder, salt, cumin, chilli powder, coriander, Paprika and stir thoroughly
2. Put the chicken pieces and toss to mix evenly
3. Add half of the Oil into a pan and place under a medium heat
4. Add the chicken, cook for 3 minutes on each side before transferring to the bowl
5. Heat the pan with the remaining Oil, add bell peppers and onions and cook for 6 minutes
6. Take the chicken back to the pan and put additional pepper and salt
7. Serve onto plates and top with avocado, lime wedges and Cilantro

Nutrition Values:

Calories: 240, Protein 20, Carbs 5, Fiber 2, Fat 10

332. Oven Baked Chicken

Preparation Time: 30 minutes
Servings: 4 people

Ingredients

- Coconut aminos – 1 ounce
- Coconut Oil – 2 tablespoons
- Ranch dressing – 4 ounces
- Bacon strips – 4
- Chopped green onions – 3
- Chicken breast – 4
- Cheddar Cheese grated – 4 ounces

Directions:

1. Pour Oil in a pan and place over high heat
2. Add the chicken breast and cook for 8 minutes
3. Turn and cook for an additional 8 minutes
4. Get a separate container and place over

medium heat
5. Put the Bacon and cook until it's crispy
6. Get it transferred to the paper towel, drain grease and crumble
7. Arrange the chicken breast to a baking dish.
8. Add the coconut, and Cheese crumbled Bacon and green onions on top
9. Place it in an oven
10. Set on the broiler and cook at high temperature for 5 minutes
11. Shared between plates and serve hot

Nutrition Values:

Protein 60, Calories 450, Fat 24, Fiber 0, Carbs 3

333. Chicken with Green Onion Sauce

Preparation Time: 37 minutes
Servings: 4 people

Ingredients:

- Ghee – 2 tablespoons
- Sour cream – 2 ounces
- Salt and black pepper
- Chopped green onion – 1
- Skinless and boneless chicken breast halves – 4

Directions:

1. Put the ghee in a pan and place over a medium heat
2. Put the chicken and add salt and pepper
3. Reduce the heat and cook for 10 minutes
4. Turn the chicken and simmer for an additional 10 minutes
5. Put the green onion and cook for 2 minutes
6. Remove it from the heat, add more salt and pepper if the need arises
7. Cook for 5 minutes too
8. Stir it to serve well

Nutrition Value:

Fat 7, Fiber 2, Protein 8, Calories 200, Carbs 1

334. Whole30 Chicken Casserole

Preparation Time: 55 minutes
Servings: 4 people

Ingredients:

- Chicken Stock – 1/3 cup
- Mayo – 1 cup
- Lemon juice – 1
- Melted coconut oil – 1 tablespoon
- Grated cheddar cheese – 3 cups
- Skinless, boneless, cooked, cubed – 3 chicken breast
- Chicken Stock – 1/3 cup
- Brocolli florets – 10 ounces

Directions:

1. Add Oil to a baking dish to grease it
2. Arrange the chicken pieces on the bottom
3. Arrange the broccoli florets and then add half of the Cheese
4. Get a medium- size bowl, add in the mayo with stock, pepper, salt and lemon juice
5. Pour the mixture over the chicken, add the rest of the Cheese, cover dish tin foil and bake in the oven at 350 degrees F for 30 minutes
6. Remove the foil and bake for 20 minutes

Nutrition Values:

Protein 25, Calories 250, Carbs 6, Fat 5

335. Italian Chicken Recipe

Preparation time: 30 minutes
Servings: 4 people

Ingredients

- Olive Oil – ¼ cup
- Chopped red onion – 1
- Chopped Anchovy Fillets – 4
- Salt and black pepper
- Skinless, boneless chicken breast6 – 4
- Minced garlic cloves – 4
- Chopped tomatoes – 4
- Pitted and chopped Italian olives – ½ cup
- Chopped Capers – 1 tablespoon
- Red chilli flakes – ½ teaspoon

Directions:

1. Add the salt and pepper to the chicken and rub with half of the Oil
2. Put in a pan that has been preheated, turn and cook for 2 minutes

3. Arrange the chicken breast in an oven at 450 degrees bake for 8 minutes
4. Remove the chicken out of the oven and divide between plates
5. Heat the remaining Oil over the medium heat
6. Add the onion, garlic, capers, olives, anchovies, chilli flakes, stir and cook for 1 minute
7. Put the tomatoes, pepper, salt and cook for 2 minutes

Nutrition Values:

Protein 7, Calories 400, Carbs 2, Fat 20, Fiber 1

336. Parmesan Crusted Chicken

Preparation time: 45 minutes
Servings: 4 people

Ingredients:

- Avocado Oil – ½ cup
- Garlic powder - ½ teaspoon
- Whisked Egg – ½ teaspoon
- Salt and Pepper
- Shredded Asia go Cheese – 1 Cup
- Grated Parmesan cheese – 1 cup
- Water – 1 tablespoon
- Cooked and crumbled bacon slices – 4
- Whisked Egg – 1

Directions:

1. Get a bowl, mix the Parmesan with Cheese, salt, garlic and pepper to stir
2. Pour the whisked egg in another bowl and mix with water
3. Add salt and pepper to each chicken and dip each piece into egg, and later deep into the cheese mix
4. Heat the pan with Oil over medium heat, add chicken breast, cook until they are golden on both sides and transfer to the baking pan
5. Place in an oven of 350 degrees and bake for 2 minutes
6. Add Bacon and Asia go Cheese to the top of the chicken, introduce to the oven
7. Turn on the broiler and broil for a couple of minutes

Nutrition Values:

Fiber 1, Protein 47, Calories 400, Fat 22

337. Baked Salsa Chicken

Preparation time: 1 hour 25 minutes
Servings: 6 people

Ingredients:

- Jarred Salsa – 2 cups
- Salt and black pepper
- Vegetable Cooking Spray –
- Shredded cheddar cheese – 1 cup
- Skinless and boneless – 6 chicken breasts

Instructions

1. Add some cooking oil o a baking dish
2. Place the breast on it
3. Add salt and pepper and pour the Salsa over it
4. Bake for 1 hour at 425degrees
5. Spread the Cheese and bake for 15 minutes
6. Divide between plates and serve

Nutrition Values:

Calories 120, Carbs 6, Protein 10, Fat 2

338. Chicken in Sour Cream Sauce

Preparation Time: 50 minutes
Servings: 4 people

Ingredients:

- Onion powder – 1 teaspoon
- Sweet Paprika – 2 tablespoons
- Sour cream – ¼ cup
- Sweet Paprika – 2 tablespoons
- Chicken thighs – 4

Directions:

1. Get a medium-sized bowl and mix in the salt, onion powder, pepper and stir thoroughly
2. Add Paprika mix to the chicken pieces
3. Arrange them on a lined baking sheet and bake at 400 degrees for 40 minutes
4. Divide chicken on plates and leave aside
5. Pour the juices in the pan to a bowl and add the sour cream
6. Stir this sauce until it's evenly mixed and drizzle over the chicken

Nutrition Values:

Fat 31, Carbs 1, Protein 33, Fat 31, Calories 384

339. Balsamic Chicken

Preparation Time: 30 minutes
Servings: 4 people

Ingredients:

- Coconut Oil – 3 Tablespoons
- Thinly sliced tomato – 1
- Salt and pepper
- Ste via – 3 tablespoons
- Chicken stock – 1 cup
- Balsamic Vinegar – ½ cup
- Chopped basil for serving
- Mozzarella slices – 6
- Minced garlic cloves – 3

Directions:

1. Pour Oil into the pan and place over a medium heat
2. Add the chicken pieces, season with salt and pepper
3. Cook until they got brown on both sides and reduce heat
4. Put the Vinegar, stock, stevia, garlic and stir thoroughly, simmer for 10 minutes
5. Arrange the mozzarella slices on top
6. Broil in the oven over medium heat until the cheese melts
7. Arrange the tomato slices over chicken pieces
8. Divide between plates and serve

Nutrition Values:

Protein 27, Calories 240, Carbs 4, Fat 12

340. Chicken Casserole Sauce

Preparation time: 50 minutes
Servings: 8 people

Ingredients:

- Shredded Mozzarella – 6 ounces
- Egg – 1
- Almond flour – 1 cup
- Grated Parmesan – ¼ cup
- Avocado Oil – 4 tablespoons
- Fresh Basil chopped for serving

- Dried Parsley – 1½ Teaspoon
- Already cooked spaghetti squash – 4 cups
- Whole30 Marinara Sauce – 1½ Cups
- Garlic powder – ½ teaspoon
- Skinless and boneless chicken breast – 1½ pounds
- Salt and Black pepper
- Dried Basil – ½ teaspoon

Directions:

1. Get a medium-size bowl and mix in the almond flour with salt, garlic powder, pepper, 1 teaspoon parsley and stir
2. Get another bowl and whisk the egg adding salt and pepper
3. Dip the chicken in egg and then in the almond flour mix
4. Pour 3 tablespoon of Oil and place over a medium heat
5. Add the chicken and cook until they turn golden on both sides
6. Transfer to the paper towels
7. In a bowl, add the spaghetti squash with salt, pepper, 1 tablespoon oil, dried basil and the rest of the Parsley and stir thoroughly
8. Arrange this into a heatproof dish, add the chicken and also marinara sauce
9. Put shredded Mozzarella and place in an oven at 375 degrees and bake for 30 minutes
10. Sprinkle the fresh basil, leave the casserole aside to cool down

Nutrition Values:

Fat 6, Protein 28, Calories 300, Carbs 5

341. Easy Chicken Stir-Fry Recipe

Preparation time: 22 minutes
Servings: 2 people

Ingredients:

- Sesame Oil – 1 tablespoon
- Skinless, boneless chicken thighs – 2
- Broccoli florets – 2 cups
- Water – ½ cup
- Onion powder – 1 teaspoon
- Tamari sauce – ½ cup
- Red Pepper flakes – ½ teaspoon

- Grated ginger – ½ teaspoon
- Chopped scallions – ½ cup
- Ste via – 1 tablespoon
- Xanthan gum – ½ teaspoon
- Garlic powder – ½ teaspoon

Instruction:

1. Put the Oil in a pan and place under medium heat
2. Put the chicken and ginger, stir well and simmer for 3 minutes
3. Add the tamari sauce, garlic powder, pepper flakes, water, onion powder, stevia, xanthan gum stir thoroughly and cook for 5 minutes
4. Put the broccoli, scallions
5. Stir thoroughly and cook for 2 minutes

Nutrition Values:

Fiber 3, Calories 210, Protein 20, Fat 10, Carbs 5

342. Mexican Styled Chicken Soup

Preparation time: 4 hours 10 minutes
Servings: 6 people

Ingredients:

- Chicken Stock – 15 ounces
- Canned Chunky Salsa – 15 ounces
- Skinless, boneless, cubed chicken thighs – 1½ pounds
- Monterrey jack – 8 ounces

Directions:

1. Mix chicken with stock, Salsa and Cheese and placed under a low cooker
2. Stir thoroughly and cook on high for 4 hours
3. Uncover the pot, stir soup and divide into bowls

Nutrition Values:

Fat 22, Protein 38, Calories 400, Carbs 6

343. Cheesy Chicken Meatloaf

Preparation Time: 50 minutes
Servings: 8 people

Ingredients:

- Minced garlic cloves – 4
- Italian Seasonings – 2 teaspoons

- Onion powder – 2 teaspoons
- Whole30 marinara sauce – 1 cup
- Chopped Parsley – 2 tablespoons
- Ground chicken meat – 2 pounds
- Salt and black pepper

For the crust:

- Minced garlic clove
- Shredded Mozzarella – 1 cup
- Chopped chives – 2 teaspoons
- Ricotta cheese – ½ cup
- Grated Parmesan – 1 cup
- Chopped Parsley – 2 tablespoons

Directions:

1. Get a bowl and mix in the chicken with half of the marinara sauce, pepper, salt, Italian Seasoning, onion powder, 4 garlic cloves and 2 tablespoons of Parsley. Ensure you stir very well
2. In a different bowl, mix the ricotta with half of the parmesan, I garlic clove, pepper, half of Mozzarella, pepper and 2 tablespoons of Parsley and stir well
3. Get half of the chicken and mix into a loaf pan and spread evenly
4. Put the cheese filling and ensure it's spread
5. Make use of the rest of the meat to top it and spread
6. Arrange the meatloaf in the oven at 400 degrees and bake for 20 minutes
7. Put the meatloaf out of the oven, spread the rest of the parmesan, marinara and Mozzarella and bake for 20 minutes
8. Put down the meatloaf to cool down, slice and divide between plates to serve

Nutrition Values:

Fat 14, Carbs 4, Protein 28, Calories 273

344. Duck Breast Salad

Preparation time: 30 minutes
Servings: a person

Ingredients:

- Sage – ¼ teaspoon
- Orange extract – ¼ teaspoon
- Baby spinach – 1 cup
- Heavy cream – 1 tablespoon
- Salt and black pepper

- Ghee – 2 tablespoons
- Swerve – 1 tablespoon
- Skin scored duck breast – 1 medium

Directions:

1. Put the ghee in a pan and place over medium heat
2. Add the swerve once it melts and stirs until the ghee gets brown
3. Put the orange extract and sage
4. Cook for an additional 2 minutes
5. Put the heavy cream and stir one more time
6. Get a separate pan over medium heat, add the skin side down, the duck breast and cook for 5 minutes
7. Flip and cook the other side for another 3 minutes
8. Add the orange sauce the duck breast
9. Put some spinach to the where you have made the sauce, stir and cook for some minutes
10. Remove the duck from the heat, get it sliced and arrange on a plate
11. Drizzle some orange sauce on top and add spinach on the side

Nutritional Value:

Fat 56, Carbs 0, Protein 35, Fiber 0, Calories 567

345. Healthy Chicken Fajita Stuffed Peppers

Preparation time: 50 minutes
Servings: 3 people

Ingredients:

- Water – 2/3 cup
- Fajita seasoning – 2 tablespoons
- Ghee – 1 tablespoon
- Cauliflower florets – 2 cups
- Salt and pepper
- Chopped small yellow onion – 1
- Tops cut off and seed removed bell peppers – 6
- Skinless, boneless, cooked and shredded chicken breast – 2 chicken

Directions:

1. Arrange the cauliflower in food processor
2. Add the salt, pepper and pulse well before

transferring into a bowl

3. Put some ghee into a pan and heat over medium heat
4. Add the cauliflower, simmer for 3 minutes
5. Add salt, pepper, chicken and water. Stir and cook for 2 minutes
6. Arrange the bell peppers on a lined baking sheet, stuff each with chicken mix
7. Place in an oven and bake for 30 minutes
8. Divide and serve

Nutrition Values:

Fiber 3, Calories 200, Carbs 6, Protein 14, Fat 6

346. Chicken Wrapped with Bacon

Preparation Time: 45 minutes
Servings: 4

Ingredients:

- Bacon slices, 12
- Cream cheese, 8 oz.
- Salt
- De-boned chicken breasts, 2 lbs.
- Black pepper
- Chopped chives, 1 tbsp.

Directions:

1. Set up a pan with bacon to cook slightly over medium heat then drain excess fat in a paper towel.
2. Combine chives, cheese cream and seasonings in a mixing bowl.
3. Hammer the chicken breasts using a meat tenderizer.
4. Divide the cream cheese mix roll the chicken breast then wrap it in the cooked bacon slice.
5. Set the wrapped chicken breasts into a baking tray.
6. Set the oven for 10 minutes at 3750F to bake the chicken breasts.
7. Set the wrapped chicken breasts into plates to serve.
8. Enjoy.

Nutrition Values:

Calories: 700, Fat: 45, Fiber: 4, Carbs: 5, Protein: 45

347. Vegetable Chicken

Stroganoff

Preparation Time: 4 hours 20 minutes
Servings: 4

Ingredients:

- Salt
- Minced garlic cloves, 2.
- Ground celery seeds, ¼ tsp.
- Chicken stock, 1 c.
- Sliced chicken breasts, 1 lb.
- Black pepper
- Chopped parsley, 2 tbsps.
- Sliced zucchinis, 4.
- Roughly chopped mushrooms, 8 oz.
- Dried thyme, 1½ tsp.
- Coconut milk, 1 c.
- Chopped yellow onion, 1.

Directions:

1. Set the chicken into a slow cooker.
2. Stir in onion, mushrooms, celery seeds, coconut milk, seasonings, thyme and half of the parsley.
3. Cook for four hours on High in a covered pot.
4. Open the pot, taste and adjust the seasonings as required then add the remaining parsley to stir.
5. Set up the pan on fire to boil water and salt over medium heat.
6. Add zucchini pasta to cook for 1 minute and drain it.
7. Set zucchini pasta into plates topped up with chicken mix to serve.

Nutrition Values:

Calories: 364, Fat: 22, Fiber: 2, Carbs: 4, Protein: 24

348. Instant Pot Whole Chicken

Preparation Time: 50 minutes
Servings: 12

Ingredients:

- Italian seasoning, 1 tsp.
- Onion powder, ½ tsp.
- Garlic powder, ½ tsp.
- Whole chicken, 1.
- Black pepper

- Guar, 2 tsp.
- Chicken stock, 1½ c.
- Salt
- Coconut oil, 2 tbsps.

Directions:

1. Rub the chicken Italian seasoning, with salt, pepper, onion powder and half of the oil.
2. Set the remaining oil into an instant pot and add chicken.
3. Add stock to the pot to cook on High for 40 minutes.
4. Set the chicken to a platter and reserve.
5. Adjust the instant pot on a Sauté mode and add guar.
6. Stir and cook the mixture to thicken.
7. Add sauce to the chicken and serve.
8. Enjoy.

Nutrition Values:

Calories: 450, Fat: 30, Fiber: 1, Carbs: 1, Protein: 34

349. Baked Zucchini Chicken

Preparation Time: 60 minutes
Servings: 4

Ingredients:

- Black pepper
- Minced garlic, 1 tsp.
- Chicken breasts, 3 lbs.
- Cooked and crumbled bacon, ½ c.
- Cubed cheddar cheese, 4 oz.
- Cubed Muenster cheese, 2 oz.
- Cubed provolone cheese, 2 oz.
- Shredded zucchini, 1.
- Salt
- Cream cheese, 2 oz.

Directions:

1. Rub the zucchini with seasonings and reserve.
2. Squeeze the zucchini and set it into a bowl.
3. Stir in cream cheese, Muenster cheese, garlic, bacon, provolone cheese and seasonings.
4. Make cuts on the chicken breasts then add the seasonings and fill with zucchini and cheese mix then set on a lined baking sheet.
5. Set the oven for 45minutes at 4000F, allow

to bake
6. Set on plates to serve.
7. Enjoy.

Nutrition Values:

Calories: 455, Fat: 20, Fiber: 0, Carbs: 2, Protein: 57

350. Mixed Veggies and Chicken Stew

Preparation Time: 40 minutes
Servings: 6

Ingredients:

- Chopped yellow onion, ½ c.
- Bay leaf, 1.
- Chopped thyme, 3 tsp.
- Ghee, 3 tbsps.
- Chopped mushrooms, 3oz.
- Green snap beans, 1 c.
- Salt
- De-boned and shredded rotisserie chicken pieces, 40 oz.
- Whipping cream, 2c.
- Canned chicken stock, 29 oz.
- Trimmed asparagus, 17 oz.
- Black pepper
- Chopped red peppers, ¾ c.

Directions:

1. Set the pan on fire to heat the cream for 7 minutes over medium heat
2. In the meantime, set another pan on fire to melt the ghee for frying onion and pepper for 3 minutes over medium heat.
3. Stir in the seasonings, stock, and bay leaf
4. Allow to boil and simmer for 10 minutes
5. Stir in the green beans, asparagus, and mushrooms to cook for 7 minutes
6. Mix in the chicken pieces to cook for 3 minutes
7. Stir in the seasonings, cream, and thyme
8. Remove the bay leaf then set the stew into bowls and serve

Nutrition Values:

Calories: 500, Fat: 27, Fiber: 3, Carbs: 4, Protein: 47

351. Cheesy Chicken Stuffed Mushrooms

Preparation Time: 20 minutes
Servings: 6

Ingredients:

- Cooking spray
- Chopped carrot, ¼ c.
- Hot sauce, 4 tbsps.
- Crumbled blue cheese, ¾ c.
- Chopped and cooked chicken meat, ½ c.
- Button mushroom caps, 16 oz.
- Chopped red onion, ¼ c.
- Ranch seasoning mix, 1 tsp.
- Black pepper
- Cream cheese, 4 oz.
- Salt

Directions:

1. Combine hot sauce, cream cheese, blue cheese, pepper, ranch seasoning, carrot, chicken, salt, and red onion in a mixing bowl.
2. Fill each mushroom cap with this mix and set them on a lined baking tray then spray with cooking spray
3. Set the oven for 10 minutes at 4250F, allow to bake
4. Set on plates to serve.
5. Enjoy.

Nutrition Values:

Calories: 200, Fat: 4, Fiber: 1. Carbs: 2, Protein: 7

352. Garlic and Peanut Grilled Chicken

Preparation Time: 30 minutes
Servings: 8

Ingredients:

- Black pepper
- Apple cider vinegar, 1 tbsp.
- Red pepper flakes
- Peanut butter, 1/3 c.
- Coconut aminos, 1 tbsp.
- Salt
- Ground ginger, ½ tsp.
- Minced garlic clove, 1.
- Warm water, ½ c.
- Chicken thighs and drumsticks, 2½ lbs.

Directions:

1. Plug in and switch on the blender to process together water, peanut butter, pepper, aminos, salt, ginger, pepper flakes, garlic and vinegar until done.
2. Pat dry chicken pieces then set them on a pan topped with the peanut butter marinade.
3. Mix to coat evenly then refrigerate for 1 hour.
4. Grill the chicken pieces with the skin facing down on a preheated grill for 10 minutes over medium-high heat.
5. Turn the chicken, brush with the marinade then bake for another 10 minutes
6. Set on plates to serve and enjoy.

Nutrition Values:

Calories: 375, Fat: 12, Fiber: 1, Carbs: 3, Protein: 4

353. Avocado And Cucumber Salad with Cilantro

Preparation Time: 10 minutes
Servings: 4

Ingredients:

- cherry tomatoes - 1 pound; halved
- Avocados - 2; pitted, peeled and chopped.
- small red onion - 1; sliced
- Cucumber - 1; sliced
- olive oil - 2 tablespoons
- Cilantro - 1/4 cup; chopped.
- 2 tablespoons lemon juice
- Salt and black pepper to the taste.

Directions:

1. Mix tomatoes with cucumber, onion and avocado in a large salad bowl and stir.
2. Drizzle some oil, and add some salt, pepper as well as lemon juice
3. Then toss to coat well.
4. Serve cold with cilantro as toppings. .

Nutrition Values:

Calories: 140; Fat : 4; Fiber : 2; Carbs : 4; Protein : 5

354. Coconut Orange Chicken

Preparation Time: 25 minutes
Servings: 4

Ingredients:

- Black pepper
- Coconut flour, ¼ c.
- De-boned and sliced chicken thighs, 2 lbs.
- Coconut oil, 3 tbsps.
- Salt

For the sauce:

- Sesame seeds, ¼ tsp.
- Water, 1c.
- Ste via, 2 tsp.
- Chopped scallions, 2 tbsps.
- Orange zest, 1 tbsp.
- Orange juice, ¼ c.
- Orange extract, 1½ tsp.
- Ground coriander, ½ tsp.
- Gluten free soy sauce, 2 tbsps.
- Fish sauce, 2 tbsps.
- Grated ginger, 1 tbsp.
- Red pepper flakes, ¼ tsp.

Directions:

1. Set up a mixing bowl to combine the seasonings and coconut flour.
2. Coat the chicken pieces with the mixture
3. Set the pan on fire to heat the oil for browning the chicken pieces over medium heat on both sides. Reserve on the bowl
4. Set up the blender to process fish sauce, orange juice, ginger, stevia, soy sauce, water, orange extract, and coriander until done.
5. Heat up the mixture on a pan over medium heat.
6. Stir in the chicken to cook for 2 minutes.
7. Mix in the scallions, sesame seeds, pepper flakes, and orange zest to cook for 2 minutes then remove from heat
8. Set on plates to serve.
9. Enjoy.

Nutrition Values:

Calories: 423, Fat: 20, Fiber: 5, Carbs: 6, Protein: 45

355. Spicy Baked Chicken Breast

Preparation Time: 40 minutes
Servings: 4

Ingredients:

- Avocado oil, 1 tbsp.

- Dried oregano, ½ tsp.
- Chopped tomato, 1.
- Chopped zucchini, 1.
- Black pepper
- Garlic powder, 1tsp.
- Dried basil, ½ tsp.
- Shredded mozzarella cheese, ½ c.
- De-boned and sliced chicken breasts, 2.
- Salt

Directions:

1. Rub the chicken with garlic powder, salt, and pepper.
2. Set the pan on fire with oil to brown the chicken on both sides then set them on a baking tray.
3. Set the pan on fire again to cook tomato, zucchini, oregano, pepper, basil, and salt for 2 minutes over medium heat.
4. Pour the mixture over chicken.
5. Set the oven for 20 minutes at 3250F, allow to bake.
6. Once the timer is up, sprinkle mozzarella over the chicken then bake for 5 more minutes.
7. Set on plates to serve.
8. Enjoy.

Nutrition Values:

Calories: 235, Fat: 4, Fiber: 1, Carbs: 2, Protein: 35

356. Tasty Pepperoni Chicken

Preparation Time: 1 hour 5 minutes
Servings: 6

Ingredients:

- Black pepper
- Sliced pepperoni, 2 oz.
- Garlic powder, 1 tsp.
- Coconut oil, 1 tbsp.
- Low carb pizza sauce, 14 oz.
- De-boned medium chicken breasts, 4.
- Dried oregano, 1 tsp.
- Salt
- Sliced mozzarella, 6 oz.

Directions:

1. Allow the pizza sauce to boil in the pot for

20 minutes over medium heat then remove from heat

2. Stir together chicken with oregano, garlic powder, pepper, and salt in a mixing bowl.
3. Set the pan on fire with coconut oil to cook the chicken pieces for 2 minutes each side over medium heat then set them on a baking tray.
4. Top with mozzarella slices then spread sauce, and the pepperoni slices.
5. Set the oven for 30 minutes at 4000F, allow to bake
6. Set on plates to serve.
7. Enjoy.

Nutrition Values:

Calories: 320, Fat: 10, Fiber: 6, Carbs: 3, Protein: 27

356. Avocado Stuffed Chicken

Preparation Time: 10 minutes
Servings: 2

Ingredients:

- Black pepper
- Cayenne pepper, ¼ tsp.
- Cooked and shredded chicken, 1½ c.
- Mayonnaise, ¼ c.
- Dried thyme, 1 tsp.
- Cream cheese, 2 tbsps.
- Lemon juice, 2 tbsps.
- Salt
- Sliced and pitted avocados, 2.
- Paprika, 1 tsp.
- Onion powder, ½ tsp.
- Garlic powder, ½ tsp.

Directions:

1. Remove the insides of your avocado halves and set them in a bowl.
2. Reserve avocado cups for later use.
3. Stir the chicken to avocado flesh.
4. Stir in cayenne, garlic, seasonings, thyme, onion, paprika, mayo, lemon juice and cream cheese.
5. Fill avocados with chicken mix.
6. Serve and enjoy.

Nutrition Values:

Calories: 230, Fat: 40, Fiber: 11, Carbs: 5, Protein:

24

358. Garlicky Chicken Nuggets

Preparation time: 15 minutes
Cooking time: 15 minutes
Servings: 2

Ingredients:

- ½ cup coconut flour
- 1 egg
- 2 chicken breasts, diced
- 2 tbsp. garlic powder
- Salt and black pepper ground, to taste
- ½ cup butter

Directions:

1. Mix coconut flour with garlic powder, pepper, and salt in a shallow bowl.
2. Whisk the egg well in another bowl and keep it next to the flour mixture.
3. Add butter to a skillet and set it over medium heat.
4. First, dip each chicken cubes in the egg then dredge it through the flour mixture to coat well.
5. Place the coated chicken in the melted butter and cook for 5 minutes per side.
6. Once done, transfer the nuggets to a plate lined with paper towels.
7. Serve warm.

Nutrition Value:

Calories –1171, Fat –74.9g, Fiber–13.3g, Carbs – 26.3g, Protein – 94.1g

359. Spicy Wings with Mint Sauce

Preparation time: 20 minutes
Cooking time: 25 minutes
Servings: 6

Ingredients:

- 1 tbsp. cumin
- 18 chicken wings, cut in half
- 1 tbsp. turmeric
- 1 tbsp. coriander
- 1 tbsp. fresh ginger, finely grated
- 2 tbsp. olive oil
- 1 tbsp. paprika
- A pinch of cayenne pepper

- Salt and black pepper ground, to taste
- Chutney/ Sauce:
- 1 cup fresh mint leaves
- Juice of ½ lime
- ¾ cup cilantro
- 1 Serrano pepper
- 1 tbsp. water
- 1 small ginger piece, peeled and finely chopped
- 1 tbsp. olive oil
- Salt and black pepper ground, to taste

Directions:

1. Mix cumin with paprika, turmeric, 1 tbsp. ginger, coriander, pepper, salt, 2 tbsp. oil and cayenne in a large bowl.
2. Toss in all the chicken wings and mix well to coat.
3. Cover these coated wings and marinate them for 20 minutes in the refrigerator.
4. Meanwhile, set a greased grill pan over high heat.
5. Place the marinated wings in the pan and cook them for 25 minutes.
6. Continue flipping the wings after every 5 minutes for even cooking.
7. Add cilantro, lime juice, ginger, mint, 1 tbsp. olive oil, salt, water, pepper and Serrano pepper to a blender.
8. Blend these ingredients well to form a smooth paste.
9. Serve the grilled wings with this green sauce.

Nutrition Value:

Calories – 452, Fat – 15.3g, Fiber – 1.1g, Carbs – 2g, Protein – 72.7g

360. Sautéed Pork

Preparation time: 4 hours
Cooking time: 1 hour and 20 minutes
Servings: 4

Ingredients:

- 2 pounds pork shoulder, boneless and cubed
- 1 teaspoon ginger, grated
- ⅓ cup white vinegar
- 1 teaspoon cumin seeds
- 10 black peppercorns
- 4 garlic cloves, peeled and minced
- ½ teaspoon turmeric
- 3 red chili peppers
- 2 green chili peppers
- 1 teaspoon black mustard seeds
- ⅓ cup olive oil
- 1¼ cup water
- 1 teaspoon cinnamon powder
- 1 yellow onion, peeled and sliced
- A pinch of salt and black pepper

Directions

1. Heat a pot with the oil over medium high heat, add the pork, salt, pepper, cumin, mustard seeds and peppercorns, stir and cook for 5-6 minutes. Add the ginger, the vinegar, garlic and all the chili peppers, stir and cook for 6 minutes. Add the onion, cinnamon and the water, stir, cover the pot, reduce heat to low and simmer for 1 hour. Divide into bowls and serve.

Nutrition Value: Calories - 321, Fat - 4, Fiber - 4, Carbs - 7, Protein - 10

361. Beef and Apple Soup

Preparation time: 10 minutes
Cooking time: 1 hour and 35 minutes
Servings: 6

Ingredients:

- 2 carrots, peeled and chopped
- 1 onion, peeled and chopped
- 1 tablespoon olive oil
- 1 apple, peeled, cored, and chopped
- 4 teaspoons curry powder
- 5 cups vegetable stock
- 1 cup cooked beef meat, minced
- A pinch of salt and black pepper
- 14 ounces canned diced tomatoes

Directions

1. Heat a pot with the oil over medium heat, add the onion, carrots, and apple, stir, and cook them for a few minutes. Add the curry powder, the stock, tomatoes, salt, and pepper. Bring to a boil, reduce heat to low, cover, and simmer for 1 hour and 30 minutes, stirring from time to time. Strain the liquid, return it to the pot, add the beef, stir, heat up over medium heat. Bring to a boil, cook for 5 minutes, ladle into bowls, and serve.

Nutrition Value: Calories - 214, Fat - 3, Fiber - 3, Carbs - 6, Protein - 10

362. Thai Grilled Beef

Preparation time: 15 minutes
Cooking time: 15 minutes
Servings: 4

Ingredients:

- 1 cup green onion, sliced
- 2 tablespoons coconut aminos
- ½ cup water
- ½ cup balsamic vinegar
- ¼ cup sesame seeds
- 5 garlic cloves, peeled and minced
- 1 teaspoon ground black pepper
- 1 pound lean beef steaks

Directions

1. In a bowl, mix the onion with the aminos, water, vinegar, garlic, sesame seeds, and pepper and stir well. Place meat in a large dish, pour the marinade over, cover, and leave aside for 10 minutes. Place on a preheated kitchen grill, and cook for 15

minutes, flipping once. Divide the meat on plates and serve.

Nutrition Value: Calories - 214, Fat - 4, Fiber - 4, Carbs - 7, Protein - 10

363. Pork and Papaya Stir-fry

Preparation time: 15 minutes
Cooking time: 10 minutes
Servings: 4

Ingredients:

- 1 teaspoon avocado oil
- 2 teaspoons coconut aminos
- ½ teaspoon fresh ginger, grated
- 1 pound papaya, peeled and cubed
- 3 garlic cloves, peeled and minced
- ½ pound pork tenderloin, cut into strips
- Juice of 1 lime
- ¼ cup fresh parsley, chopped

Directions

1. Heat a large pan with the oil over medium-high heat, add the pork, and cook for 2-3 minutes. Add the aminos, garlic, ginger, lime juice and parsley, stir, cook for 5 minutes, take of the heat, add the papaya, toss, divide into bowls and serve.

Nutrition Value: Calories - 306, Fat - 4, Fiber - 7, Carbs - 12, Protein - 20

364. Chinese Beef Mix

Preparation time: 4 hours
Cooking time: 20 minutes
Servings: 6

Ingredients:

- 3 tablespoons olive oil
- ¼ cup tamari sauce
- 1½ teaspoons sesame oil
- 1 teaspoon ginger, grated
- 2 garlic cloves, peeled and chopped
- 2 pounds beef meat, cubed
- 2 scallions, chopped

Directions

1. In a bowl, mix the olive oil with the tamari, ginger, garlic, and the oil, whisk well, add the beef, toss to coat, and keep in the

refrigerator for 4 hours. Heat a kitchen grill over medium heat, add the beef, cook for 8 minutes, turning from time to time. Divide between plates, sprinkle the scallions on top and serve.

Nutrition Value: Calories - 150, Fat - 4, Fiber - 3, Carbs - 7, Protein - 12

365. Spiced Beef Stew

Preparation time: 30 minutes
Cooking time: 1 hour
Servings: 8

Ingredients:

For the spice mix:

- ¼ teaspoon ground nutmeg
- ½ teaspoon cumin seeds, toasted
- 1 teaspoon fenugreek seeds, toasted
- ¼ teaspoon turmeric powder
- ½ teaspoon black pepper
- 4 tablespoons red chili flakes
- 1 teaspoon ground ginger
- 2 tablespoons sweet paprika
- 2 teaspoons dried onion flakes
- ¼ teaspoon allspice
- ½ teaspoon garlic powder
- 1 teaspoon coriander
- ½ teaspoon ground cloves
- ½ teaspoon ground cinnamon

For the stew:

- 3 tablespoons olive oil
- 3 pounds beef, cubed
- 2 garlic cloves, peeled and minced
- 1 onion, peeled and chopped
- 2 tablespoons tomato paste
- Salt and ground black pepper, to taste
- 2 cups vegetable stock

Directions

1. In a bowl, mix the nutmeg with the cumin seeds, fenugreek, turmeric, black pepper, chili flakes, ginger, paprika, onion flakes, allspice, coriander, garlic powder, cloves and cinnamon stir well. Transfer 3 teaspoons of this mix to another bowl, add the meat, toss and keep in the fridge for 30 minutes. Heat a pot with the oil over

medium-high heat, add the onion, stir well, cook for 3-4 minutes. Add the meat, the garlic, tomato paste, the stock, salt and pepper, toss, cover the pot, and simmer over medium heat for about 1 hour. Divide between plates and serve.

Nutrition Value: calories-214, fat-7, fiber-5, carbs-14, protein-11

366. Cardamom Beef

Preparation time: 10 minutes
Cooking time: 10 minutes
Servings: 6

Ingredients:

- 1 and ½ pounds beef tenderloin, trimmed and cubed
- 1 teaspoon cardamom powder
- 6 teaspoons cayenne pepper
- 4 tablespoons coconut oil, melted
- Salt and ground black pepper, to taste
- ¼ teaspoon onion powder
- ¼ teaspoon garlic powder

Directions

1. Heat a pan with the oil over medium high heat, add the beef and brown it for 2-3 minutes. Add salt, pepper, cayenne, cardamom, onion powder and garlic powder, toss. Cook for 8 minutes more, divide between plates and serve with a side salad.

Nutrition Value: Calories - 120, Fat - 3, Fiber - 3, Carbs - 4, Protein - 6

367. Beef Chuck and Celery Soup

Preparation time: 10 minutes
Cooking time: 1 hour and 20 minutes
Servings: 8

Ingredients:

- 1 pound beef chuck, cubed
- 2 tablespoons olive oil
- 3 celery stalks, chopped
- 1 onion, peeled and chopped
- Salt and ground black pepper, to taste
- 6 garlic cloves, peeled and chopped
- 32 ounces canned beef stock

- 1½ teaspoons parsley, dried
- 1 teaspoon dried oregano
- 28 ounces canned diced tomatoes
- ¼ cup fresh cilantro, minced

Directions

1. Heat a pot with the oil over medium-high heat; add the beef, stir, and brown for 8 minutes. Add the celery, garlic, onion, oregano, and dried parsley, stir, and cook for 10 minutes more. Add the stock, salt, pepper and tomatoes, bring to a boil, reduce heat to medium, and cook for 1 hour. Add parsley, stir, ladle into soup bowls, and serve.

Nutrition Value: Calories - 241, Fat - 4, Fiber - 4, Carbs - 5, Protein - 9

368. Pork and Basil Soup

Preparation time: 10 minutes
Cooking time: 1 hour and 10 minutes
Servings: 6

Ingredients:

- 1 onion, peeled and chopped
- 1 tablespoon olive oil
- 3 teaspoons fresh basil, chopped
- 3 garlic cloves, diced
- Salt and ground black pepper, to taste
- 1 carrot, peeled and chopped
- 1 pound pork chops, bone-in
- 3 cups chicken stock
- 2 tablespoons tomato paste
- 2 tablespoons lime juice
- 1 teaspoon red chili flakes

Directions

1. Heat a pot with the oil over medium-high heat, add the garlic, onion, basil, salt and pepper, stir well, and cook for 6 minutes. Add the carrots and the pork chops, stir and brown for 5 minutes. Add the tomato paste, salt, pepper and stock, stir well, bring to a boil, reduce heat to medium, and simmer for 50 minutes. Transfer the pork to a plate, discard the bones, shred it, return to soup, add the chili flakes, and lime juice, stir, ladle into bowls, and serve.

Nutrition Value: Calories - 321, Fat - 4, Fiber - 4, Carbs - 7, Protein - 17

369. Meatballs and Hoisin Sauce

Preparation time: 10 minutes
Cooking time: 10 minutes
Servings: 4

Ingredients:

For the meatballs:

- 1 pound ground beef
- ⅓ cup fresh cilantro, chopped
- 1 cup onion, chopped
- 4 garlic cloves, peeled and chopped
- 1 tablespoon fresh ginger, grated
- 1½ tablespoon coconut aminos
- 1 Serrano chili pepper, chopped
- 2 tablespoons olive oil

For the sauce:

- 2 tablespoons coconut aminos
- ¼ cup hoisin sauce
- 1 tablespoon fish sauce
- 2 tablespoons water
- 1 Serrano chili pepper, chopped

Directions

1. In a bowl, mix the beef with the onion, garlic, cilantro, ginger, aminos and chili, stir well and shape medium meatballs out of this mix. Heat up a pan with the oil over a medium-high heat, add the meatballs, cover, cook for 5 minutes on each side and transfer them to a platter. In a bowl, mix the hoisin sauce with the fish sauce, aminos, water and Serrano chili, whisk well and drizzle over the meatballs.

Nutrition Value: Calories - 245, Fat - 4, Fiber - 4, Carbs - 7, Protein - 9

370. Beef and Walnut Mix

Preparation time: 10 minutes
Cooking time: 20 minutes
Servings: 4

Ingredients:

- 2 tablespoons lime juice
- 2 tablespoons coconut aminos
- 5 garlic cloves, peeled and minced

- 3 tablespoons olive oil
- 1 onion, peeled and cut into wedges
- 1½ pound beef tenderloin, cubed
- 3 tablespoons walnuts, toasted and chopped
- 2 scallions, sliced

Directions

1. Heat a pan with the oil over medium high heat, add the beef and brown it for 3 minutes on each side. Add the garlic and the onion, stir and cook for 2 minutes more. Add the lime juice, the aminos and the walnuts, toss, cook for 10 minutes over medium low heat. Divide into bowls, sprinkle the scallions on top and serve.

Nutrition Value: Calories - 300, Fat - 3, Fiber - 4, Carbs - 6, Protein - 12

371. Lemongrass Beef Bowls

Preparation time: 30 minutes
Cooking time: 2 hours
Servings: 4

Ingredients:

- 2 pounds beef, boneless and cubed
- 3 tablespoons coconut aminos
- 1 stalk lemongrass, chopped
- 1½ teaspoons five spice powder
- 2½ tablespoons fresh ginger, grated
- 3 tablespoons olive oil
- 1 onion, peeled and chopped
- 2 cups tomatoes, chopped
- 1 pound carrots, peeled and chopped
- Salt and ground black pepper, to taste
- 3 cups water
- 2 tablespoons cilantro, chopped

Directions

1. In a bowl, mix the coconut aminos with the lemongrass, 5 spice powder, ginger, and beef, cover, and set aside for 30 minutes. Heat a pot with the oil over medium-high heat, add the beef, stir, cook for 3-4 minutes and transfer to a plate. Heat the pot again over medium heat, add the onions, and cook for 5 minutes, stirring often. Add the tomato, salt, pepper, the

water, the carrots, return the beef and the lemongrass mix. Stir, cover, and cook for 15 minutes. Reduce the heat to low and simmer the stew for 1 hour and 30 minutes. Add the cilantro, stir, divide into bowls and serve.

Nutrition Value: Calories - 320, Fat - 4, Fiber - 4, Carbs - 7, Protein - 12

372. Garlic Rib Eye Steaks

Preparation time: 30 minutes
Cooking time: 10 minutes
Servings: 4

Ingredients:

- 11 ounces rib eye steak, sliced
- 4 garlic cloves, peeled and chopped
- 2 tablespoons olive oil
- 1 red bell pepper, seeded and cut into strips
- A pinch of salt and black pepper
- 2 tablespoons fish sauce
- ½ cup vegetable stock
- 4 green onions, sliced

Directions

1. In a bowl, mix the beef with the oil, garlic, black pepper, and bell pepper. Stir, cover, and keep in the refrigerator for 30 minutes. Heat a pan over medium-high heat, add the beef, the marinade, fish sauce and the stock, stir, and cook for 8 minutes. Add the green onions, cook for 1-2 minutes, divide between plates, and serve.

Nutrition Value: Calories - 321, Fat - 4, Fiber - 5, Carbs - 7, Protein - 15

373. Pork and Spinach Soup

Preparation time: 10 minutes
Cooking time: 20 minutes
Servings: 4

Ingredients:

- 2 inches ginger piece, grated
- ½ pound pork loin, cubed
- 1 onion, peeled and cut in half
- 2 tablespoons fish sauce
- 1 cup baby spinach
- 6 cups vegetable soup

Directions

1. Put the stock in a pot and bring to a simmer over medium heat. Add the pork, fish sauce and ginger, stir and simmer for 20 minutes. Add the spinach, stir, take off the heat, cover, set aside for 2-3 minutes, ladle into bowls and serve.

Nutrition Value: Calories - 254, Fat - 3, Fiber - 3, Carbs - 6, Protein - 10

374. Pork, Shrimp and Pickled Veggie Salad

Preparation time: 10 minutes
Cooking time: 2 hours
Servings: 4

Ingredients:

- 2 jars pickled root vegetables, drained and chopped
- 3 cups pickled carrots, drained
- 1 bunch mint leaves, chopped
- 1 bunch cilantro, chopped
- ½ pound pork shoulder
- ½ pound shrimp, cooked, peeled and deveined
- 2 teaspoons walnuts, roasted and ground
- 2 tablespoons shallots
- ½ cup fish sauce

Directions

1. Put the pork shoulder in a pot, add the water to cover and a pinch of salt, bring to a boil over medium heat, cook for 2 hours, drain, shred, and set aside. Put the pickled vegetables and carrots in a salad bowl, add the sliced pork, shrimp, cilantro, mint, shallots, walnuts, and fish sauce. Toss everything to coat, and serve.

Nutrition Value: Calories - 230, Fat - 4, Fiber - 4, Carbs - 6, Protein - 10

375. Bacon and Sausage Stew

Preparation time: 30 minutes
Cooking time: 3 hours
Servings: 12

Ingredients:

- 4 sausages, sliced

- 1 pound bacon, sliced
- 4 heads green cabbage, chopped
- 2 yellow onions, peeled and sliced
- 5 pounds sweet potatoes, chopped
- 4 ounces garlic, minced
- Ground black pepper, to taste
- 4 cups water
- 3 tablespoons coconut oil, melted

Directions

1. Heat a pot with the oil over medium-high heat, add the onions and garlic, stir, and cook for 5 minutes. Add the black pepper, $\frac{1}{3}$ of the cabbage and half of the potatoes. Add the 2 cups water and half of the sausages and stir. Add $\frac{1}{3}$ of cabbage, the other half of the potatoes, the rest of the cabbage, sausages, garlic, and 2 cups water. Stir again, cover, cook for 3 hours, divide into bowls and serve.

Nutrition Value: Calories - 232, Fat - 4, Fiber - 3, Carbs - 6, Protein - 12

376. Apple and Ginger Pork Chops

Preparation time: 20 minutes
Cooking time: 20 minutes
Servings: 6

Ingredients:

- $\frac{1}{2}$ cup natural apple juice
- 1 tablespoon coconut aminos
- 4 tablespoons olive oil
- Salt and ground black pepper, to taste
- $\frac{1}{2}$ teaspoon fresh ginger, grated
- $\frac{1}{2}$ cup water
- 6 boneless pork chops

Directions

1. Heat a pan with the oil over medium heat, add the aminos, apple juice, ginger, salt, and pepper, stir, bring to a simmer, cook for 10 minutes and take off the heat. Brush the pork chops with this half of mixture, place them on a preheated grill over medium heat, and cook for 10 minutes, turning them once. Divide the pork chops on plates serve with the rest of the sauce on top.

Nutrition Value: Calories - 231, Fat - 4, Fiber - 3, Carbs - 5, Protein - 9

377. Pork and Kimchi Soup

Preparation time: 10 minutes
Cooking time: 10 minutes
Servings: 2

Ingredients:

- $\frac{1}{8}$ pound pork loin, sliced
- Ground black pepper, to taste
- 1 cup Kimchi, chopped
- 1 green onion, sliced
- $\frac{1}{4}$ cup mushrooms, chopped
- 3 tablespoons green chili peppers, sliced
- $1\frac{1}{2}$ cup vegetable soup
- 1 tablespoon olive oil
- 4 teaspoons red chili flakes
- 2 teaspoons chili paste
- 4 teaspoons coconut aminos
- $\frac{1}{2}$ teaspoon garlic, minced

Directions

1. Heat pot with the oil over medium-high heat, add the Kimchi, cook for 5 minutes, and transfer to a bowl. In another bowl, mix the chili flakes with the chili paste, aminos, garlic, and black pepper. Add the Kimchi, green onion, green chili peppers, and mushrooms. Transfer everything to the pot, add the stock and the meat. Stir, bring to a boil over medium-high heat, simmer everything for 5 minutes, ladle into bowls, and serve.

Nutrition Value: Calories - 130, Fat - 1, Fiber - 5, Carbs - 7, Protein - 10

378. Baked Pork with Blueberry Sauce

Preparation time: 10 minutes
Cooking time: 30 minutes
Servings: 4

Ingredients:

- 1 cup blueberries
- $\frac{1}{2}$ teaspoon dried thyme
- 2 pounds pork loin
- 1 tablespoon balsamic vinegar

- ½ teaspoon red chili flakes
- 1 teaspoon ground ginger
- Ground black pepper, to taste
- 2 tablespoon water

Directions

1. Heat a pan over medium heat, add the blueberries, vinegar, water, thyme, black pepper, chili flakes, and ginger, stir, cook for 5 minutes, and take off the heat. Put the pork in a baking dish, pour the sauce all over, place in the oven at 375°F, bake for 25 minutes. Slice the meat, divide it between plates, drizzle the sauce all over and serve.

Nutrition Value: Calories - 335, Fat - 5, Carbs - 6, Fiber - 1, Protein - 14

379. Braised Pork with Grapes

Preparation time: 10 minutes
Cooking time: 1 hour and 30 minutes
Servings: 4

Ingredients:

- 2 pounds pork loin roast, boneless
- 3 tablespoons olive oil
- Salt and ground black pepper, to taste
- 2 cups chicken stock
- 2 garlic cloves, peeled and minced
- 1 teaspoon fresh thyme, chopped
- 1 tablespoon rosemary, chopped
- ½ onion, peeled and chopped
- ½ pound grapes, halved

Directions

1. Put the pork in a baking dish. Add the oil, salt, pepper, stock, garlic, thyme, rosemary, onion and grapes, cover, and bake in the oven at 380°F for 1 hour and 30 minutes. Slice the roast, divide it and the grapes mix between plates and serve.

Nutrition Value: Calories - 321, Fat - 3, Fiber - 3, Carbs - 6, Protein - 10

380. Lamb Chops with Apples

Preparation time: 10 minutes
Cooking time: 20 minutes
Servings: 4

Ingredients:

- 1½ cups pearl onions
- 2 cups apple, cut in wedges
- 1 tablespoon olive oil
- Salt and ground black pepper, to taste
- 2 teaspoons fresh rosemary, chopped
- 4 medium lamb chops
- ½-cup vegetable stock

Directions

1. Heat a pan with oil over medium high heat, add the lamb chops, salt, pepper and the rosemary, cook for 4 minutes on each side, take off heat, add the stock, the apple and the onions. Place the pan in the oven and bake at 400°F for 10 minutes more. Divide everything between plates and serve.

Nutrition Value: Calories - 240, Fat - 10, Fiber - 3, Carbs - 10, Protein - 18

381. Pork Roll

Preparation time: 10 minutes
Cooking time: 35 minutes
Servings: 4

Ingredients:

- 1 pound pork tenderloin
- Salt and ground black pepper, to taste
- 1 teaspoon olive oil
- ¾ cup apple, peeled and chopped
- ¾ cup onion, chopped
- 2 teaspoons garlic, minced
- 1 teaspoon fresh rosemary, chopped
- 1 tablespoon white vinegar
- 1 teaspoon Dijon mustard
- ⅓ cup chicken stock

Directions

1. Heat a pan with the oil over medium-high heat, add the apple, onion, and garlic, stir, and cook for 5 minutes. Add the vinegar and rosemary, stir, and transfer to a bowl. Butterfly the pork lengthwise, butterfly each half lengthwise, cover with the plastic, and flatten a bit using a meat tenderizer. Season the pork with salt and pepper, arrange with the apple mixture, and roll up. Heat the same pan over medium heat; add

the pork roulade, brown for 4 minutes, place in the oven at 425°F, and bake for 15 minutes. Slice the pork and arrange on a platter. Heat the pan again over medium-high heat, add the stock and the mustard, stir, bring to a boil, cook for 2 minutes, drizzle over pork roll, and serve.

Nutrition Value: Calories - 181, Fat - 4, Fiber - 2, Carbs - 9, Protein - 24

382. Lamb Stew

Preparation time: 10 minutes
Cooking time: 7 hours
Servings: 4

Ingredients:

- 2 pounds lamb meat, cubed
- Salt and ground black pepper, to taste
- 2 cups vegetable stock
- 2 tablespoons olive oil
- 2 bay leaves
- ¼ cup tapioca flour
- 1 onion, peeled and chopped
- 2 tablespoons fresh thyme, chopped
- 4 garlic cloves, peeled and minced
- 16 ounces mushrooms, chopped
- 3 carrots, peeled and chopped
- 3 celery stalks, chopped
- 28 ounces canned crushed tomatoes
- ½ cup fresh parsley, chopped

Directions

1. In a bowl, mix the beef with the salt, pepper and coat in tapioca flour. Heat a pan with the oil over medium-high heat, add the meat, brown it for a few minutes, and transfer to a slow cooker. Add the stock, bay leaves, onion, thyme, garlic, mushrooms, carrots, celery and tomatoes. Cover, cook on Low for 7 hours, add the parsley, stir, divide into bowls and serve.

Nutrition Value: Calories - 240, Fat - 7, Fiber - 4, Carbs - 15, Protein - 13

383. Beef, Watercress and Radish Salad

Preparation time: 10 minutes
Cooking time: 0 minutes

Servings: 4

Ingredients:

- ½ cup olive oil
- Salt and ground black pepper, to taste
- 2 tablespoon balsamic vinegar
- 2 teaspoons mustard
- 4 ounces cherry tomatoes, cut in half
- 4 ounces baby plum tomatoes, cut in quarters
- 2 tablespoons sun-dried tomatoes in oil, drained and chopped
- 4 ounces radishes, chopped
- 4 ounces watercress
- 8 slices roast beef, cut into thin strips
- 4 green onions, sliced

Directions

1. In a salad bowl, mix the beef with green onions, watercress, radishes, sun-dried tomatoes, plum tomatoes, cherry tomatoes, mustard, vinegar, salt, pepper and the oil, toss and serve.

Nutrition Value: Calories - 154, Fat - 4, Fiber - 3, Carbs - 8, Protein - 10

384. Beef Brisket with Tomato Sauce

Preparation time: 10 minutes
Cooking time: 7 hours and 20 minutes
Servings: 6

Ingredients:

- 1 pound onions, peeled and chopped
- 4 pounds beef brisket
- 1 pound carrots, peeled and chopped
- 8 Earl Grey tea bags
- ½ pound celery, chopped
- Salt and ground black pepper, to taste
- 4 cups water

For the sauce:

- 16 ounces canned diced tomatoes
- ½ pound celery, chopped
- 1 ounce garlic, minced
- 4 ounces olive oil
- 1 pound onions, peeled and chopped
- 1 cup white vinegar

Directions

1. Put the water in a pot, add 1 pound onion, carrot, ½-pound celery, salt, and pepper, stir, and bring to a simmer over medium-high heat. Add the beef brisket and the tea bags, stir, cover, reduce heat to low, and cook for 7 hours. Heat a pan with the olive oil over medium-high heat; add 1 pound onion, stir, and sauté for 10 minutes. Add the garlic, ½ pound celery, tomatoes, vinegar, salt and pepper, stir, bring to a simmer and cook for 20 minutes Transfer the beef brisket to a cutting board, set aside to cool down, slice, divide between plates. Drizzle the tomato sauce all over and serve.

Nutrition Value: Calories - 400, Fat - 12, Fiber - 4, Carbs - 18, Protein - 3

385. Pork Chops and Tomato Sauce

Preparation time: 10 minutes
Cooking time: 1 hour and 20 minutes
Servings: 4

Ingredients:

- 4 pork chops
- ½ teaspoon ground cinnamon
- ¼ teaspoons ground black pepper

For the sauce:

- 30 ounces canned tomato sauce
- 2 tablespoons cumin. ground
- 10 garlic cloves, peeled and minced
- Ground black pepper, to taste
- 2 tablespoons dry mustard
- ¼ teaspoons red pepper flakes
- ½ teaspoon ground cinnamon
- ½ cup red vinegar

Directions

1. Rub the ribs with a mixture of cloves, pepper, and ½-teaspoon cinnamon, rub with the oil. Place on preheated grill and cook over medium high heat for 7 minutes on each side. In a pan, mix the tomato sauce with the cumin, garlic, black pepper, mustard, pepper flakes, ½-teaspoon cinnamon, and vinegar. Stir, bring to a boil over medium heat, and simmer for 1 hour

covered. Divide the ribs between plates, drizzle the sauce all over and serve.

Nutrition Value: Calories - 242, Fat - 4, Fiber - 2, Carbs - 5, Protein - 10

386. Beef and Beets Salad

Preparation time: 10 minutes
Cooking time: 5 minutes
Servings: 4

Ingredients:

- 3 red beetroot, peeled and sliced
- Juice of 1 lemon
- 2 sirloin steaks
- 2 tablespoons olive oil
- 1 small bunch fresh dill, chopped
- 4 ounces coconut cream
- 2 tablespoon olive oil
- Salt and ground black pepper, to taste

Directions

1. In a salad bowl, mix the beetroot with half of the lemon juice and toss to coat, then set aside. Heat a kitchen grill over medium-high heat, add the steaks, season with salt and pepper, rub them with half of the olive oil, cook for 2 minutes on each side. Slice, and put in a bowl. In another bowl, mix the dill with the coconut cream, the rest of the lemon juice, and remaining olive oil then whisk. Mix the beetroot and apple slices with the beef slices, divide between plates, drizzle with the dressing, and serve.

Nutrition Value: Calories - 234, Fat - 2, Fiber - 4, Carbs - 5, Protein - 10

387. Pork Rib Stew

Preparation time: 10 minutes
Cooking time: 2 hours and 20 minutes
Servings: 6

Ingredients:

- 8 cups water
- 4 ounces tomatillos, husked
- 2 cups cilantro leaves
- 2 jalapeños
- 4 garlic cloves, peeled
- 6 garlic cloves, peeled and minced

- 1 teaspoon dried oregano
- 2 pounds baby back pork ribs, ribs divided
- Salt and ground black pepper, to taste
- 1 onion, peeled and cut in wedges

Directions

1. Put the tomatillos and jalapeños in a pan, add water to cover, heat up over high heat, bring to a boil, cook for 5 minutes, drain. Transfer to a blender, add the cilantro and whole garlic cloves and pulse very well. Put the pork ribs in a pot, add 4 cups water, bring to a boil, and cook for 1 hour and 15 minutes. Add the onion, cilantro, oregano and the tomatillo sauce, stir, and cook for another 15 minutes. Add the remaining water, stir, bring to a boil, and reduce the heat to low, and cook pork for 30 minutes. Season with salt and pepper, stir, divide between bowls, and serve.

Nutrition Value: Calories - 231, Fat - 2, Fiber - 3, Carbs - 7, Protein - 10

388. Pork Chops and Green Chillies

Preparation time: 10 minutes
Cooking time: 30 minutes
Servings: 4

Ingredients:

- 4 pork chops, boneless
- 1 teaspoon ancho chili powder
- 1 teaspoon cumin
- Salt and ground black pepper, to taste
- ¾ cup chicken stock
- 3 tablespoons jarred jalapeños, chopped
- 4 ounces canned green chilies, chopped
- 1 tablespoon white vinegar
- 1 yellow onion, peeled and sliced
- 3 tablespoons olive oil

Directions

1. In a bowl, mix the chili powder with the salt, pepper, and cumin and stir. Sprinkle this over the pork chops, place them in a preheated pan with 2 tablespoons oil over medium heat, and cook for 4 minutes on each side and transfer to a bowl. In a food processor, mix the stock with the

jalapeños, green chilies, and vinegar and pulse well. Heat a pan over medium-high heat, add the rest of the oil and the onions, stir, and cook for 4 minutes. Add the green chili mixture, salt and pepper, stir, bring to a boil, and simmer for 8 minutes. Divide the pork chops on plates, drizzle the sauce over them, and serve.

Nutrition Value: Calories - 312, Fat - 4, Fiber - 4, Carbs - 6, Protein - 10

389. Beef Patties

Preparation Time: 10 minutes
Cooking Time: 45 minutes
Serve: 4

Ingredients:

- 10 oz beef minced
- 1 tsp tomato puree
- 1 tsp garlic puree
- 1/4 tsp ginger puree
- 1 1/2 tsp mixed herbs
- 1 tsp basil
- 1/2 tsp mustard
- Pepper
- Salt

Directions:

1. Add all ingredients into the large bowl and mix until well combined.
2. Make patties from bowl mixture and place into the air fryer basket.
3. Cook at 400 F/ 200 C for 25 minutes.
4. Turn patties to other side and cook at 350 F/ 180 C for 20 minutes more.
5. Serve and enjoy.

Nutritional Value (Amount per Serving):
Calories 173
Fat 7.2 g
Carbohydrates 0.8 g
Sugar 1.9 g
Protein 24.7 g
Cholesterol 35 mg

390. Meatloaf

Preparation Time: 10 minutes
Cooking Time: 25 minutes
Serve: 4

Ingredients:

- 1 lb ground beef
- 2 oz chorizo sausage, chopped
- 3 tbsp almond flour
- 1 egg, lightly beaten
- 3 mushrooms, sliced
- 1/2 tbsp thyme, chopped
- 1 small onion, chopped
- Pepper
- Salt

Directions:

1. Preheat the air fryer to 400 F/ 200 C.
2. Add all ingredients into the large bowl and mix until well combined.
3. Transfer bowl mixture into the baking dish and place into the air fryer basket.
4. Cook for 25 minutes.
5. Serve and enjoy.

Nutritional Value (Amount per Serving):

Calories 409
Fat 22.8 g
Carbohydrates 7.9 g
Sugar 2.2 g
Protein 43.7 g
Cholesterol 51 mg

391. Sirloin Steak

Preparation Time: 10 minutes
Cooking Time: 15 minutes
Serve: 4

Ingredients:

- 1 lb pork steaks, boneless
- 1 tsp garam masala
- 3 garlic cloves
- 1 tbsp ginger, sliced
- 1/2 onion, diced
- 1 tsp cayenne
- 1/4 tsp ground cardamom
- 1/2 tsp cinnamon
- 1 tsp ground fennel
- 1 tsp salt

Directions:

1. Add all ingredients except meat into the blender and blend until smooth paste form.

2. Add meat into the bowl. Pour blended mixture over the meat and mix well.
3. Place meat into the fridge for overnight.
4. Spray air fryer basket with cooking spray.
5. Place marinated meat into the air fryer basket and cook at 330 F/ 165 C for 15 minutes. Turn halfway through.
6. Slice and serve.

Nutritional Value (Amount per Serving):

Calories 260
Fat 18.3 g
Carbohydrates 4.3 g
Sugar 0.7 g
Protein 20.7 g
Cholesterol 0 mg

392. Beef Meatballs

Preparation Time: 10 minutes
Cooking Time: 20 minutes
Serve: 12

Ingredients:

- 1 lb ground beef
- 2 tbsp fresh parsley, chopped
- 4 tbsp mushrooms, chopped
- 1/2 cup almond flour
- 1/4 cup onion, chopped
- 1/4 tsp pepper
- 1 tsp salt

Directions:

1. In a bowl, mix together ground beef, parsley, onions, and mushrooms.
2. Add remaining ingredients and mix until well combined.
3. Make small balls from the mixture.
4. Spray air fryer basket with cooking spray.
5. Place prepared meatballs in the air fryer basket and cook at 350 F/ 180 C for 20 minutes.
6. Serve and enjoy.

Nutritional Value (Amount per Serving):

Calories 79
Fat 2.9 g
Carbohydrates 0.6 g
Sugar 0.2 g
Protein 11.8 g
Cholesterol 0 mg

393. Spicy Pork Chops

Preparation Time: 10 minutes
Cooking Time: 10 minutes
Serve: 4

Ingredients:

- 4 pork chops
- 1 1/2 tsp olive oil
- 1/4 tsp dried sage
- 1/2 tsp cayenne pepper
- 1/4 tsp black pepper
- 1/2 tsp ground cumin
- 1/2 tsp garlic salt
- 1 tsp smoked paprika

Directions:

1. Preheat the air fryer to 400 F/ 200 C.
2. In a small bowl, mix together paprika, garlic salt, sage, pepper, cayenne pepper, and cumin.
3. Rub pork chops with spice mixture and place into the air fryer basket.
4. Spray pork chops with cooking spray.
5. Cook for 10 minutes. Turn halfway through.
6. Serve and enjoy.

Nutritional Value (Amount per Serving):

Calories 276
Fat 21.8 g
Carbohydrates 1 g
Sugar 0.2 g
Protein 18.2 g
Cholesterol 0 mg

394. Spice Steak

Preparation Time: 10 minutes
Cooking Time: 9 minutes
Serve: 3

Ingredients:

- 1 lb ribeye steak
- 1/2 tsp paprika
- 1/2 tsp onion powder
- 1/4 tsp garlic powder
- 1/4 tsp chili powder
- 1/8 tsp cocoa powder
- 1/8 tsp coriander powder
- 1/4 tsp chipotle powder
- 1/4 tsp black pepper
- 1 tsp coffee powder
- 1 1/2 tsp sea salt

Directions:

1. In a small bowl, mix together all ingredients except steak.
2. Rub spice mixture all over the steak and let sit the steak for 20 minutes.
3. Spray air fryer basket with cooking spray.
4. Preheat the air fryer to 400 F/ 200 C.
5. Place steak in the air fryer basket and cook for 9 minutes.
6. Serve and enjoy.

Nutritional Value (Amount per Serving):

Calories 305
Fat 7.6 g
Carbohydrates 0.9 g
Sugar 0.2 g
Protein 54.8 g
Cholesterol 65 mg

395. Simple Lamb Chops

Preparation Time: 10 minutes
Cooking Time: 30 minutes
Serve: 2

Ingredients:

- 4 lamb chops
- 1 tbsp fresh oregano, chopped
- 1 1/2 tbsp olive oil
- 2 garlic cloves, minced
- Pepper
- Salt

Directions:

1. Preheat the air fryer to 400 F/ 200 C.
2. Mix together garlic, olive oil, oregano, pepper, and salt and rub over lamb chops.
3. Place lamb chops into the air fryer basket and cook for 30 minutes.
4. Serve and enjoy.

Nutritional Value (Amount per Serving):

Calories 736
Fat 62.6 g
Carbohydrates 1.3 g
Sugar 0.1 g

Protein 38.2 g

Cholesterol 0 mg

396. Rosemary Beef Roast

Preparation Time: 10 minutes

Cooking Time: 45 minutes

Serve: 6

Ingredients:

- 2 lbs beef roast
- 1 tbsp olive oil
- 2 tsp rosemary
- 1/4 tsp pepper
- 1 tsp salt

Directions:

1. Preheat the air fryer to 350 F/ 180 C.
2. Mix together oil, rosemary, pepper, and salt and rub all over the meat.
3. Place meat in the air fryer and cook for 45 minutes.
4. Serve and enjoy.

Nutritional Value (Amount per Serving):

Calories 302

Fat 11.8 g

Carbohydrates 0.2 g

Sugar 0 g

Protein 45.9 g

Cholesterol 46 mg

397. Sausage Meatballs

Preparation Time: 10 minutes

Cooking Time: 15 minutes

Serve: 4

Ingredients:

- 4 oz sausage meat
- 1/2 tsp garlic paste
- 1/2 small onion, diced
- 3 tbsp almond flour
- 1/2 tsp sage
- Pepper
- Salt

Directions:

1. Preheat the air fryer to 350 F/ 180 C.
2. Spray air fryer basket with cooking spray.
3. Add all ingredients into the mixing bowl

and mix until well combined.
4. Make balls from bowl mixture and place into the air fryer basket and cook for 15 minutes.
5. Serve and enjoy.

Nutritional Value (Amount per Serving):

Calories 211

Fat 17.6 g

Carbohydrates 6 g

Sugar 1.3 g

Protein 9.5 g

Cholesterol 3 mg

398. Rosemary Thyme Lamb Chops

Preparation Time: 10 minutes

Cooking Time: 20 minutes

Serve: 4

Ingredients:

- 1 lb lamb chops
- 1 tsp oregano
- 1 1/2 tsp thyme
- 1 tsp rosemary
- 2 tbsp fresh lemon juice
- 2 tbsp olive oil
- 1/2 tsp coriander
- 1 tsp salt

Directions:

1. Add all ingredients except lamb chops into the zip-lock bag.
2. Add lamb chops to the bag. Seal bag and shake well and place in the fridge for overnight.
3. Place marinated lamb chops into the air fryer basket and cook at 390 F/ 198 C for 3 minutes.
4. Turn lamb chops to other side and cook for 4 minutes more.
5. Serve and enjoy.

Nutritional Value (Amount per Serving):

Calories 276

Fat 15.5 g

Carbohydrates 0.8 g

Sugar 0.2 g

Protein 32 g

Cholesterol 0 mg

399. Easy Air Fryer Steak

Preparation Time: 10 minutes
Cooking Time: 10 minutes
Serve: 2

Ingredients:

- 2 sirloin steaks
- 2 tbsp steak seasoning
- 2 tsp olive oil
- Pepper
- Salt

Directions:

1. Preheat the air fryer to 350 F/ 180 C.
2. Brush steak with olive oil and season with steak seasoning.
3. Spray air fryer basket with cooking spray and place steak in the air fryer basket.
4. Cook for 10 minutes. Turn halfway through.
5. Cut into slices and serve.

Nutritional Value (Amount per Serving):

Calories 262
Fat 12.7 g
Carbohydrates 1 g
Sugar 0 g
Protein 36 g
Cholesterol 0 mg

400. Tasty Kabab

Preparation Time: 10 minutes
Cooking Time: 10 minutes
Serve: 4

Ingredients:

- 1 lb ground beef
- 1 1/2 tbsp kabab spice mix
- 3 garlic cloves, minced
- 1/4 cup fresh parsley, chopped
- 1 tbsp olive oil
- 1 tsp salt

Directions:

1. Add all ingredients into the mixing bowl and mix until well combined.
2. Place in refrigerator for 30 minutes.
3. Divide mixture into the four portions and make sausage shape kabab.

4. Spray air fryer basket with cooking spray.
5. Place kabab into the air fryer basket and cook at 375 F/ 190 C for 10 minutes.
6. Serve and enjoy.

Nutritional Value (Amount per Serving):

Calories 245
Fat 10.5 g
Carbohydrates 0.9 g
Sugar 0.1 g
Protein 34.6 g
Cholesterol 0 mg

401. Garlic Lamb Chops

Preparation Time: 5 minutes
Cooking Time: 12 minutes
Serve: 4

Ingredients:

- 4 lamb chops
- 3 garlic cloves, minced
- 3 tbsp olive oil
- 1 1/2 tbsp dried thyme
- Pepper
- Salt

Directions:

1. Preheat the air fryer to 400 F/ 200 C.
2. In a small bowl, mix together thyme, oil, and garlic.
3. Season lamb chops with pepper and salt and rub with thyme mixture.
4. Place lamb chops into the air fryer basket and cook for 12 minutes. Turn halfway through.
5. Serve and enjoy.

Nutritional Value (Amount per Serving):

Calories 414
Fat 36.6 g
Carbohydrates 1 g
Sugar 0 g
Protein 19.2 g
Cholesterol 0 mg

402. Pesto Pork Chops

Preparation Time: 10 minutes
Cooking Time: 18 minutes
Serve: 5

Ingredients:

- 5 pork chops
- 2 tbsp basil pesto
- 2 tbsp almond flour
- 1 tbsp olive oil
- Pepper
- Salt

Directions:

1. Brush pork chops with oil.
2. Season pork chops with pepper and salt.
3. Spread basil pesto on top of each pork chops and sprinkle with almond flour.
4. Place pork chops into the air fryer basket and cook at 350 F/ 180 C for 18 minutes.
5. Serve and enjoy.

Nutritional Value (Amount per Serving):

Calories 320
Fat 25.5 g
Carbohydrates 2.4 g
Sugar 0.4 g
Protein 20.4 g
Cholesterol 40 mg

Carbohydrates 6.8 g
Sugar 2.7 g
Protein 35.2 g
Cholesterol 16 mg

403. Tasty Beef with Broccoli

Preparation Time: 10 minutes
Cooking Time: 10 minutes
Serve: 4

Ingredients:

- 1 lb beef cubes
- 1 tsp garlic powder
- 1/2 lb broccoli florets, steamed
- 1 tsp olive oil
- 1/2 small onion, diced
- 1/2 tsp onion powder

Directions:

1. Spray air fryer basket with cooking spray.
2. Add all ingredients except broccoli into the large bowl and toss well.
3. Add bowl mixture into the air fryer basket and cook at 350 F/ 180 C for 10 minutes.
4. Serve with broccoli and enjoy.

Nutritional Value (Amount per Serving):

Calories 227
Fat 6 g

404. Jicama and Cabbage Salad

Preparation time: 10 minutes
Cooking time: 0 minutes
Servings: 4

Ingredients:

- 2 tablespoons lime juice
- 1 garlic clove, peeled and minced
- 1 red chili pepper, sliced
- 2 teaspoons coconut aminos
- 1 grapefruit, peeled, and cut into segments
- 1 Jicama bulb, cut into sticks
- 2 cups napa cabbage, shredded
- ½ cup fresh cilantro, chopped
- ¼ cup cashews, roasted and crushed
- 2 tablespoons shallots, chopped

Directions:

1. In a bowl, mix the Jicama with the cabbage, shallots, grapefruit, chili pepper and garlic. Add lime juice, aminos, cashews and cilantro, toss and serve.

Nutrition Value: Calories - 124, Fat - 1, Fiber - 1, Carbs - 2, Protein - 4

405. Green and Fruit Salad

Preparation time: 10 minutes
Cooking time: 0 minutes
Servings: 4

Ingredients:

- 1 tablespoon avocado oil
- A pinch of black pepper
- 3 plums, pitted and sliced
- 1 tablespoon balsamic vinegar
- 8 cups mixed greens
- 2 nectarines, peeled and sliced
- 2 apricots, pitted and sliced
- 2 peaches, pitted and sliced
- ¾ cup cherries, pitted and cut in half

Directions:

1. In a bowl, mix the greens with the plums, nectarines, apricots, peaches, cherries, and

almonds. Add vinegar, black pepper and oil, toss to coat, and serve.

Nutrition Value: Calories - 110, Fat - 2, Fiber - 1, Carbs - 1, Protein - 4

406. Baked Rosemary Zucchini

Preparation time: 10 minutes
Cooking time: 20 minutes
Servings: 4

Ingredients:

- 1 onion, sliced
- 4 zucchinis, chopped
- 1 tablespoon lemon rind, grated
- 1 tablespoon olive oil
- ¼ cup lemon juice
- 2 tablespoon rosemary, chopped
- Salt and ground black pepper, to taste

Directions:

1. Put the zucchini in a baking dish, add salt, pepper, onion, lemon juice, oil, and lemon rind, toss, place in the oven at 400°F, and bake for 18 minutes. Divide between plates, sprinkle rosemary on top, and serve.

Nutrition Value: Calories - 100, Fat - 2, Fiber - 3, Carbs - 4, Protein - 4

407. Parsnip and Pear Mix

Preparation time: 10 minutes
Cooking time: 1 hour
Servings: 4

Ingredients:

- 4 parsnips, peeled and cut into medium wedges
- 1 onion, cut into wedges
- 1 red pear, cored and cut into wedges
- ⅓ cup sage leaves
- ¼ teaspoon red chili flakes
- 2 tablespoons olive oil
- A pinch of salt and ground black pepper

Directions:

1. In a bowl, mix the pear with the parsnips,

onion, sage, chili flakes, oil salt and black pepper. Toss to coat, arrange on a lined baking sheet, place in the oven at 300ºF, and bake for 1 hour. Divide between plates and serve hot.

Nutrition Value: Calories - 200, Fat - 2, Fiber - 3, Carbs - 6, Protein - 8

408. Celeriac and Olive Salad

Preparation time: 10 minutes
Cooking time: 0 minutes
Servings: 4

Ingredients:

- 1 celeriac, peeled and cut into sticks
- 2 tablespoons lemon juice
- 4 oranges, peeled and sliced
- 10 green olives, pitted and sliced
- 1 onion, peeled and sliced
- 2 ounces baby spinach
- ⅓ cup orange juice
- 1 tablespoon balsamic vinegar
- Salt and ground black pepper, to taste
- 2 teaspoons olive oil

Directions:

1. In a bowl, mix the orange slices, baby spinach, onion, olives and celeriac. In a smaller bowl, mix the orange juice with the olive oil, lemon juice, salt, pepper, and vinegar, whisk well. Drizzle this dressing over salad, toss to coat, and serve.

Nutrition Value: Calories - 121, Fat - 2, Fiber - 2, Carbs - 5, Protein - 8

409. Peach Salsa

Preparation time: 10 minutes
Cooking time: 0 minutes
Servings: 3

Ingredients:

- 2 jalapeños, chopped
- 1-inch lemongrass, minced
- 3 peaches, pitted and chopped
- 1 tablespoon fresh basil, chopped
- Salt and ground black pepper, to taste
- 1 tablespoon balsamic vinegar

- 2 tablespoons olive oil

Directions:

1. In a bowl, mix the lemongrass with the jalapeños and stir. In a bowl, mix the peaches with the basil, lemongrass mixture, salt, pepper, vinegar, and oil, toss well, and serve.

Nutrition Value: Calories - 100, Fat - 2, Fiber - 1, Carbs - 1, Protein - 2

410. Cold Garlic Mushroom Mix

Preparation time: 4 hours and 10 minutes
Cooking time: 0 minutes
Servings: 6

Ingredients:

- 5 pounds mushrooms, sliced
- 2 cups olive oil
- 2 bunches fresh parsley, chopped
- 1 cup lemon juice
- 8 garlic cloves, peeled and minced
- Salt and ground black pepper, to taste

Directions:

1. In a bowl, mix the oil with the parsley, lemon juice, salt, black pepper, garlic and mushrooms. Toss well and keep in the refrigerator for 4 hours before serving.

Nutrition Value: Calories - 90, Fat - 1, Fiber - 2, Carbs - 3, Protein - 3

411. Balsamic Beet Mix

Preparation time: 10 minutes
Cooking time: 50 minutes
Servings: 4

Ingredients:

- 4 red beets
- 1 avocado, pitted and cubed
- 1 tablespoon + 1 teaspoon olive oil
- 1 teaspoon balsamic vinegar
- 2 teaspoon lemon juice
- Sea Salt and black pepper
- ½ bunch fresh parsley, chopped

Directions:

1. Rub the beets with 1 tablespoon olive oil. Arrange in a pan, cover with the aluminum

foil, place in the oven at 400°F, and bake for 50 minutes. Peel, cool down, cut into small pieces and put in a bowl. In a smaller bowl, mix the lemon juice with the salt, pepper, and 1 teaspoon olive oil and stir well. Add the avocado, the beets and the parsley, toss and serve

Nutrition Value: Calories - 127, Fat - 2, Fiber - 1, Carbs - 4, Protein - 6

412. Mustard and Gold Potato Salad

Preparation time: 10 minutes
Cooking time: 25 minutes
Servings: 4

Ingredients:

- 2 pounds gold potatoes, cut into quarters
- 3 tablespoons vegetable stock
- ¼ cup balsamic vinegar
- 1 teaspoon Dijon mustard
- A pinch of salt and black pepper
- ⅓ cup green onions, chopped

Directions:

1. Put the potatoes in a pot, add the water to cover, bring to a boil over medium heat. Cook for 25 minutes, drain, peel them, cut into medium-sized pieces and put them in a bowl. Add mustard, stock, vinegar, salt, and pepper, and green onions, toss and serve cold.

Nutrition Value: Calories - 110, Fat - 3, Fiber - 2, Carbs - 5, Protein - 9

413. Avocado and Asparagus Soup

Preparation time: 5 minutes
Cooking time: 0 minutes
Servings: 2

Ingredients:

- 8 ounces mushrooms, chopped
- 12 asparagus spears, trimmed
- 1 avocado, pitted and peeled
- A pinch of salt and white pepper
- 1 yellow onion, peeled and chopped
- 3 cups vegetable stock

Directions:

1. In a blender, mix the mushrooms with the asparagus, avocado, onion, stock, salt, and pepper and puree well. Ladle into soup bowls and serve.

Nutrition Value: Calories - 124, Fat - 2, Fiber - 2, Carbs - 4, Protein - 5

414. Carrot Cream

Preparation time: 10 minutes
Cooking time: 5 minutes
Servings: 2

Ingredients:

- 1 garlic clove, peeled and minced
- 2 celery stalks, chopped
- 1 avocado, pitted, peeled, and chopped
- 4 carrots, peeled and chopped
- A pinch of salt and black pepper
- 4 tablespoons + ½ teaspoon olive oil
- 1 green onion, chopped
- 1½ cups water
- 1 tomato, cored and chopped

Directions:

1. In a blender, mix the celery with the avocado, carrots, garlic, salt, 4 tablespoons oil, onion, and water, pulse well, transfer this to a pot. Stir, heat for a few minutes over medium heat, ladle into soup bowls, garnish with the tomato and drizzle the rest of the oil all over and serve.

415. Tomato Gazpacho

Preparation time: 5 minutes
Cooking time: 0 minutes
Servings: 2

Ingredients:

- 1 red bell pepper, seeded and chopped
- 3 tomatoes, cored and chopped
- 4 tablespoons sesame paste
- 2 carrots, peeled and chopped
- Juice of 1 lime
- 1 teaspoon chili pepper
- A pinch of sea salt and black pepper
- 1 garlic clove, peeled and minced
- 1 tablespoon olive oil

- 4 tablespoons celery, chopped

Directions:

1. In a blender, mix the bell pepper with the tomatoes, sesame paste, carrots, lime juice, chili pepper, salt, pepper, garlic, oil and celery, pulse well, divide into bowls and serve cold.

Nutrition Value: Calories - 110, Fat - 1, Fiber - 2, Carbs - 4, Protein - 1

416. Mango and Squash Soup

Preparation time: 10 minutes
Cooking time: 0 minutes
Servings: 2

Ingredients:

- 3 cups orange juice
- 2 cups butternut squash, peeled, seeded and chopped
- 1 mango, chopped
- A pinch of ground nutmeg
- A pinch of ground cinnamon

Directions:

1. In a blender, mix the squash with orange juice, mango, nutmeg and cinnamon, pulse well, divide into bowls and serve.

Nutrition Value: Calories - 121, Fat - 1, Fiber - 2, Carbs - 4, Protein - 6

417. Tomato and Olive Salad

Preparation time: 10 minutes
Cooking time: 0 minutes
Servings: 4

Ingredients:

- 2 tomatoes, cored and cut into small wedges
- 2 bell peppers, seeded and chopped
- 1 cucumber, chopped
- 1 small onion, sliced thin
- ½ cup Kalamata olives, pitted and sliced
- ¼ cup lemon juice
- ½ cup olive oil
- 1 tablespoon fresh oregano, chopped
- Salt and ground black pepper, to taste
- 2 garlic cloves, peeled and minced

Directions:

1. In a bowl, mix the tomatoes with the bell peppers, cucumber, onion, olives, lemon juice, oil, oregano, salt, pepper and garlic, toss well and serve.

Nutrition Value: Calories - 165, Fat - 3, Fiber - 1, Carbs - 2, Protein - 4

418. Spinach and Bacon Salad

Preparation time: 10 minutes
Cooking time: 0 minutes
Servings: 4

Ingredients:

- Salt and ground black pepper, to taste
- 6 bacon slices, cooked and crumbled
- 2 tablespoons red vinegar
- 2 tablespoons extra virgin olive oil
- 2 scallions, chopped
- 6 cups baby spinach

Directions:

1. In a salad bowl, mix the spinach with the scallions, vinegar, oil, salt, pepper and the bacon, toss and serve.

Nutrition Value: Calories - 156, Fat - 4, Fiber - 2, Carbs - 2, Protein - 1

419. Rosemary Potato Wedges

Preparation time: 10 minutes
Cooking time: 45 minutes
Servings: 8

Ingredients:

- 3 pounds assorted potatoes, cut into medium wedges
- Salt and ground black pepper, to taste
- 1 garlic head
- 1 tablespoon fresh rosemary, chopped
- 3 tablespoons olive oil

Directions:

1. Place the potatoes in a baking pan, add the garlic, sprinkle the rosemary, season with salt and pepper, drizzle with the oil, toss well, and bake in the oven at 400°F for 45 minutes. Transfer the potatoes to a platter, squeeze garlic on top, and serve.

Nutrition Value: Calories - 142, Fat - 1, Fiber - 2, Carbs - 3, Protein - 4

420. Japanese Seaweed Salad

Preparation time: 10 minutes
Cooking time: 5 minutes
Servings: 4

Ingredients:

- 2 tablespoons dried wakame seaweed
- 3 tablespoons coconut aminos
- 2 tablespoons balsamic vinegar
- 1 tablespoon olive oil
- 2 garlic cloves, peeled and minced
- 1 tablespoon arrowroot powder
- 1 teaspoon fresh ginger, grated
- 2 teaspoons sesame seeds

Directions:

1. Put the seaweed in a bowl, add the hot water to cover, set aside for a few seconds. Drain, rinse and put it in a pot. In a blender, mix the vinegar with the coconut aminos, ginger, and garlic and blend well. Add the dressing over the seaweed, bring to a boil over medium-high heat, simmer for 1 minute, add the arrowroot powder, simmer for 4 minutes more. Transfer to a bowl, sprinkle sesame seeds and oil and serve cold.

Nutrition Value: Calories - 140, Fat - 1, Fiber - 1, Carbs - 1, Protein - 5

421. Coconut Zucchini Soup

Preparation time: 10 minutes
Cooking time: 12 minutes
Servings: 4

Ingredients:

- 2 tablespoons olive oil
- 2 tablespoons green curry paste
- 1 cup shallots, chopped
- 6 zucchinis, chopped
- 1 cup coconut milk
- 1 cup water
- Juice of 1 lime
- Salt and ground black pepper, to taste
- Roasted cherry tomatoes, for serving

- 1 tablespoon fresh cilantro, chopped, for serving

Directions:

1. Heat a pan with the olive oil over medium-high heat, add the shallots, salt, and pepper, stir, and cook for 2 minutes. Add the curry paste, and the zucchini, stir, and cook for 10 minutes. Add the coconut milk, lime juice, water, stir, bring to a simmer, and ladle into soup bowls. Serve with roasted tomatoes and chopped cilantro on top.

Nutrition Value: Calories - 140, Fat - 1, Fiber - 1, Carbs - 2, Protein - 6

422. Tomato Soup

Preparation time: 10 minutes
Cooking time: 35 minutes
Servings: 6

Ingredients:

- 2 cups yellow onion, sliced
- 2 cups tomatoes, diced
- 4 teaspoons olive oil
- A pinch of salt and ground black pepper
- 2 and ⅔ cups tomato juice
- 2 cups vegetable stock
- 2 tablespoons fresh basil, chopped
- 2 teaspoons fresh oregano, chopped

Directions:

1. Heat a pot with the oil over medium-high heat, add the onion, stir, and cook for 6 minutes. Add the water, tomato juice, salt and black pepper, basil, and oregano, stir, bring to a boil, reduce the heat to medium-low, and simmer for 20 minutes. Add the tomatoes, stir, cook for 10 minutes, ladle into soup bowls and serve.

Nutrition Value: Calories - 140, Fat - 1, Fiber - 1, Carbs - 0, Protein - 5

423. Tomato and Citrus Soup

Preparation time: 10 minutes
Cooking time: 1 hour and 10 minutes
Servings: 4

Ingredients:

- 1½ pounds small tomatoes, cut in halves

- 4 tablespoons extra virgin olive oil
- 2 garlic cloves, diced
- 2 yellow onions, diced
- Salt and ground black pepper, to taste
- 2 carrots, diced
- 1 celery stalk, chopped
- 3 ounces orange juice
- 20 ounces vegetable stock
- Zest of 1 orange

Directions:

1. Arrange the tomatoes on a lined baking sheet, spread garlic, drizzle half of the oil, add the salt and pepper, place in the oven at 350ºF and bake for 45 minutes. Heat a pot with the rest of the oil over medium heat, add the onions, celery, and carrots, stir, reduce heat to low, and cook for 20 minutes. Add the roasted tomatoes and garlic, the stock and orange juice, stir well, bring to a boil, cook for 2 minutes. Take off the heat, transfer to a blender, pulse well, return it to the pot, heat up the soup again for a few minutes, ladle into bowls, and serve with the orange zest on top.

Nutrition Value: Calories - 140, Fat - 2, Fiber - 1, Carbs - 4, Protein - 6

424. Baked Eggplant Soup

Preparation time: 10 minutes
Cooking time: 35 minutes
Servings: 4

Ingredients:

- 2 pounds eggplants, pricked
- 2 cups yellow onion, sliced
- 5 tablespoons olive oil
- 6 garlic cloves, peeled and minced
- Salt and ground black pepper, to taste
- 4 tablespoons lemon juice
- ½ teaspoon lemon zest
- 6 cups vegetable stock
- 2 tablespoons fresh parsley, minced

Directions:

1. Arrange the eggplants on a baking sheet, place in a broiler, and cook them for 4 minutes on each side. Peel, chop, and transfer them to a bowl. Heat a pot with the 3 tablespoons oil over medium-high heat, add the onion, salt, and pepper, stir, and cook for 7 minutes. Add the garlic, eggplant, and the stock, bring to a boil, reduce heat to medium, and simmer for 10 minutes. Transfer the soup to a blender, pulse well, return to pot, add the lemon juice, stir again and ladle into bowls. In a bowl, mix the lemon zest with the rest of the olive oil, and whisk. Drizzle this over the soup, sprinkle parsley on top, and serve.

Nutrition Value: Calories - 180, Fat - 3, Fiber - 3, Carbs - 5, Protein - 9

425. Creamy Mushroom Stew

Preparation time: 10 minutes
Cooking time: 20 minutes

Servings: 3

Ingredients:

- 1 teaspoon olive oil
- 1 garlic clove, peeled and chopped
- 1 onion, sliced
- 1-inch fresh ginger, peeled and grated
- 1 green chili pepper, chopped
- ½ teaspoon garam masala
- ¼ teaspoon ground cinnamon
- 5 ounces coconut milk
- 1 teaspoon almonds, flaked
- 6 ounces mushrooms, sliced
- Salt and ground black pepper, to taste

Directions:

1. Heat a pan with the oil over a low heat, add the onion, chili, ginger, garlic, salt, pepper, garam masala and cinnamon, stir, and cook for 3 minutes. Add the milk, cook for 7 minutes, transfer to a blender, pulse well, and set aside. Heat the same pan at a medium temperature, add the mushrooms, and cook for 2-3 minutes. Add the coconut sauce, stir, cook for 8 minutes, divide into bowls and serve with almond flakes on top.

Nutrition Value: Calories - 173, Fat - 4, Fiber - 5, Carbs - 10, Protein - 12

426. Simple Veggie Stir-fry

Preparation time: 10 minutes
Cooking time: 35 minutes
Servings: 2

Ingredients:

- 9 ounces beet, chopped
- 12 ounces butternut squash, chopped
- 1 onion, peeled and chopped
- 1 garlic clove, peeled and chopped
- ¼ teaspoon cumin seeds
- ½ teaspoon ground cinnamon
- 1 tablespoon olive oil
- 3 ounces green beans, cut in half
- ounces spinach, chopped
- A small bunch fresh parsley, chopped
- Salt and ground black pepper, to taste
- 1-cup veggie stock

Directions:

1. Heat a large pan with the oil over medium-high heat, add the onion and the garlic, stir and cook for 5 minutes. Add the cumin seeds, the cinnamon, salt and pepper, stir and cook for 5 minutes more. Add the beets, the squash, green beans, and the stock, toss, cover the pan, reduce heat to low and cook for 20 minutes. Add the spinach and the parsley, toss, cook for 5 minutes more, divide between plates and serve.

Nutrition Value: Calories - 220, Fat - 3, Fiber - 3, Carbs - 10, Protein - 12

427. Baked Potato Salad

Preparation time: 10 minutes
Cooking time: 25 minutes
Servings: 4

Ingredients:

- 4 gold potatoes, chopped
- 2 rosemary sprigs, chopped
- 1 tablespoon balsamic vinegar
- 2 teaspoons mustard
- 1 teaspoon shallot, sliced
- 1 teaspoon fresh parsley, chopped
- 2 tablespoons olive oil
- Salt and ground black pepper, to taste
- 1 onion, peeled and chopped
- 2 leaf lettuce heads, leaves separated
- 2 tomatoes, cored and cut into wedges

Directions:

1. Arrange the potatoes on a baking sheet, add half of the oil and rosemary sprigs, toss, and place in the oven at 375 ° F, bake for 25 minutes and transfer to a salad bowl. Add the tomatoes and the lettuce and toss. Add the vinegar, the mustard, shallot, onion, salt, pepper, parsley and the rest of the oil, toss and serve.

Nutrition Value: Calories - 241, Fat - 7, Fiber - 4, Carbs - 10, Protein - 14

428. Coconut Pumpkin Soup

Preparation time: 10 minutes
Cooking time: 15 minutes
Servings: 4

Ingredients:

- 2 tablespoons coconut oil, melted
- 1 cup onion, chopped
- 2 garlic cloves, peeled and minced
- 1½ cups vegetable stock
- 2 cups pumpkin puree
- ½ cup coconut cream
- Salt and ground black pepper, to taste
- ¼ cup parsley, chopped

Directions:

1. Heat a pot with the oil over medium heat, add the garlic, stir, and cook for 4 minutes. Add the stock, pumpkin puree, coconut cream, salt, and black pepper. Bring to a boil, and simmer for 10 minutes. Ladle into bowls, sprinkle parsley on top, and serve.

Nutrition Value: Calories - 100, Fat - 3, Fiber - 4, Carbs - 11, Protein - 4

429. Broccoli and Mayonnaise Salad

Preparation time: 10 minutes
Cooking time: 0 minutes
Servings: 6

Ingredients:

- ¼ cup homemade avocado mayonnaise
- 1 garlic clove, peeled and minced
- 6 cups broccoli florets, chopped
- 3 slices bacon, cooked and crumbled
- 2 teaspoons white vinegar
- ¼ cup coconut cream
- 3 tablespoons dried cranberries
- Salt and ground black pepper, to taste

Directions:

1. In a bowl, mix the mayonnaise with the garlic, vinegar, and coconut cream and whisk well. In a salad bowl, mix the broccoli with cranberries, bacon, salt, and pepper and toss. Add the mayonnaise mix, toss to coat, and serve cold.

Nutrition Value: Calories - 92, Fat - 5, Fiber - 2, Carbs - 11, Protein - 3

430. Bell Peppers and Chives

Preparation time: 10 minutes
Cooking time: 20 minutes
Servings: 4

Ingredients:

- 1 pound red bell peppers, cut into wedges
- 1 cup veggie stock
- 1 tablespoon chives, chopped
- 1 tablespoon sweet paprika
- 1 tablespoon chives, chopped

Directions:

1. In your instant pot, mix the bell peppers with the rest of the ingredients except the chives, put the lid on and cook on High for 20 minutes.
2. Release the pressure naturally for 10 minutes, divide the mix between plates and serve with the chives sprinkled on top.

Nutrition Value: calories 70, fat 1.8, fiber 1.1, carbs 1.4, protein 0.6

431. Cayenne Peppers and Sauce

Preparation time: 5 minutes
Cooking time: 20 minutes
Servings: 4

Ingredients:

- 1 pound mixed bell peppers, cut into wedges
- ½ cup chicken stock
- ½ cup heavy cream
- A pinch of cayenne pepper
- A pinch of salt and black pepper
- 1 tablespoon cilantro, chopped

Directions:

1. In your instant pot, combine the bell peppers with the stock and the rest of the ingredients, put the lid on and cook on High for 15 minutes.
2. Release the pressure fast for 5 minutes, divide the mix between plates and serve.

Nutrition Value: calories 63, fat 5.7, fiber 0.4, carbs 2.8, protein 0.7

432. Bell Peppers and Brussels Sprouts

Preparation time: 5 minutes
Cooking time: 15 minutes
Servings: 4

Ingredients:

- 1 pound mixed bell peppers, cut into wedges
- ½ pound Brussels sprouts, halved
- 1 cup veggie stock
- 1 tablespoon ghee, melted
- 1 teaspoon smoked paprika
- 1 teaspoon cumin, ground
- 1 tablespoon chives, chopped

Directions:

1. Set the instant pot on Sauté mode, add the ghee, heat it up, add the peppers and the sprouts and cook for 3 minutes.
2. Put the lid on, cook on High for 12 minutes, release the pressure fast for 5 minutes, divide the mix between plates and serve.

Nutrition Value: calories 68, fat 4.2, fiber 2.3, carbs 3.4, protein 2.4

433. Bell Peppers and Mustard Greens

Preparation time: 5 minutes

Cooking time: 20 minutes
Servings: 4

Ingredients:

- 1 pound mixed bell peppers, cut into wedges
- ½ pound mustard greens
- A pinch of salt and black pepper
- 1 cup chicken stock
- 1 tablespoon sweet paprika
- 1 teaspoon chives, chopped

Directions:

1. In your instant pot, combine the bell peppers with the rest of the ingredients, put the lid on and cook on High for 20 minutes.
2. Release the pressure naturally for 5 minutes, divide the mix between plates and serve.

Nutrition Value: calories 32, fat 3.4, fiber 2.3, carbs 2.9, protein 2.3

434. Parmesan Radish

Preparation time: 10 minutes
Cooking time: 10 minutes
Servings: 4

Ingredients:

- 1 pound radishes, sliced
- Juice of 1 lemon
- 1 teaspoon chili powder
- A pinch of salt and black pepper
- 1 cup chicken stock
- 3 tablespoons parmesan, grated

Directions:

1. In your instant pot, combine the radishes with the lemon juice and the rest of the ingredients, put the lid on and cook on High for 10 minutes.
2. Release the pressure naturally for 10 minutes, divide mix between plates and serve.

Nutrition Value: calories 38, fat 1.5, fiber 0.2, carbs 0.4, protein 2.5

435. Cheddar Tomatoes

Preparation time: 10 minutes

Cooking time: 20 minutes
Servings: 4

Ingredients:

- 1 and ½ pounds tomatoes, cut into wedges
- 1 cup cheddar cheese, grated
- 1 cup chicken stock
- A pinch of salt and black pepper
- 1 tablespoon dill, chopped
- 1 teaspoon sweet paprika
- 1 tablespoon chives, chopped

Directions:

1. In your instant pot, mix tomatoes with the rest of the ingredients except the cheese and toss.
2. Sprinkle the cheese on top, put the lid on and cook on High for 20 minutes.
3. Release the pressure naturally for 10 minutes, divide the mix between plates and serve.

Nutrition Value: calories 161, fat 10.1, fiber 3.1, carbs 4.5, protein 9.6

436. Creamy Tomatoes

Preparation time: 10 minutes
Cooking time: 10 minutes
Servings: 4

Ingredients:

- 2 cups cherry tomatoes, halved
- 2 spring onions, chopped
- 1 cup coconut cream
- A pinch of salt and black pepper
- 2 tablespoons garlic, minced
- 1 tablespoon dill, chopped

Directions:

1. In your instant pot, mix the tomatoes with the spring onions and the rest of the ingredients, put the lid on and cook on High for 10 minutes.
2. Release the pressure naturally for 10 minutes, divide the mix between plates and serve.

Nutrition Value: calories 165, fat 14.5, fiber 2.8, carbs 6.4, protein 2.7

437. Garlic Celery and Kale

Preparation time: 10 minutes
Cooking time: 14 minutes
Servings: 4

Ingredients:

- 2 celery stalks, toughly chopped
- 1 pound kale, torn
- 1 tablespoon olive oil
- 4 garlic cloves, minced
- 1 cup chicken stock
- A pinch of salt and black pepper
- 1 tablespoon parsley, chopped

Directions:

1. Set your instant pot on Sauté mode, add the oil, heat it up, add the garlic and brown for 2 minutes.
2. Add the rest of the ingredients, put the lid on and cook on High for 12 minutes more.
3. Release the pressure naturally for 10 minutes, divide the mix between plates and serve.

Nutrition Value: calories 95, fat 3.7, fiber 1.9, carbs 2.4, protein 3.8

438. Creamy Eggplant Mix

Preparation time: 10 minutes
Cooking time: 15 minutes
Servings: 4

Ingredients:

- 2 tablespoons rosemary, chopped
- 2 eggplants, sliced
- A pinch of salt and black pepper
- 1 cup heavy cream
- 1 teaspoon turmeric powder
- 1 tablespoon dill, chopped

Directions:

1. In your instant pot, mix the eggplants with the rest of the ingredients, put the lid on and cook on High for 15 minutes.
2. Release the pressure naturally for 10 minutes, divide the mix between plates and serve.

Nutrition Value: calories 181, fat 11.8, fiber 4.2, carbs 5.9, protein 3.6

439. Spicy Eggplant and Kale Mix

Preparation time: 10 minutes
Cooking time: 15 minutes
Servings: 4

Ingredients:

- 4 small eggplants, sliced
- ¼ cup chicken stock
- 1 tablespoon chili powder
- ½ pound kale, torn
- A pinch of salt and black pepper

Directions:

1. In your instant pot, mix the eggplants with the stock and the rest of the ingredients, put the lid on and cook on High for 15 minutes.
2. Release the pressure naturally for 10 minutes, divide the mix between plates and serve.

Nutrition Value: calories 65, fat 1.5, fiber 0.3, carbs 0.9, protein 2.8

440. Tomato and Dill Sauté

Preparation time: 10 minutes
Cooking time: 15 minutes
Servings: 4

Ingredients:

- 1 pound tomatoes, cubed
- 1 tablespoon dill, chopped
- 1 teaspoon garlic, minced
- A pinch of salt and black pepper
- ½ cup chicken stock
- 1 tablespoon parsley, chopped

Directions:

1. In your instant pot, mix the tomatoes with the dill and the rest of the ingredients, put the lid on and cook on High for 15 minutes.
2. Release the pressure naturally for 10 minutes, divide the mix between plates and serve.

Nutrition Value: calories 25, fat 1.9, fiber 0.5, carbs 1.4, protein 1.4

441. Mustard Greens and Cabbage Sauté

Preparation time: 10 minutes

Cooking time: 15 minutes
Servings: 4

Ingredients:

- 2 cups mustard greens
- 1 red cabbage, shredded
- 1 tablespoon tomato passata
- A pinch of salt and black pepper
- ¼ cup chicken stock
- 1 tablespoon dill, chopped

Directions:

1. In your instant pot, mix the mustard greens with the cabbage and the rest of the ingredients, put the lid on and cook on High for 15 minutes.
2. Release the pressure naturally for 10 minutes, divide the mix between plates and serve.

Nutrition Value: calories 36, fat 1.4, fiber 0.2, carbs 0.4, protein 2

442., Dill Zucchini, Tomatoes and Eggplants

Preparation time: 10 minutes
Cooking time: 15 minutes
Servings: 4

Ingredients:

- 2 cups zucchinis, sliced
- 1 cup tomatoes, cubed
- 1 cup eggplants, sliced
- A pinch of salt and black pepper
- 1 cup tomato passata
- 2 tablespoon dill, chopped

Directions:

1. In your instant pot, mix the zucchinis with the tomatoes and the rest of the ingredients, put the lid on and cook on High for 15 minutes.
2. Release the pressure naturally for 10 minutes, divide the mix between plates and serve.

Nutrition Value: calories 41, fat 1.2, fiber 0.2, carbs 0.6, protein 2.4

443. Balsamic Okra

Preparation time: 10 minutes

Cooking time: 15 minutes
Servings: 4

Ingredients:

- 2 cups okra
- 2 spring onions, chopped
- ½ cup chicken stock
- A pinch of salt and black pepper
- 1 tablespoon balsamic vinegar
- 1 tablespoon dill, chopped

Directions:

1. In your instant pot, mix the okra with the spring onions and the rest of the ingredients, put the lid on and cook on High for 15 minutes.
2. Release the pressure naturally for 10 minutes, divide the mix between plates and serve.

Nutrition Value: calories 26, fat 1.2, fiber 0.2, carbs 0.7, protein 1.4

444. Creamy Okra and Collard Greens

Preparation time: 10 minutes
Cooking time: 20 minutes
Servings: 4

Ingredients:

- 1 pound collard greens, trimmed
- 1 cup okra
- 1 cup heavy cream
- ½ cup chicken stock
- 1 tablespoon sweet paprika
- A pinch of salt and black pepper
- 1 tablespoon cilantro, chopped

Directions:

1. In your instant pot, combine the collard greens with the okra and the rest of the ingredients, put the lid on and cook on High for 20 minutes.
2. Release the pressure naturally for 10 minutes, divide the mix between plates and serve.

Nutrition Value: calories 151, fat 12.2, fiber 4.3, carbs 6.8, protein 4

445. Balsamic Savoy Cabbage

Preparation time: 10 minutes

Cooking time: 20 minutes

Servings: 4

Ingredients:

- 1 Savoy cabbage, shredded
- ½ cup chicken stock
- 1 tablespoon dill, chopped
- A pinch of salt and black pepper
- 1 tablespoon balsamic vinegar

Directions:

1. In your instant pot, mix the Savoy cabbage with the chicken stock and the rest of the ingredients, put the lid on and cook on High for 20 minutes.
2. Release the pressure naturally for 10 minutes, divide the mix between plates and serve.

Nutrition Value: calories 61, fat 1.3, fiber 0.8, carbs 1, protein 3.2

446. Cilantro Red Cabbage and Artichokes

Preparation time: 10 minutes

Cooking time: 20 minutes

Servings: 4

Ingredients:

- ½ cup canned artichoke hearts, drained and chopped
- 3 garlic cloves, minced
- 2 small red cabbage heads, shredded
- A pinch of salt and black pepper
- 1 cup chicken stock
- ½ cup tomato passata
- 1 tablespoon cilantro, chopped

Directions:

1. In your instant pot, combine the artichokes with the garlic and the rest of the ingredients except the cilantro, put the lid on and cook on High for 20 minutes.
2. Release the pressure naturally for 10 minutes, divide the mix between plates and serve with the cilantro sprinkled on top.

Nutrition Value: calories 141, fat 1.5, fiber 0.2, carbs 1.2, protein 7.3

447. Dill Fennel and Brussels Sprouts

Preparation time: 10 minutes

Cooking time: 15 minutes

Servings: 4

Ingredients:

- 2 fennel bulbs, cut into wedges
- 1 pound Brussels sprouts, halved
- A pinch of salt and black pepper
- 1 cup chicken stock
- 1 tablespoon dill, chopped
- ¼ cup tomato passata

Directions:

1. In your instant pot, mix the fennel with the sprouts and the rest of the ingredients, put the lid on and cook on High for 15 minutes.
2. Release the pressure naturally for 10 minutes, divide the mix between plates and serve.

Nutrition Value: calories 96, fat 1.4, fiber 0.8, carbs 1, protein 5.6

448. Cinnamon Green Beans Mix

Preparation time: 10 minutes

Cooking time: 15 minutes

Servings: 4

Ingredients:

- 1 pound green beans, trimmed
- A pinch of salt and black pepper
- ½ cup chicken stock
- 1 teaspoon chili powder
- 1 tablespoon rosemary, chopped
- ½ teaspoon cinnamon powder

Directions:

1. In your instant pot, combine the green beans with the stock and the rest of the ingredients, put the lid on and cook on High for 15 minutes.
2. Release the pressure naturally for 10 minutes, divide the mix between plates and serve.

Nutrition Value: calories 41, fat 1.4, fiber 0.1, carbs 0.5, protein 2.3

449. Okra and Olives Mix

Preparation time: 10 minutes
Cooking time: 15 minutes
Servings: 4

Ingredients:

- 2 cups okra
- 1 cup kalamata olives, pitted and sliced
- A pinch of salt and black pepper
- Juice of ½ lime
- ½ cup veggie stock
- 2 tablespoons tomato passata
- 2 tablespoons parsley, chopped

Directions:

1. In your instant pot, mix the okra with the olives and the rest of the ingredients, put the lid on and cook on High for 15 minutes.
2. Release the pressure naturally for 10 minutes, divide the mix between plates and serve.

Nutrition Value: calories 64, fat 4, fiber 2.8, carbs 3, protein 1.4

450. Olives, Capers and Kale

Preparation time: 10 minutes
Cooking time: 20 minutes
Servings: 4

Ingredients:

- 1 cup black olives, pitted and sliced
- 2 spring onions, chopped
- 1 tablespoon capers, drained
- ½ cup chicken stock
- 1 pound kale, torn
- A pinch of salt and black pepper
- 1 tablespoon parsley, chopped

Directions:

1. In your instant pot, combine kale with the olives, capers and the rest of the ingredients, put the lid on and cook on High for 20 minutes.
2. Release the pressure naturally for 10 minutes, divide the mix between plates and serve.

Nutrition Value: calories 99, fat 3.7, fiber 2.3,

carbs 3, protein 4

451. Eggplants and Cabbage Mix

Preparation time: 5 minutes
Cooking time: 15 minutes
Servings: 4

Ingredients:

- 1 big eggplant, peeled and sliced
- 2 garlic cloves, minced
- A pinch of salt and black pepper
- 1 green cabbage, shredded
- 1 cup chicken stock
- 1 tablespoon dill, chopped
- 1 teaspoon cumin, ground

Directions:

1. In your instant pot, mix the eggplant with the garlic, cabbage and the rest of the ingredients, put the lid on and cook on High for 15 minutes.
2. Release the pressure fast for 5 minutes, divide the mix between plates and serve.

Nutrition Value: calories 94, fat 1.5, fiber 0.4, carbs 1, protein 4.5

452. Eggplants, Cucumber and Olives

Preparation time: 10 minutes
Cooking time: 12 minutes
Servings: 4

Ingredients:

- 2 and ½ cups eggplant, sliced
- 1 tablespoon avocado oil
- 2 cucumbers, cubed
- 1 shallot, minced
- 1 cup black olives, pitted and sliced
- A pinch of salt and black pepper
- ½ cup chicken stock

Directions:

1. Set the instant pot on Sauté mode, add the oil, heat it up, add the shallot and cook for 2 minutes.
2. Add the eggplant and the rest of the ingredients, put the lid on and cook on High for 10 minutes.
3. Release the pressure naturally for 10

minutes, divide the mix between plates and serve.

Nutrition Value: calories 83, fat 4.4, fiber 2.3, carbs 3.4, protein 2

453. Lemon Peppers and Bok Choy

Preparation time: 10 minutes
Cooking time: 20 minutes
Servings: 4

Ingredients:

- 1 pound mixed bell peppers, cut into wedges
- 1 cup bok choy, chopped
- 2 tablespoons sweet paprika
- A pinch of salt and black pepper
- ½ cup chicken stock
- ¼ cup lemon juice
- 1 tablespoon cilantro, chopped

Directions:

1. In your instant pot, mix the bell peppers with the bok choy and the rest of the ingredients except the cilantro, put the lid on and cook on High for 20 minutes.
2. Release the pressure naturally for 10 minutes, divide the mix between plates, sprinkle the cilantro on top and serve.

Nutrition Value: calories 34, fat 1, fiber 0.2, carbs 0.5, protein 1.3

454. Tomato Bok Choy Mix

Preparation time: 10 minutes
Cooking time: 15 minutes
Servings: 4

Ingredients:

- 1 pound bok choy, torn
- 1 cup cherry tomatoes, halved
- 2 tablespoons lime juice
- ½ cup chicken stock
- 1 tablespoon ginger, grated
- 1 tablespoon chives, chopped
- 1 tablespoon oregano, chopped
- 1 tablespoon olive oil

1. **Directions:**

2. Set the instant pot on Sauté mode, add the oil, heat it up, add the ginger and sauté for 2 minutes.
3. Add the rest of the ingredients, put the lid on and cook on High for 12 minutes.
4. Release the pressure naturally for 10 minutes, divide the mix between plates and serve.

Nutrition Value: calories 62, fat 4.1, fiber 2.3, carbs 3, protein 2.5

455. Garlic Cabbage and Watercress

Preparation time: 10 minutes
Cooking time: 16 minutes
Servings: 4

Ingredients:

- 1 pound red cabbage, shredded
- 2 garlic cloves, chopped
- 1 tablespoon ghee, melted
- 1 cup chicken stock
- 1 bunch watercress, trimmed
- 1 tablespoon cilantro, chopped

Directions:

1. Set your instant pot on Sauté mode, add the ghee, heat it up, add the garlic, stir and cook for 2 minutes.
2. Add the cabbage and the rest of the ingredients, put the lid on and cook on High for 14 minutes.
3. Release the pressure naturally for 10 minutes, divide the mix between plates and serve.

Nutrition Value: calories 63, fat 3.5, fiber 2, carbs 3.1, protein 2

456. Mint and Basil Eggplant

Preparation time: 10 minutes
Cooking time: 20 minutes
Servings: 4

Ingredients:

- 1 pound eggplants cubed
- 2 spring onions, chopped
- 1 cup chicken stock
- 1 tablespoon olive oil

- 1 tablespoon mint, chopped
- 1 tablespoon basil, chopped
- 1 teaspoon sweet paprika
- A pinch of salt and black pepper

Directions:

1. Set your instant pot on Sauté mode, add the oil, heat it up, add the onions and sauté for 2 minutes.
2. Add the eggplants and the rest of the ingredients, put the lid on and cook on High for 18 minutes.
3. Release the pressure naturally for 10 minutes, divide the mix into bowls and serve.

Nutrition Value: calories 76, fat 3.7, fiber 0.5, carbs 1.2, protein 0.5

457. Smoked Ham and Split Pea soup

Ingredients:

- Water; 6 cups
- ½ cup of split pea
- 1 sliced jelapeno pepper
- 4 Oz of diced smoked ham
- 2 carrots; chopped
- 2 tomatoes; peeled and sliced
- 1 diced sweet onion
- 1 sliced parsnip
- 2 cups of vegetable stock
- 1 juiced lemon
- Olive oil; 2 tablespoons
- 2 carrots; sliced
- 2 cloves; sliced
- 2 red bell pepper; cored and sliced
- Creme fraiche to serve

Directions:

1. Get a soup pot and heat your olive oil, then pour in your ham and cook for 5 minutes, then pour the rest of your Ingredients: therein.
2. Add pepper and salt to taste, then cook for 30 minutes with low heat.
3. Serve your warm soup topped with creme fraiche and enjoy.

458. Red Beet soup

Ingredients:

- Vegetable stock; 4 cups
- Water; 2 cups
- 2 sliced carrots
- Olive oil; 2 tablespoons
- 2 sliced leeks
- 1 sliced parsnip
- Shredded cabbage; 2 cups
- 2 peeled and sliced red beets
- A sprig of rosemary
- 1 sliced celery stalk

- A sprig of thyme
- Diced tomatoes; 1 cup
- 1 bay leaf
- Pepper and salt to taste

Directions:

1. Get a soup pot and heat your olive oil, then add in your sliced celery, leeks, parsnip, carrots, beets and your shredded cabbage and cook for 5 minutes.
2. Now, add the rest of your Ingredients: with pepper and salt to taste and cook for 20-25 minutes.
3. Serve and enjoy when cooled.

459. Green Bean Minestrone soup

Ingredients:

- Chilli powder; ½ teaspoon
- 2 carrots; sliced
- Dried basil; ½ teaspoon
- Water; 5 cups
- Dried oregano; ½ teaspoon
- Olive oil; 3 tablespoons
- ½ cup of short pasta
- 2 tablespoons of sliced parsley
- Vegetable stock; 4 cups
- 2 sliced sweet onion
- Diced tomatoes; 1 can
- 1 pound of sliced green beans
- Pepper and salt to taste

Directions:

1. Get a soup pot and heat your olive oil, add in your sliced onion, carrot and celery and cook for 5 minutes.
2. Add your tomatoes, pasta, green beans, stock and water.
3. Add pepper and salt to taste with oregano, basil and chilli powder and cook for 25 minutes.
4. Pour in your sliced parsley and serve when cooled

460. Seafood Tomato soup

Ingredients:

- Diced tomatoes; 1 can
- 2 diced cod fillet
- ¼ cup of white wine
- Water; 3 cups
- Worcestershire sauce; 1 teaspoon
- 2 cups of vegetable stock
- ½ pound rinsed scallops
- 4 sliced cloves
- 1 sliced celery stalk
- Olive oil; 2 tablespoons
- 1 sliced sweet onion
- Lemon juice; 2 tablespoons
- 1 jelapeno pepper; sliced
- 1 pound of peeled and deveined shrimp
- Pepper and salt to taste

Directions:

1. Get a soup pot and heat your olive oil, then pour in your jelapeno, clove, celery then cook for 5 minutes.
2. Add your stock, diced tomatoes, wine and water, then add pepper and salt to taste and cook for 15 minutes.
3. Now, add the remaining Ingredients: and cook for another 10 minutes.
4. Serve and enjoy your soup

461. Creamy Parsnip soup

Ingredients:

- 4 peeled and sliced parsnip
- 1 peeled and sliced green apple
- ¼ cup of heavy cream
- 2 sliced sweet onion
- Olive Oil; 3 tablespoons
- 2 sliced leeks
- Water; 2 cups
- Vegetable stock; 2 cups
- 1 chopped celery stalk
- Pepper and salt to taste

Directions:

1. Get a soup pot and heat your olive oil, then pour in your sliced leeks, onions, apple, parsnip and celery with stock and water.
2. Add pepper and salt to taste, then cook for

20 minutes.

3. After 20 minutes, add in your heavy cream and blend the soup in an immersion blender.
4. Serve and enjoy

462. Italian meatball Soup

Ingredients:

- Ground chicken; 1 pound
- Chicken stock; 4 cups
- Chopped parsley; 2 tablespoons
- 1 juiced lemon
- 1 sliced shallot
- Water; 4 cups
- ½ teaspoon of dried oregano
- White rice; 2 tablespoons
- Tomato juice; 1 cup
- 1 sliced carrot
- 2 cored and sliced red bell pepper
- 2 sliced tomatoes
- 1 sliced celery stalk
- Dried basil; 1 teaspoon
- Pepper and salt to taste

Directions:

1. Get a soup pot and add your sliced tomatoes, bell pepper, celery, stock, basil, carrot, oregano, tomato juice, shallot and water together, then add pepper and salt to taste and cook for 10 minutes.
2. Create meatballs by combining your white rice, chicken and parsley together.
3. Create small meatballs and drop them in the soup, then cook for another 15 minutes.
4. Add lemon juice.
5. Serve and enjoy.

463. Kale and White Beans soup

Ingredients:

- 2 chopped celery stalk
- 1 sliced fennel bulb
- A sprig of thyme
- 8 shredded kale leaves
- Dried marjoram; ½ teaspoon
- 2 sliced carrots

- Chilli powder; ¼ teaspoon
- Vegetable stock; 4 cups
- 2 cloves; sliced
- 4 cups of water
- Olive Oil; 2 tablespoons
- Drained cannelloni beans; 2 cans
- 1 diced sweet onion
- Pepper and salt to taste

Directions:

1. Get a soup pot and heat your olive oil, then pour in your chopped celery, fennel, onion, clove and carrot, then cook for 5 minutes.
2. Add chilli powder, stock, beans, water, marjoram, pepper and salt to taste and cook for another 20 minutes.
3. Add the kale and cook for 5 minutes, then serve and enjoy your warm soup.

464. Veal Shank Barley soup

Ingredients:

- ½ cup of rinsed barley pearls
- 1 sliced sweet onion
- 2 sliced carrots
- 2 peeled and sliced tomatoes
- Vegetable stock; 4 cups
- Olive Oil; 3 tablespoons
- 2 cored and sliced red bell pepper
- Chopped parsley for serving
- 4 sliced veal shank
- 2 chopped celery stalk
- 1 sliced parsnip
- Water; 4 cups
- Pepper and salt to taste

Directions:

1. Get a soup pot and heat your olive oil, then pour in your sliced veal shank and cook for 10 minutes, then add in your stock with water and cook for 10 minutes.
2. Now, add your the rest of your Ingredients: except the chopped parsley.
3. Cook for another 30 minutes on low heat then add pepper and salt to taste.
4. Serve and enjoy your soup topped with parsley.

465. Creamy Carrot Coriander soup

Ingredients:

- 6 chopped carrots
- ½ cup of heavy cream
- Coriander seeds; ½ teaspoon
- Vegetable stock; 2 cups
- 2 sliced shallots
- Water; 2 cups
- Olive Oil; 2 tablespoons
- 2 cloves; sliced
- 1 sliced red pepper
- Pepper and salt to taste

Directions:

1. Get a soup pot and heat your olive oil, then add in your sliced carrot, shallot, garlic with your coriander seeds and cook for 5 minutes.
2. Add in your stock, red pepper, water with pepper and salt to taste then cook for another 10-15 minutes on low heat.
3. Now take the soup off heat and add your cream then blend the soup in an immersion blender.
4. Serve and enjoy when cooled

466. Yoghurt Sweet Corn soup

Ingredients:

- 4 cloves; sliced
- Drained sweet corn; 2 cans
- Water; 1 cup
- Plain yoghurt; 1 cup
- ½ sliced red pepper
- Olive Oil; 2 tablespoons
- Dried basil; ½ teaspoon
- 2 sweet onions; diced
- Dried oregano;½ teaspoon
- Vegetable stock; 2 cups
- Pepper and salt to taste

Directions:

1. Get a soup pot and heat your olive oil, then add in your red pepper, cloves and onions then cook for 5 minutes.
2. Add the remaining Ingredients: except

yoghurt and cook for 15 minutes

3. Blend your soup in an immersion blender then pour in your yoghurt.
4. Serve and enjoy

467. Tuscan Cabbage soup

Ingredients:

- 1 shredded cabbage
- 2 diced sweet onion
- A sprig of oregano
- Water; 2 cups
- Olive oil; 2 tablespoons
- 1 sliced celery stalk
- 1 sprig of thyme
- 1 sprig of basil
- Vegetable stock; 2 cups
- 2 grated carrot
- 1 juiced lemon
- Diced tomatoes; 1 can
- Pepper and salt to taste

Directions:

1. Get a soup pot and heat your olive oil, then add in your celery, carrots and onions then cook for 5 minutes before adding the rest of your Ingredients:.
2. Add pepper and salt to taste then cook for 25 minutes on low heat.
3. Serve and enjoy

468. Spicy Tortilla Soup

Ingredients:

- 1 sliced sweet onion
- ½ teaspoon of chilli flakes
- Drained kidney beans; 1 can
- 2 grated carrots
- Olive Oil; 3 tablespoons
- Tomato paste; 2 tablespoons
- 1 juiced lime
- Water; 4 cups
- Sliced parsley; ¼ cup
- Vegetable stock; 1 cup
- Diced tomatoes; 1 cup
- 2 sliced cloves
- 1 sliced celery stalk

- 1 cup of drained sweet corn
- ½ teaspoon of cumin powder
- 1 peeled and sliced avocado
- Pepper and salt to taste

Directions:

1. Get a soup pot and heat your olive oil, then add in your cloves, chilli flakes, onion, cumin powder, carrots and celery then cook for 5 minutes.
2. Now, add the rest of the Ingredients: except your sliced avocado, lime juice and parsley and cook for 20-25 minutes.
3. Thereafter, add your sliced avocado, lime juice, and parsley.
4. Serve and enjoy.

469. Potato Vegetable soup

Ingredients:

- 2 peeled and diced potatoes
- Dried oregano; ½ teaspoon
- 2 sliced cloves
- 2 peeled and sliced tomatoes
- Dried basil; ½ teaspoon
- Vegetable stock; 2 cups
- Water; 6 cups
- 1 sliced sweet onions
- Olive Oil; 2 tablespoons
- 1 sliced celery stalk
- Broccoli florets; 2 cups
- 1 sliced parsnip
- 2 sliced carrots
- Pepper and salt to taste

Directions:

1. Get a soup pot and heat your olive oil, then add in your parsnip, carrot, cloves, onion and celery then cook for 5 minutes while stirring all the time.
2. Add in your broccoli, potatoes, tomatoes, stock and water with your dried basil and oregano.
3. Cook for 25 minutes on low heat.
4. Serve and enjoy.

470. Chickpea Soup with yoghurt

Cooking and

Preparation: 45 minutes

Servings: 4

Ingredients:

- Water – 2 cups
- Chopped shallot – 1
- Greek yogurt – ½ cup
- Diced celery stalk – 1
- Crushed tomatoes – 1 can
- Drained chickpeas – 1 can
- Vegetable stock – 2 cups
- Pepper and salt to taste
- Olive oil – 2 tbsps

Directions:

1. Stir in a soup pot shallot, celery and heated oil. Allow it to soften by cooking it for 2 minutes.
2. Then add other Ingredients: like stock, chickpeas, water, pepper, tomatoes and salt.
3. Cook for 15 minutes on low heat.
4. Stir the soup in the yogurt after removing it from heat. Then use an immersion blender to puree the soup so that it can be smooth and creamy.
5. It's best served fresh

471. Gazpacho soup recipe

Preparation: 20 minutes

Servings: 6

Ingredients:

- Wheat bread slices - 2
- Cored and diced red bell pepper – 1
- Chopped cilantro for serving
- Sliced celery stalk – 1
- Sherry vinegar – 1 tsp
- Chopped garlic cloves - 2
- Extra virgin olive oil – 3 tbsps
- Cumin powder – 1 pinch
- Peeled and cubed tomatoes – 2 pounds
- Salt and pepper to taste

Directions:

1. In a blender, mix celery, bread, tomatoes, garlic, vinegar, bell pepper, coming and oil.
2. Use immersion blender to puree the soup

after the addition of pepper and salt to taste. Make sure it is smooth after blending.

3. Then pour the soup into serving plates immediately.

472. Creamy Pepper Soup

Preparation Time: 20 minutes

Servings: 6

Ingredients:

- Diced tomatoes – 1 can
- Chopped celery stalk – 1
- Thyme sprig - 1
- Chopped garlic clove – 1
- Chopped sweet onion - 1
- Sliced roasted red bell peppers – 2 jars
- Vegetable stock – 2 cups
- Olive oil – 2 tbsps.
- Pepper and salt to taste

Directions:

1. Stir in a soup pot celery, onion, garlic and heated oil. Then add other Ingredients: after cooking for 2 minutes.
2. On low heat, cook it for 20 minutes after adding pepper and salt.
3. First remove the thyme sprig when the soup is done. Then use immersion blender to puree it.
4. It's best served chilled or warm.

473. Gazpacho soup with watermelon

Preparation: 25 minutes. Servings: 4

Ingredients:

- Ice cubes – 1 cup
- Seedless watermelon – 6 oz.
- Juiced lime - 1
- Sherry vinegar – 1 tspn
- Peeled and cubed tomatoes – 4
- Garlic clove - 1
- Seeded red pepper - 1
- Shallot - 1
- Pepper and salt to taste

Directions:

1. In a blender, mix all the Ingredients:.

2. Make it creamy and smooth by pulsing it. But add pepper and salt first.
3. Serve it chilled in a bowl.

474. Delicious Sausage Soup

Cooking and
Preparation: 1 hour. Servings: 8

Ingredients:

- Cauliflower florets – 2 cups
- Halved chicken sausages - 4
- Chopped garlic clove - 1
- Cored and diced red bell peppers – 2
- Dried thyme – ½ tspn
- Cubed zucchini - 1
- Diced tomatoes – 1 can
- Pepper and salt to taste
- Olive oil – 2 tbsps.
- Water – 6 cups
- Dried oregano – ½ tspn
- Chopped shallots - 2
- Dried basil – ½ tspn
- Vegetable stock – 2 cups

Directions:

1. Stir in a soup pot sausages and heated oil. Then stir in other Ingredients: after cooking it for 5 minutes.
2. On low heat, cook it for 25 minutes after adding pepper and salt.
3. Best enjoyed when served fresh and warm.

475. Refreshing Chorizo Soup

Preparation Time: 50 minutes
Servings: 6

Ingredients:

- Vegetable stock – 2 cups
- Olive oil – 2 tbsps
- Chopped shallot - 1
- Cored and diced red bell peppers - 1
- Diced carrots - 2
- Cored and diced yellow bell pepper - 1
- Drained white beans – 1 can
- Chopped garlic clove - 1
- Diced tomatoes – 1 can
- Water – 6 cups

- Thyme sprig - 1
- Chopped red pepper - 1
- Pepper and salt to taste
- Sliced chorizo links - 2

Directions:

1. In a soup pot, pour the oil and heat it
2. Cook for 5 minutes after stirring in the chorizo links. Then add all other Ingredients: and season with pepper and salt.
3. On low heat, cook the soup for 25 minutes.
4. Serve the soup warm when it's done.

476. Gorgeous Kale Soup made with white bean

Cooking and Preparation: 1 hour
Servings: 8

Ingredients:

- Drained white beans – 1 can
- Shredded kale – 1 bunch
- Chopped shallot – 1
- Water – 6 cups
- Chopped garlic cloves - 2
- Diced carrots - 2
- Lemon juice – 2 tbsps
- Diced tomatoes – 1 can
- Chopped red pepper - 1
- Vegetable stock – 2 cups
- Pepper and salt to taste
- Olive oil – 2 tbsps
- Diced celery stalk - 1

Directions:

1. Stir in a soup pot celery, garlic, carrots, shallot, red pepper and heated oil. Soften it by cooking for 2 minutes.
2. Add other Ingredients: and season with pepper and salt.
3. On low heat, cook the soup for 30 minutes.
4. Enjoy the soup as you serve it chill or warm.

477. Spicy Cod Soup

Cooking and

Preparation: 45 minutes

Servings: 6

Ingredients:

- Cored and diced yellow bell pepper - 2
- Sliced chorizo links – 2
- Cod fillets - 4
- Chopped shallot - 1
- Diced carrot - 1
- Vegetable stock – 2 cups
- Sliced leek - 1
- Water – 4 cups
- For serving, chopped parsley
- Thyme sprig – 1
- Olive oil – 2 tbsps
- Pepper and salt to taste
- Diced tomatoes – 1 can

Directions:

1. Stir in a soup pot chorizo links, heated oil and allow it to cook for 5 minutes.
2. Add other Ingredients: apart from cod fillets.
3. Cook it for 15 minutes after seasoning with pepper and salt.
4. Cook for extra 5 minutes after adding cod
5. Use chopped parsley to top the soup and serve warm.

478. Tomato spiced Haddock Soup recipe

Cooking and

Preparation: 30 minutes

Servings: 6

Ingredients:

- Peeled and diced tomatoes - 4
- Sherry vinegar – 1 tspn
- Bay leaf - 1
- Chopped shallot - 1
- Diced celery stalk - 1
- Water – 2 cups
- Cubed haddock fillets – 4
- Minced garlic cloves - 2
- Thyme sprig - 1
- Dried oregano – ½ tspn
- Olive oil – 2 tbsps.

- Pepper and salt to taste
- Vegetable stock – 2 cups

Directions:

1. Stir in a soup pot garlic, shallot and heated oil. Then make it fragrant by cooking it for 2 minutes.
2. Add vinegar, oregano, stock, celery, thyme, tomatoes, water, bay leaf, pepper and salt.
3. Also add haddock after cooking for 15 minutes and with a lid, cover the pot.
4. On low hear, cook for extra 10 minutes.
5. Serve it fresh and warm.

479. Gazpacho soup made with yoghurt and cucumber

Preparation: 20 minutes.   Servings: 6

Ingredients:

- Seedless white grapes – 1 cup
- Partially peeled cucumbers - 4
- Sliced almonds – 2 tbsps.
- Garlic cloves – 2
- Ice cubes – 1 cup
- Chopped dill – 1 tbsp.
- Plain yogurt – ½ cup
- Cream cheese – 2 tbsps.
- Extra virgin olive oil – 2 tbsps.
- Lemon juice 1 tbsp.
- Pepper and salt to taste

Directions:

1. In a blender, add all the Ingredients: and combine with cucumbers.
2. Make it creamy and smooth by pulsing it after the addition of pepper and salt.
3. Serve when it's still very fresh.

Fast Delicious Avocado Soup

Preparation: 20 minutes Servings: 6

Ingredients:

- Mint leaves – 2
- Peeled cucumbers – 4
- Chopped shallot - 1
- Water – 1 cup
- Plain yogurt – ½ cup
- Lemon juice – 2 tbsps.

- Fresh basil leaves – 2
- Garlic cloves - 2
- Extra virgin olive oil – 2 tbsps.
- Peeled and pitted avocados - 2
- Pepper and salt to taste

Directions:

1. In a blender, add and mix all the Ingredients:.
2. Make it creamy and smooth by pulsing it after the addition of pepper and salt.
3. Serve the soup immediately after pouring into bowls.

481. Roasted Vegetable Soup With Cream

Cooking and
Preparation: 45 minutes Servings: 8

Ingredients:

- Dried oregano – 1 tsp.
- Sliced potatoes - 2
- Garlic cloves - 2
- Dried basil – 1 tsp.
- Sliced tomatoes - 2
- Pepper and salt to taste
- Vegetable stock – 4 cups
- Sliced zucchini - 1
- Water – 8 cups
- Bay leaf – 1
- Sliced red onions - 2
- Thyme sprig – 1
- Olive oil – 2 tbsps.

Directions:

1. In a deep dish baking pan, mix basil, potatoes, onions, garlic, oil, zucchini, potatoes, oil and oregano.
2. Preheat an oven at 400F. Then season with pepper and salt and cook until it turn golden brown or for 30 minutes.
3. In a soup pot, first pour the vegetables and then add water and stock.
4. Cook for 15 minutes after stirring in the thyme sprig and bay leaf.
5. Wait till it's done. Then remove the bay leaf and thyme sprig and Immerse in a blender to puree the soup.

6. Freshly serve the food when it's still warm.

482. Vegetable Chicken Soup

Preparation Time: 1 ¾ hours Servings: 8

Ingredients:

- Chopped sweet onion – 1
- Whole chicken – 1 (cut into smaller pieces)
- Sliced celery stalks - 2
- Cored and diced red bell peppers – 2
- Sliced carrots - 2
- Cubed zucchini - 1
- Peeled and diced tomatoes – 2
- Vegetable stock – 2 cups
- Peeled and cubed potatoes - 2
- Water – 8 cups
- Lemon juice – 1 tbsp.
- Pepper and salt to taste
- Chopped parsley – 2 tbsps. (for serving)

Directions:

1. In a pot, mix the stock, chicken and water together. Then cook on low heat after adding pepper and salt for 40 minutes.
2. Continue cooking after adding other Ingredients: for extra 20-25 minutes.
3. When it's finally done, stir in the parsley after removing from heat.
4. Freshly serve the soup when it's still warm.

483. Delicious Mixed Barley Soup

Preparation Time: 1 hour Servings: 8

Ingredients:

- Barley – ¼ cup
- Chopped shallots – 2
- Extra virgin olive oil – 2 tbsps.
- Cubed zucchini – 1
- Chopped garlic cloves - 2
- Diced carrots - 2
- Cored and diced yellow bell pepper – 1
- Diced and cored red bell pepper - 1
- Peeled and cubed potatoes - 2
- Drained canned corn – ½ cup
- Diced tomatoes – 1 can
- Bay leaf - 1
- Dried tarragon – ½ tsp.

- Water – 7 cups
- Vegetable stock – 2 cups
- Pepper and salt to taste

Directions:

1. Make it fragrant by stirring garlic, shallots and heated oil in a soup pot for 2 minutes. then add other Ingredients:.
2. On low heat, cook for 30 minutes after seasoning with pepper and salt.
3. Freshly serve the soup warm.

481. Tasty Tomato Soup For Rice

Cooking and
Preparation: 45 minutesServings: 6

Ingredients:

- Chopped shallot – 1
- Olive oil – 2 tbsps.
- Chopped garlic cloves - 2
- Sliced celery stalk – 1
- Peeled and tomatoes - 4
- Tomato paste – 2 tbsps.
- Water – 2 cups
- Vegetable stock – 2 cups
- Rinsed white rice – ½ cup
- Thyme sprig – 1
- Bay leaf - 1
- Cumin powder - ¼ tsp.
- Pepper and salt to taste
- Mustard seeds – ¼ tsp.

Directions:

1. Make it fragrant by stirring garlic, shallots, tomatoes and heated oil in a soup pot for 5 minutes. Then add other Ingredients:.
2. On low heat, cook for 25 minutes.
3. Serve chilled or slightly warm.

485. Whitish Bean Soup with cream

Preparation Time: 40 minutesServings: 6

Ingredients:

- Chopped garlic cloves – 2
- Olive oil – 2 tbsps.
- Chopped shallots - 2
- Drained white beans – 1 can

- Sliced celery stalk - 1
- Chicken stock – 2 cups
- Pepper and salt to taste
- Thyme sprig – 1
- Water – 2 cups
- Lemon juice – 1 tbsp.

Directions:

1. Soften it by stirring garlic, shallots, celery and heated oil in a soup pot for 2 minutes. then add other Ingredients:.
2. On low heat, cook for 20 minutes.
3. Wait till it's done. Then remove the thyme sprig and Immerse in a blender to puree the soup
4. Freshly serve the soup warm.

486. Whitish Bean Soup delicacy

Cooking and
Preparation: 50 minutesServings: 8

Ingredients:

- Baby spinach – 2 cups
- Diced carrots – 2
- Chopped shallots – 2
- Sliced celery stalks - 2
- Chopped garlic cloves – 2
- Cored and diced yellow bell peppers - 2
- Drained white beans – 1 can
- Thyme sprig – 1
- Cubed zucchini - 1
- Rosemary sprig - 1
- Chicken stock – 2 cups
- Diced tomatoes – 1 can
- Water – 6 cups
- Olive oil – 2 tbsps.
- Pepper and salt to taste

Directions:

1. In a soup pot, heat the oil and stir in the peppers, shallots, garlic, carrots and celery.
2. Add other Ingredients: after cooking for 10 minutes on low heat and season with pepper and salt.
3. Allow soup to cook for extra 20 minutes.
4. Freshly serve the soup warm.

487. Zucchini Salad

Preparation time: 10 minutes
Cooking time: 1 hour
Servings: 24

Ingredients:

- 2 tablespoons olive oil
- 3 zucchinis, sliced
- 3 tomatoes, cubed
- 2 tablespoons basil, chopped
- 2 tablespoons mint, chopped
- Salt and black pepper to the taste

Directions:

1. In your slow cooker, mix the oil with zucchini, tomatoes, basil, mint, salt and pepper, toss, cover and cook on High for 1 hour.
2. Divide into small bowls and serve as an appetizer.
3. Enjoy!

Nutrition Value: calories 241, fat 3, fiber 3, carbs 14, protein 8

488. Salmon Patties

Preparation time: 10 minutes
Cooking time: 2 hours
Servings: 4

Ingredients:

- 2 garlic cloves, minced
- 1 yellow onion, chopped
- 1 pound wild salmon, boneless and minced
- ¼ cup chives, chopped
- 1 egg
- 2 tablespoons Dijon mustard
- 1 tablespoon coconut flour
- A pinch of salt and black pepper

For the sauce:

- 4 garlic cloves, minced
- 2 tablespoons olive oil
- 2 tablespoons Dijon mustard
- Juice of 1 lemon

- 2 cups coconut cream
- 2 tablespoons chives, chopped

Directions:

1. In a bowl, mix onion, 2 garlic cloves, salmon, ¼-cup chives, coconut flour, salt, pepper, 2 tablespoons mustard and egg and stir well.
2. Shape medium cakes, put them in your slow cooker, add 4 garlic cloves, 2 tablespoons oil, 2 tablespoons mustard, lemon juice, coconut cream and chives, cover and cook on High for 2 hours.
3. Arrange salmon meatballs on a platter and serve as an appetizer.
4. Enjoy!

Nutrition Value: calories 271, fat 5, fiber 1, carbs 6, protein 7

489. Chili Salmon Bites

Preparation time: 30 minutes
Cooking time: 1 hour
Servings: 4

Ingredients:

- 4 salmon fillets, skinless, boneless and cubed
- 1 tablespoon olive oil
- A pinch of salt and black pepper
- 1 teaspoon cumin, ground
- 1 teaspoon sweet paprika
- ½ teaspoon ancho chili powder
- 1 teaspoon onion powder
- 2 tablespoons cilantro, chopped
- 3 tablespoons lime juice

Directions:

1. In a bowl, mix salt, pepper, chili powder, onion powder, paprika and cumin.
2. Rub salmon with this mix, drizzle the oil, transfer to your slow cooker, add cilantro and lime juice, toss, cover and cook on High for 1 hour.
3. Divide into small bowls and serve as an appetizer.
4. Enjoy!

Nutrition Value: calories 280, fat 14, fiber 4, carbs 11, protein 16

490. Shrimp and Orange Vinaigrette

Preparation time: 10 minutes
Cooking time: 1 hour
Servings: 4

Ingredients:

- 1 pound shrimp, deveined
- 4 spring onions, chopped
- A drizzle of olive oil
- 1 small slice of ginger, minced
- Salt and black pepper to the taste
- Juice of 2 oranges

Directions:

1. In your slow cooker, mix shrimp with spring onions, oil, ginger, salt, pepper and orange juice, toss, cover, cook on High for 1 hour, arrange on a platter, drizzle orange vinaigrette all over and serve as an appetizer.
2. Enjoy!

Nutrition Value: calories 200, fat 5, fiber 7, carbs 16, protein 6

491. Salmon Salad

Preparation time: 5 minutes
Cooking time: 2 hours
Servings: 2

Ingredients:

- 2 wild salmon fillets, boneless and cut into strips
- A pinch of salt and black pepper
- ½ cup cauliflower rice
- 1 cup chicken stock
- 2 carrots, sliced
- 2 celery stalks, chopped
- 2 yellow onions, chopped
- 2 tomatoes, cut into cubes
- A pinch of saffron

Directions:

1. In your slow cooker, mix the salmon with salt, pepper, cauliflower rice, stock, carrots, celery, onions, tomatoes and saffron, toss,

cover, cook on High for 2 hours, divide into small bowls and serve cold as an appetizer.

2. Enjoy!

Nutrition Value: calories 261, fat 4, fiber 8, carbs 39, protein 16

492. Salmon and Shrimp Bites

Preparation time: 10 minutes
Cooking time: 2 hours and 30 minutes
Servings: 6

Ingredients:

- 8 ounces salmon fillets, skinless, boneless and cut into medium cubes
- 8 ounces shrimp, deveined
- 1 yellow onion, chopped
- 13 ounces potatoes, peeled and cubed
- 13 ounces coconut milk
- Salt and black pepper to the taste

Directions:

1. In your slow cooker, mix salmon with onion, potatoes, coconut milk, salt and pepper, cover and cook on High for 2 hours.
2. Add shrimp, cover, cook on High for 30 minutes more, divide into small bowls and serve cold.
3. Enjoy!

Nutrition Value: calories 200, fat 7, fiber 8, carbs 28, protein 6

493. Shrimp Cocktail and Raspberry Sauce

Preparation time: 10 minutes
Cooking time: 2 hours
Servings: 6

Ingredients:

- 2 pounds shrimp, deveined
- 2 tablespoons olive oil
- 2 garlic cloves, minced
- 2 tablespoons parsley, chopped
- 2 tablespoons lemon juice
- Salt and white pepper to the taste
- 1/3 cup dill, chopped
- 2 pints red raspberries

Directions:

1. In your slow cooker, mix shrimp with oil, garlic, parsley, lemon juice, salt, pepper, dill and raspberries, cover, cook on Low for 2 hours, divide into cups and serve cold.
2. Enjoy!

Nutrition Value: calories 311, fat 4, fiber 7, carbs 17, protein 6

494. Tuna Appetizer Bowls

Preparation time: 10 minutes
Cooking time: 1 hour
Servings: 4

Ingredients:

- 8 ounces zucchini noodles
- ½ cup red onion, chopped
- 1 tablespoon extra virgin olive oil
- 1 cup veggie stock
- 14 ounces canned tomatoes, chopped
- A pinch of salt and black pepper
- 14 ounces canned tuna, drained and flaked
- 1 tablespoon parsley, chopped

Directions:

1. Grease your slow cooker with the oil, add zucchini noodles, onion, stock, tomatoes, salt, pepper, tuna and parsley, toss, cover, cook on High for 1 hour, divide into small cups and serve cold as an appetizer.
2. Enjoy!

Nutrition Value: calories 261, fat 7, fiber 7, carbs 29, protein 17

495. Radicchio and Mussels Salad

Preparation time: 10 minutes
Cooking time: 2 hours
Servings: 4

Ingredients:

- 2 pounds mussels, cleaned and scrubbed
- 2 radicchios, cut into thin strips
- 1 white onion, chopped
- 1 pound baby spinach
- 1 cup veggie stock
- 1 garlic clove, crushed
- A drizzle of extra virgin olive oil

Directions:

1. In your slow cooker, combine mussels with radicchios, onion, stock, garlic and the oil, toss a bit, cover and cook on High for 2 hours.
2. Add spinach, toss, divide between appetizer plates and serve.
3. Enjoy!

Nutrition Value: calories 162, fat 4, fiber 9, carbs 18, protein 4

496. Seafood Appetizer

Preparation time: 10 minutes
Cooking time: 2 hours and 30 minutes
Servings: 4

Ingredients:

- 12 shell clams
- 12 mussels
- 1 and ½ pounds big shrimp, peeled and deveined
- 1 cup ghee, melted
- 2 yellow onions, chopped
- 3 garlic cloves, minced
- ½ cup parsley, chopped
- 20 ounces canned tomatoes, chopped
- 1 tablespoon basil, dried
- Salt and black pepper to the taste

Directions:

1. Put the ghee in your slow cooker, add clams, mussels, onions, garlic, tomatoes, basil, salt and pepper, toss, cover and cook on High for 2 hours.
2. Add shrimp and parsley, cover, cook on High for 30 minutes more, divide between bowls and serve as an appetizer.
3. Enjoy!

Nutrition Value: calories 271, fat 6, fiber 8, carbs 18, protein 18

497. Chicken Appetizer

Preparation time: 10 minutes
Cooking time: 4 hours
Servings: 4

Ingredients:

- 1 bunch lemongrass, trimmed and chopped

- 1 ginger slice, chopped
- 4 garlic cloves, minced
- 3 tablespoons coconut aminos
- 1 teaspoon Chinese five spice
- 1 pound chicken breasts, skinless, boneless and cut into strips
- 1 cup coconut milk
- Salt and black pepper to the taste
- 1 teaspoon ghee
- ¼ cup cilantro, chopped
- 1 tablespoon lime juice

Directions:

1. In your food processor, mix lemongrass with ginger, garlic, aminos, five spice and coconut milk and pulse well.
2. Add the ghee to your slow cooker, add lemongrass mix, also add chicken strips, cilantro and limejuice, toss, cover and cook on Low for 4 hours.
3. Arrange chicken strips on a platter and serve.
4. Enjoy!

Nutrition Value: calories 261, fat 4, fiber 7, carbs 18, protein 18

498. Turkey Meatballs

Preparation time: 10 minutes
Cooking time: 4 hours
Servings: 8

Ingredients:

- 1 pound turkey meat, ground
- 1 yellow onion, minced
- 4 garlic cloves, minced
- ¼ cup parsley, chopped
- Salt and black pepper to the taste
- 1 teaspoon oregano, dried
- 1 egg, whisked
- ¼ cup almond milk
- 2 teaspoons coconut aminos
- 12 cremini mushrooms, chopped
- 1 cup chicken stock
- 2 tablespoons olive oil
- 2 tablespoons ghee

Directions:

1. In a bowl, mix turkey meat with salt, pepper, onion, garlic, parsley, oregano, egg and aminos, stir and shape medium meatballs out of this mix.
2. Add the oil and the ghee to your slow cooker, add almond milk, mushrooms, stock and the meatballs, cover and cook them on Low for 4 hours.
3. Arrange meatballs on a platter drizzle the mushroom sauce all over and serve as an appetizer.
4. Enjoy!

Nutrition Value: calories 291, fat 6, fiber 7, carbs 28, protein 16

499. Sausage Dip

Preparation time: 10 minutes
Cooking time: 2 hours
Servings: 6

Ingredients:

- 8 ounces coconut cream
- A pinch of salt and black pepper
- 2 jalapenos, chopped
- 15 ounces canned tomatoes, chopped
- 1 pound Italian sausage, ground
- ¼ cup green onions, chopped

Directions:

1. In your slow cooker, mix the coconut cream with salt, pepper, jalapenos, tomatoes, sausage and green onions, toss, cover and cook on High for 2 hours.
2. Divide the mix into bowls and serve as a party dip.
3. Enjoy!

Nutrition Value: calories 244, fat 12, fiber 1, carbs 23, protein 8

500. Black Olives and Tomato Dip

Preparation time: 10 minutes
Cooking time: 2 hours
Servings: 6

Ingredients:

- 8 black olives, pitted and chopped
- A pinch of salt and black pepper
- 2 tablespoons sun-dried tomatoes, blended
- 14 pepperoni slices, chopped

- 1 tablespoons basil, chopped

Directions:

1. In your slow cooker, combine the olives with salt, pepper, blended tomatoes, pepperoni and basil, stir, cover, cook on Low for 2 hours, stir once again, divide into bowls and serve.
2. Enjoy!

Nutrition Value: calories 210, fat 10, fiber 6, carbs 14, protein 8

501. Jalapeno Dip

Preparation time: 10 minutes
Cooking time: 2 hours
Servings: 4

Ingredients:

- 3 bacon slices, chopped
- ¼ teaspoon onion powder
- Salt and black pepper to the taste
- 3 jalapeno peppers, chopped
- 1 cup coconut cream
- ½ teaspoon parsley, dried
- ¼ teaspoon garlic powder

Directions:

1. In your slow cooker, mix the bacon with onion powder, salt, pepper, jalapenos, cream parsley and garlic powder, toss, cover and cook on High for 2 hours.
2. Stir the mix one more time, divide into bowls and serve as a party dip.
3. Enjoy!

Nutrition Value: calories 221, fat 18, fiber 8, carbs 22, protein 9

502. Italian Dip

Preparation time: 10 minutes
Cooking time: 3 hours
Servings: 4

Ingredients:

- 1 cup coconut cream
- A pinch of salt and black pepper
- 1/2 cup tomato sauce
- ¼ cup mayonnaise
- 1 tablespoon green bell pepper, chopped
- 6 pepperoni slices, chopped

- ½ teaspoon Italian seasoning
- 4 green olives, pitted and chopped

Directions:

1. In your slow cooker, combine the coconut cream with salt, pepper, tomato sauce, bell pepper, pepperoni, seasoning and olives, toss, cover and cook on High for 3 hours.
2. Add mayo, toss, divide into bowls and serve.
3. Enjoy!

Nutrition Value: calories 260, fat 14, fiber 4, carbs 16, protein 8

503. Zucchini Chips

Preparation time: 10 minutes
Cooking time: 3 hours
Servings: 8

Ingredients:

- 3 zucchinis, very thinly sliced
- Salt and black pepper to the taste
- 2 tablespoons olive oil
- 2 tablespoons balsamic vinegar

Directions:

1. In a bowl, mix oil with vinegar, salt and pepper and whisk well.
2. Add zucchini slices, toss to coat well, add them to your slow cooker, cover, cook on Low for 3 hours, cool them down, divide into bowls and serve.
3. Enjoy!

Nutrition Value: calories 140, fat 3, fiber 7, carbs 13, protein 6

504. Hot Celery Snack

Preparation time: 10 minutes
Cooking time: 2 hours
Servings: 8

Ingredients:

- 6 celery stacks, halved
- 3 tablespoons hot tomato sauce
- ¼ cup mayonnaise
- Salt and black pepper to the taste
- ½ teaspoon garlic powder

Directions:

1. In your slow cooker, mix the celery with the tomato sauce, mayo, salt, pepper and garlic powder, toss, cover and cook on High for 2 hours.
2. Arrange celery stick on a platter and serve them as a snack.
3. Enjoy!

Nutrition Value: calories 261, fat 2, fiber 3, carbs 11, protein 8

505. Avocado Salsa

Preparation time: 10 minutes
Cooking time: 1 hour
Servings: 4

Ingredients:

- 1 small red onion, chopped
- 2 avocados, pitted, peeled and chopped
- 3 jalapeno pepper, chopped
- Salt and black pepper to the taste
- 2 tablespoons parsley, chopped
- 1 tablespoon sweet paprika
- 2 tablespoons lime juice
- ½ tomato, chopped

Directions:

1. In your slow cooker, combine the onion with avocados, salt, pepper, paprika, lime juice, tomato and parsley, toss, cover, cook on High for 1 hour, divide into cups and serve as an appetizer.
2. Enjoy!

Nutrition Value: calories 140, fat 8, fiber 2, carbs 14, protein 4

506. Cod Spread

Preparation time: 10 minutes
Cooking time: 3 hours
Servings: 4

Ingredients:

- 1 pound cod fillets, boneless and skinless
- 3 teaspoons water
- 2 tablespoons lemon juice
- Salt and black pepper to the taste
- 4 tablespoons coconut cream
- 2 tablespoons mayonnaise
- 1 teaspoon dill, chopped

- 1 tablespoon olive oil

Directions:

1. In your slow cooker, mix cod with water, lemon juice, salt, pepper, cream and oil, toss, cover and cook on High for 3 hours.
2. Flake the cod, add mayo and dill, whisk well, divide into bowls and serve as a party spread.
3. Enjoy!

Nutrition Value: calories 204, fat 12, fiber 4, carbs 16, protein 11

507. Oysters Platter

Preparation time: 10 minutes
Cooking time: 1 hour and 20 minutes
Servings: 3

Ingredients:

- 6 big oysters, shucked
- 3 garlic cloves, minced
- Juice of 1 lemon
- 1 tablespoon parsley, chopped
- 2 teaspoons sweet paprika
- 2 tablespoons melted ghee

Directions:

1. In your slow cooker, mix the oysters with garlic, lemon juice, parsley, paprika and ghee, cover and cook on High for 1 hour and 20 minutes.
2. Transfer oysters to a platter, drizzle some of the sauce from the pot over them and serve.
3. Enjoy!

Nutrition Value: calories 160, fat 4, fiber 4, carbs 16, protein 8

508. Tuna Cakes

Preparation time: 10 minutes
Cooking time: 1 hour and 30 minutes
Servings: 12

Ingredients:

- 15 ounces canned tuna, drain well and flaked
- 3 eggs
- ½ teaspoon dill, dried
- 1 teaspoon parsley, dried

- ½ cup red onion, chopped
- 1 teaspoon garlic powder
- A pinch of salt and black pepper
- 2 tablespoons olive oil
- 1 cup tomato sauce

Directions:

1. In a bowl, mix tuna with salt, pepper, dill, parsley, onion, garlic powder and eggs, stir well and shape medium cakes out of this mix.
2. Add the oil and the sauce to your slow cooker, add tuna cakes, cover and cook on High for 1 hour and 30 minutes.
3. Arrange on a platter and serve as an appetizer.
4. Enjoy!

Nutrition Value: calories 200, fat 2, fiber 4, carbs 12, protein 6

509. Shrimp and Arugula Appetizer Salad

Preparation time: 10 minutes
Cooking time: 2 hours
Servings: 2

Ingredients:

- 1 and ½ pounds shrimp, deveined
- 2 tablespoons olive oil
- A pinch of salt and black pepper
- Juice of 1 lemon
- 3 cups arugula
- 1 cup black olives, pitted and sliced
- 4 tablespoons capers, chopped
- 3 garlic cloves, chopped

Directions:

1. In your slow cooker, mix the shrimp with oil, salt, pepper, lemon juice, capers, olives and garlic, cover, cook on Low for 2 hours, transfer to a salad bowl, add arugula, toss, divide between small plates and serve as an appetizer.
2. Enjoy!

Nutrition Value: calories 220, fat 5, fiber 8, carbs 13, protein 9

510. Shrimp and Lobster Platter

Preparation time: 10 minutes
Cooking time: 0 minutes
Servings: 2

Ingredients:

- 1 tablespoon shallots, chopped
- ¼ cup white vinegar
- A pinch of salt and black pepper
- 2 tablespoons cucumber, diced
- 1 tablespoon horseradish
- ⅓ cup tomato paste, unsweetened
- ¼ teaspoon orange zest
- 4 shrimp, peeled, deveined, and steamed
- 1 lobster tail, steamed and cut in half

Directions:

1. In a bowl, mix the shallots with the vinegar, salt, pepper, horseradish, tomato paste and orange zest and whisk really well. Arrange the lobster and the shrimp on a platter; add the sauce you have just made and serve.

Nutrition Value: Calories - 176, Fat - 4, Fiber - 4, Carbs - 6, Protein - 8

511. Olive and Anchovy Spread

Preparation time: 10 minutes
Cooking time: 0 minutes
Servings: 4

Ingredients:

- 1 garlic clove, peeled and chopped
- 1 cup green olives, pitted
- 3 tablespoons capers, drained
- 5 anchovy fillets, chopped
- 2 teaspoons lemon juice

Directions:

1. In a food processor, mix the olives with the garlic, capers, anchovy and lemon juice, pulse well and serve cold.

Nutrition Value: Calories - 100, Fat - 2, Fiber - 3, Carbs - 6, Protein - 8

512. Beef and Caper Tartar

Preparation time: 45 minutes
Cooking time: 0 minutes
Servings: 2

Ingredients:

- 3 tablespoons olive oil
- 8 ounces beef tenderloin, julienned
- 1 egg yolk
- 3 tablespoons capers, soaked in water, drained and rinsed
- 1 onion, minced
- 2 tablespoons fresh parsley, minced
- A pinch of sea salt and black pepper
- 1 Serrano chili pepper, minced
- 1 teaspoon Dijon mustard
- 1 teaspoon balsamic vinegar

Directions:

1. Put the meat on a cutting board, dice finely, put it in a bowl and keep it in the fridge for 45 minutes. In a bowl, mix the egg yolk with the oil and whisk well. Add the parsley, chili pepper, capers, onion, salt, pepper, the beef and the vinegar and stir really well. Transfer to plates and serve with the Dijon mustard on top.

Nutrition Value: Calories - 140, Fat - 3, Fiber - 3, Carbs - 6, Protein - 8

513. Shrimp Spread

Preparation time: 10 minutes
Cooking time: 10 minutes
Servings: 8

Ingredients:

- 1 pound shrimp, cooked, peeled, deveined and chopped
- 2 tablespoons coconut cream
- A pinch of salt and black pepper

Directions:

1. In a bowl, mix the shrimp with the coconut cream, salt and pepper, stir well, divide into bowls and serve.

Nutrition Value: Calories - 110, Fat - 1, Fiber - 3, Carbs - 6, Protein - 8

514. Salmon Bites

Preparation time: 10 minutes
Cooking time: 0 minutes
Servings: 14

Ingredients:

- 1 cucumber, peeled and sliced thin into 42 pieces
- 2 teaspoons lemon juice
- 4 ounces coconut cream
- 1 teaspoon lemon zest
- A pinch of salt and ground black pepper
- 2 teaspoons fresh dill, chopped
- 4 ounces smoked salmon, cut into 42 strips

Directions:

1. In a bowl, mix the coconut cream with lemon zest, lemon juice, salt and pepper and stir well. Arrange the cucumber slices on a platter, top each with the salmon strips, add coconut mixture over the salmon, sprinkle the dill and serve.

Nutrition Value: Calories - 165, Fat - 4, Fiber - 5, Carbs - 7, Protein - 10

515. Tuna Platter

Preparation time: 10 minutes
Cooking time: 0 minutes
Servings: 2

Ingredients:

- 7 ounces tuna, sliced thin
- 1 tomato, cored and chopped
- 1 teaspoon lime juice
- 1 teaspoon fresh parsley, chopped
- 1 avocado, pitted and chopped
- 1 teaspoon olive oil
- A pinch of salt and black pepper

Directions:

1. In a bowl, mix the tomato with the lime juice, parsley, avocado, oil, salt and pepper and toss. Arrange the tuna on a platter, top the slices with the tomato mix and serve.

Nutrition Value: Calories - 120, Fat - 2, Fiber - 3, Carbs - 6, Protein - 8

516. Tuna Cube Salad

Preparation time: 10 minutes
Cooking time: 0 minutes
Servings: 3

Ingredients:

- 7 ounces sashimi-grade tuna, cubed

- 4 cherry tomatoes, cubed
- ⅓ cucumber, cubed
- 1 teaspoon fresh cilantro, minced
- 4 tablespoons olive oil
- A pinch of salt and ground black pepper
- 3 tablespoons white vinegar
- 1 teaspoons lemon juice

Directions:

1. In a bowl, mix the tomatoes with the cucumber, cilantro, half of the oil, salt, pepper, vinegar and half of the lemon juice and toss well. In a separate bowl, mix the tuna cubes with the rest of the oil and remaining lemon juice, toss and arrange them on a platter. Add the tomato mix on the side and serve.

Nutrition Value: Calories - 150, Fat - 5, Fiber - 4, Carbs - 5, Protein - 6

517. Eggplant Spread

Preparation time: 10 minutes
Cooking time: 35 minutes
Servings: 8

Ingredients:

- 2 tablespoons olive oil+ a drizzle
- 4 pounds eggplants, cut in half
- 2 shallots, peeled and chopped
- 1 pound tomatoes, peeled and chopped
- 4 garlic cloves, peeled and minced
- A pinch of salt and ground black pepper
- 2 tablespoons lemon juice

Directions:

1. Put the eggplant halves in a baking dish, brush them with a drizzle of olive oil, place in the oven at 350°F, bake for 30 minutes, cool them down, peel the flesh and put in a blender. Heat a pan with the rest of the oil over medium high heat, add the shallots and the garlic, stir and cook them for 5 minutes. Transfer this to the blender as well, add the tomatoes, salt, pepper and the lemon juice, pulse well, divide into bowls and serve as a dip.

Nutrition Value: Calories - 150, Fat - 4, Fiber - 5, Carbs - 6, Protein - 7

518. Olive and Roasted Pepper Tapenade

Preparation time: 10 minutes
Cooking time: 0 minutes
Servings: 8

Ingredients:

- 2 tablespoons olive oil
- ½ cup bottled roasted peppers, chopped
- ½ cup Kalamata and black olives, pitted and chopped
- 1 tablespoon lemon juice
- 1 teaspoon red pepper flakes
- A pinch of salt and black pepper
- ½ tablespoon mint leaves, chopped
- ½ tablespoon fresh parsley, chopped
- ½ tablespoon fresh oregano, chopped
- ½ tablespoon fresh basil, chopped

Directions:

1. In a bowl, mix the bell peppers with the olives, lemon juice, pepper flakes, salt, pepper, mint, parsley, oregano, basil and the oil, toss and serve cold.

Nutrition Value: Calories - 140, Fat - 4, Fiber - 4, Carbs - 7, Protein - 9

519. Chinese Tuna Skewers

Preparation time: 30 minutes
Cooking time: 10 minutes
Servings: 16

Ingredients:

- 2 tablespoons coconut aminos
- 1 pound tuna steaks, cut in 16 cubes
- 2 tablespoons balsamic vinegar
- A pinch of salt and black pepper
- 1 tablespoon sesame seeds
- 2 tablespoons olive oil
- 16 pieces pickled ginger

Directions:

1. In a bowl, mix the aminos with the vinegar and tuna, toss to coat, cover the bowl, and keep in the refrigerator for 30 minutes. Pat dry the tuna and season with the salt and black pepper, and sprinkle the sesame seeds. Heat a pan with the oil over medium

heat, add the tuna pieces, cook them for 2 minutes on each side and transfer them to a plate. Thread one ginger slice on each of the 16 skewers, continue with the tuna, arrange everything on a platter and serve.

Nutrition Value: Calories - 150, Fat - 4, Fiber - 4, Carbs - 6, Protein - 8

520. Smoked Salmon Platter

Preparation time: 10 minutes
Cooking time: 0 minutes
Servings: 4

Ingredients:

- 2 tablespoons scallions, chopped
- 2 tablespoons onion, peeled and chopped
- 1½ teaspoons lime juice
- 1 tablespoon fresh chives, minced
- 1 tablespoon olive oil
- ½ pound smoked salmon fillet, skinless and diced
- 12 cherry tomatoes, cut in half
- A pinch of salt and black pepper
- 1 tablespoon parsley, chopped

Directions:

1. In a bowl, mix the salmon with the scallions, onion, lime juice, chives, oil, tomatoes, salt, pepper and parsley, toss, arrange on a platter and serve.

Nutrition Value: Calories - 170, Fat - 3, Fiber - 4, Carbs - 6, Protein - 7

521. Carrot Spread

Preparation time: 10 minutes
Cooking time: 12 minutes
Servings: 6

Ingredients:

- 3 carrots, peeled and grated
- ¼ cup olive oil
- ⅓ cup pine nuts
- A pinch of salt and black pepper
- 2 cups coconut yogurt
- 1 shallot, minced

Directions:

1. Heat a pan with the oil over medium-high

heat, add the carrots and the shallot, stir, and cook for 6 minutes. Add the salt, pepper and pine nuts, reduce the heat, cook for 6 minutes more. Transfer this to a bowl, add the coconut yogurt, whisk and serve.

Nutrition Value: Calories - 140, Fat - 2, Fiber - 3, Carbs - 7, Protein - 8

522. Veggies and Pomegranate Salad

Preparation time: 10 minutes
Cooking time: 0 minutes
Servings: 6

Ingredients:

- 3 garlic cloves, peeled and minced
- 2 tablespoons olive oil
- ½ teaspoon red pepper flakes
- A pinch of salt and black pepper
- 2 teaspoon pomegranate seeds
- 2 tomatoes, cored and chopped
- 2 cucumbers, cubed
- 2 scallions, chopped
- 1 onion, peeled and chopped
- 1 green bell pepper, and chopped
- ½ cup cilantro, chopped
- ¼ cup mint leaves, chopped

Directions:

1. In a bowl, mix the tomatoes with the cucumber, garlic, scallions, onion, bell pepper, cilantro and mint and toss. Add the oil, pepper flakes, salt, pepper and the pomegranate seeds, toss and serve.

Nutrition Value: Calories - 120, Fat - 2, Fiber - 3, Carbs - 4, Protein - 7

523. Fresh Tomato Salad

Preparation time: 40 minutes
Cooking time: 0 minutes
Servings: 6

Ingredients:

- 1 pound tomatoes, cubed
- ¾ pound cucumbers, chopped
- 1 green bell pepper, seeded and chopped
- 1 onion, sliced thin

- ¼ cup fresh parsley, chopped
- 2 tablespoons mint leaves, chopped
- A pinch of salt and black pepper
- 3 tablespoons olive oil
- 3 tablespoons lemon juice
- 10 black olives, pitted and chopped

Directions:

1. In a salad bowl, mix the tomatoes with the cucumbers, bell pepper, onion, parsley, mint, salt, pepper, oil, lemon juice and olives, toss and serve.

Nutrition Value: Calories - 120, Fat - 2, Fiber - 3, Carbs - 5, Protein - 5

524. Zucchini and Green Onion Salad

Preparation time: 10 minutes
Cooking time: 0 minutes
Servings: 4

Ingredients:

- 4 zucchinis, spiralized
- 4 green onions, chopped
- Juice of 1 lime
- 1 tablespoon olive oil
- ½ cup fresh parsley, chopped
- ¾ cup almonds, chopped
- A pinch of salt and black pepper

Directions:

1. In a salad bowl, mix zucchini with the green onions, lime juice, oil, almonds, parsley, salt and pepper, toss and serve.

Nutrition Value: Calories - 90, Fat - 4, Fiber - 2, Carbs - 5, Protein - 7

525. Curry Cabbage Slaw

Preparation time: 1 hour
Cooking time: 0 minutes
Servings: 4

Ingredients:

- 1 green cabbage head, chopped
- ⅓ cup coconut, shaved
- ¼ cup avocado oil
- 2 tablespoons lemon juice

- 3 tablespoons sesame seeds
- ½ teaspoon curry powder
- ⅓ teaspoon turmeric powder

Directions:

1. In a bowl, mix the cabbage with the coconut, oil, lemon juice, curry powder, turmeric and sesame seeds, toss and serve after keeping the mix in the fridge for 1 hour.

Nutrition Value: Calories - 100, Fat - 2, Fiber - 5, Carbs - 5, Protein - 6

526. Papaya and Cabbage Slaw

Preparation time: 10 minutes
Cooking time: 0 minutes
Servings: 4

Ingredients:

- 2 cups green papaya, peeled and grated
- ¼ cup carrots, grated
- 2 tablespoons coconut aminos
- ¼ cup green cabbage, shredded
- 10 cherry tomatoes, cut in half
- 1 teaspoon olive oil
- 2 red chilies, chopped
- 2 garlic cloves, peeled and minced
- 1 teaspoon lemon juice
- 2 tablespoons walnuts, chopped
- A pinch of salt and black pepper

Directions:

1. In a salad bowl, mix the papaya with the carrots, tomatoes, cabbage, chilies, garlic, walnuts, salt and pepper. Add the lemon juice, oil and the aminos, toss and serve cold.

Nutrition Value: Calories - 140, Fat - 3, Fiber - 2, Carbs - 6, Protein - 8

527. Apple and Celery Appetizer Salad

Preparation time: 1 hour
Cooking time: 0 minutes
Servings: 4

Ingredients:

- 3 apples, cored and chopped

- 1 celery stalk, chopped
- 2 carrot, grated
- ¼ cup cashews, chopped
- For the salad dressing:
- 1 tablespoon lemon juice
- 2 garlic cloves, peeled and minced
- ¼ cup homemade mayonnaise
- 1 tablespoon balsamic vinegar
- 2 tablespoons water
- 3 tablespoons olive oil
- 1 tablespoon fresh parsley, chopped
- A pinch of sea salt

Directions:

1. In a bowl, mix the apples with the carrots, celery and cashews and toss. In another bowl, mix the garlic with the lemon juice, mayonnaise, vinegar, oil, parsley, salt and water, whisk well, pour over the salad, toss and serve cold.

Nutrition Value: Calories - 100, Fat - 3, Fiber - 4, Carbs - 5, Protein - 6

528. Radish Slaw

Preparation time: 10 minutes
Cooking time: 0 minutes
Servings: 4

Ingredients:

- 16 radishes, sliced
- 2 tablespoons raisins
- Juice of 2 lemons
- 1 tablespoon fresh chives, minced
- 1 tablespoon fresh parsley, chopped
- 1 tablespoon sesame seeds
- 4 handfuls spinach leaves, torn
- 4 tablespoons olive oil
- A pinch of salt and black pepper

Directions:

1. In a salad bowl, mix the radishes with the raisins, chives, parsley, lemon juice, spinach, sesame seeds, oil, salt and pepper, toss and serve cold.

Nutrition Value: Calories - 90, Fat - 2, Fiber - 2, Carbs - 4, Protein - 6

529. Oregano Tomatoes Mix

Preparation time: 10 minutes
Cooking time: 0 minutes
Servings: 4

Ingredients:

- ½ cup olive oil
- 2 pints cherry tomatoes, cut in half
- A pinch of salt and black pepper
- 1 red onion, peeled and chopped
- 3 tablespoons red vinegar
- 1 garlic clove, peeled and minced
- 1 bunch oregano, chopped

Directions:

1. In a bowl, mix the tomatoes with salt, pepper, onion, garlic, oregano, vinegar and oil, toss and serve cold.

Nutrition Value: Calories - 100, Fat - 1, Fiber - 2, Carbs - 2, Protein - 5

530. Tomato and Avocado Salad

Preparation time: 10 minutes
Cooking time: 0 minutes
Servings: 4

Ingredients:

- 1 pound tomatoes, cored and chopped
- 2 avocados, pitted and chopped
- 1 small onion, chopped
- 2 tablespoons olive oil
- 2 tablespoons lemon juice
- ¼ cup cilantro, diced
- A pinch of sea salt and black pepper

Directions:

1. In a bowl, mix the tomatoes with the avocados, onion, oil, lemon juice, cilantro, salt and pepper, toss and serve as an appetizer.

Nutrition Value: Calories - 120, Fat - 2, Fiber - 2, Carbs - 3, Protein - 4

531. Cucumber, Fennel and Chive Slaw

Preparation time: 10 minutes
Cooking time: 0 minutes
Servings: 4

Ingredients:

- 4 cucumbers, chopped
- ¾ cup fennel, sliced
- 2 tablespoons fresh chives, minced
- ½ cup walnuts, chopped
- 2 tablespoons lemon juice
- 4 tablespoons olive oil
- A pinch of salt and black pepper

Directions:

1. In a bowl, mix the cucumbers with the fennel, chives, walnuts, lemon juice, oil, salt and pepper, toss and serve cold.

Nutrition Value: Calories - 70, Fat - 1, Fiber - 1, Carbs - 1, Protein - 5

532. Endive Appetizer Salad

Preparation time: 10 minutes
Cooking time: 0 minutes
Servings: 4

Ingredients:

- 2 tablespoons lemon juice
- ¼ cup olive oil
- A pinch of salt and black pepper
- 1 teaspoon Dijon mustard
- 4 endives, shredded
- ½ cup almonds, chopped
- 2 tablespoons cilantro, chopped

Directions:

1. In a salad bowl, mix the endives with almonds, cilantro, lemon juice, oil, salt, pepper and mustard, toss and serve cold.

Nutrition Value: Calories - 100, Fat - 0, Fiber - 1, Carbs - 0, Protein - 6

533. Ginger Cilantro Dip

Preparation time: 10 minutes
Cooking time: 0 minutes
Servings: 6

Ingredients:

- ½ cup ginger, grated
- 2 bunches fresh cilantro
- 3 tablespoons balsamic vinegar
- ½ cup olive oil
- 2 tablespoons coconut aminos

Directions:

1. In a blender mix cilantro with the oil, aminos, vinegar and ginger, pulse well, divide into bowls and serve.

Nutrition Value: Calories - 89, Fat - 2, Fiber - 2, Carbs - 6, Protein - 8

534. Roasted Beet Spread

Preparation time: 3 hours and 10 minutes
Cooking time: 1 hour
Servings: 6

Ingredients:

- 3 beets
- 1 cup coconut cream
- A pinch of salt and black pepper
- 2 tablespoons mint leaves, chopped
- 2 teaspoons balsamic vinegar
- A drizzle of olive oil

Directions:

1. Place beets in a baking dish, add some hot water on the bottom of the pan, add a pinch of salt and pepper, cover the pan, place in the oven at 450°F and bake for 1 hour. Let the beets cool down, peel, chop, and transfer to a bowl. Add cream, salt, pepper, mint, vinegar and the oil, pulse using an immersion blender and serve cold after 3 hours.

Nutrition Value: Calories - 130, Fat - 4, Fiber - 5, Carbs - 8, Protein - 9

535. Red Bell Pepper Hummus

Preparation time: 10 minutes
Cooking time: 10 minutes
Servings: 4

Ingredients:

- 1 garlic clove, peeled and minced
- 3 red bell peppers, deseeded and cut into quarters
- A pinch of salt and black pepper
- 1½ tablespoons olive oil
- ¼ cup coconut cream
- 2 green onions, sliced

Directions:

1. Place the peppers on preheated grill over medium-high heat, cook for 8 minutes, transfer to a bowl, cover, leave aside for a few minutes. Peel, transfer to a food processor, add garlic, salt, pepper, oil and the cream, pulse well, divide into bowls, sprinkle the green onions on top and serve.

Nutrition Value: Calories - 176, Fat - 3, Fiber - 2, Carbs - 6, Protein - 7

536. Tomato and Dragon Fruit Platter

Preparation time: 10 minutes
Cooking time: 0 minutes
Servings: 4

Ingredients:

- 4 tomatoes, cored and sliced thin
- 1 tablespoon lemon juice
- 1 dragon fruit, skinless and cubed
- 1 teaspoon lemon zest
- 1 tablespoon balsamic vinegar
- A pinch of salt
- 1 tablespoon mint, chopped
- 4 tablespoons olive oil

1. **Directions:**
2. Arrange the tomatoes on a platter and top with the dragon fruit cubes. In a bowl, mix lemon zest with lemon juice, vinegar, salt, oil and mint, whisk well, drizzle over the tomatoes and dragon fruit and serve

Nutrition Value: Calories - 98, Fat - 1, Fiber - 2, Carbs - 3, Protein - 6

537. Mango and Tomato Salad

Preparation time: 10 minutes
Cooking time: 0 minutes
Servings: 6

Ingredients:

- 4 tomatoes, cored, seeded, and chopped
- A pinch of salt and black pepper
- ⅓ cup onion, chopped
- 1 mango, peeled, seedless, and chopped
- 2 jalapeño peppers, chopped
- ¼ cup fresh cilantro, chopped

- 3 tablespoons lime juice

Directions:

1. In a bowl, mix the tomatoes with onion, mango, jalapeno, cilantro, lime juice, salt and pepper, toss and serve.

Nutrition Value: Calories - 67, Fat - 1, Fiber - 2, Carbs - 4, Protein - 7

538. Tuna Cucumber Rounds

Preparation time: 10 minutes
Cooking time: 0 minutes
Servings: 6

Ingredients:

- 1 cucumber, sliced
- 1 tablespoon fresh cilantro, chopped
- 6 ounces canned tuna, drained and flaked
- 1 teaspoon lemon juice

Directions:

1. In a bowl, mix the tuna with lemon juice and cilantro and mash well. Spoon this mixture on each cucumber slice and serve.

Nutrition Value: Calories - 120, Fat - 1, Fiber - 2, Carbs - 5, Protein - 6

539. Tuna Salad

Preparation time: 10 minutes
Cooking time: 0 minutes
Servings: 2

Ingredients:

- 8 ounces canned tuna, drained and flaked
- 2 teaspoons olive oil
- 2 tablespoons shallots, chopped
- 4 lettuce leaves, torn
- 1 tablespoon capers, drained
- 2 tablespoons red bell pepper, seeded and chopped
- 1 tablespoon arugula leaves, torn
- 2 tablespoons hard boiled egg, peeled and chopped
- A pinch of salt and black pepper
- Juice of ½ lemon

Directions:

1. In a bowl, mix the tuna with oil, shallots,

lettuce leaves, capers, bell pepper, arugula, eggs, salt, pepper and lemon juice, toss and serve cold.

Nutrition Value: Calories - 120, Fat - 2, Fiber - 3, Carbs - 6, Protein - 8

540. Tuna and Carrot Salad

Preparation time: 10 minutes
Cooking time: 0 minutes
Servings: 4

Ingredients:

- ¼ red onion, peeled and chopped
- 4 carrots, cut into thin sticks
- 1 tablespoon avocado oil
- 6 ounces canned tuna, drained and flaked
- 1 tablespoon Dijon mustard
- 1 tablespoon red vinegar
- A pinch of salt and black pepper
- 1 tablespoon lemon juice

Directions:

1. In a large bowl, mix the onion with the carrots, tuna, oil, mustard, vinegar, salt, pepper and lemon juice, toss well and serve cold.

Nutrition Value: Calories - 140, Fat - 3, Fiber - 3, Carbs - 6, Protein - 8

541. Goji Berry Mix

Preparation time: 10 mins
Cooking time: 0 minutes
Servings: 4

Ingredients:

- 1 cup almonds
- 1 cup goji berries
- ½ cup sunflower seeds
- ½ cup pumpkin seeds
- ½ cup walnuts, halved
- 12 apricots, dried and quartered

Directions:

1. 1.In a bowl, combine the almond while using goji berries, sunflower seeds, pumpkin seeds, walnuts and apricots, toss, divide into bowls and serve.
2. Enjoy!

Nutrition Value: calories 187, fat 2, fiber 5, carbs 12, protein 6

542. Artichoke Spread

Preparation time: 10 minutes
Cooking time: fifteen minutes
Servings: 4

Ingredients:

- 10 ounces spinach, chopped
- 12 ounces canned artichoke hearts, no-salt-added, drained and chopped
- 1 cup coconut cream
- 1 cup low-fat cheddar, shredded
- A pinch of black pepper

Directions:

1. 1.In a bowl, combine the spinach with all the artichokes, cream, cheese and black pepper, stir well, transfer with a baking dish, introduce within the oven and bake at 400 degrees F for a quarter-hour.
2. 2.Divide into bowls and serve.
3. Enjoy!

Nutrition Value: calories 200, fat 4, fiber 6, carbs 14, protein 8

543. Avocado Salsa

Preparation time: 10 minutes
Cooking time: 0 minutes
Servings: 4

Ingredients:

- 1 small yellow onion, minced
- 1 jalapeno, minced
- ¼ cup cilantro, chopped
- A pinch of black pepper
- 2 avocados, peeled, pitted and cubed
- 2 tablespoons lime juice

Directions:

1. 1.In a bowl, combine the onion when using jalapeno, cilantro, black pepper, avocado and lime juice, toss and serve.
2. Enjoy!

Nutrition Value: calories 198, fat 2, fiber 5, carbs 14, protein 7

544. Onion Spread

Preparation time: 10 minutes
Cooking time: 35 minutes
Servings: 4

Ingredients:

- 2 tablespoons essential organic olive oil
- 2 yellow onions, sliced
- A pinch of black pepper
- 8 ounces low-fat cream cheese
- 1 cup coconut cream
- 2 tablespoons chives, chopped

Directions:

1. 1.Heat up a pan while using oil over low heat, add the onions along with the black pepper, stir and cook for 35 minutes.
2. 2.In a bowl, combine the onions with all the cream cheese, coconut cream and chives, stir well and serve as a celebration spread.
3. Enjoy!

Nutrition Value: calories 212, fat 3, fiber 5, carbs 14, protein 8

545. Simple Salsa

Preparation time: ten mins
Cooking time: 0 minutes
Servings: 6

Ingredients:

- 1 yellow bell pepper, cubed
- 2 tomatoes, cubed
- 1 cucumber, cubed
- 1 small red onion, cubed
- 1 tablespoon extra virgin essential olive oil
- 1 tablespoon red vinegar

Directions:

1. 1.In a bowl, combine the bell pepper with all the tomatoes, cucumber, onion, oil and vinegar, toss, divide into small cups and serve.
2. Enjoy!

Nutrition Value: calories 142, fat 4, fiber 4, carbs 6, protein 7

546. Spinach Dip

Preparation time: 10 mins

Cooking time: 0 minutes
Servings: 4

Ingredients:

- 1 tablespoon essential olive oil
- 10 ounces spinach
- 1 and ½ cups canned chickpeas, no-salt-added, drained and rinsed

Directions:

1. 1.In your blender, combine the chickpeas while using oil and also the spinach, pulse well, divide into bowls and serve.
2. Enjoy!

Nutrition Value: calories 200, fat 3, fiber 5, carbs 14, protein 6

547. Avocado Dip

Preparation time: ten mins
Cooking time: 0 minutes
Servings: 8

Ingredients:

- 4 avocados, peeled and pitted
- 1 cup cilantro leaves
- ½ cup coconut cream
- 1 jalapeno, chopped
- ¼ cup lime juice
- A pinch of black pepper

Directions:

1. 1.In your blender, combine the avocados when using cilantro, coconut cream, jalapeno, lime juice and black pepper, pulse well, divide into bowls and serve.
2. Enjoy!

Nutrition Value: calories 187, fat 3, fiber 7, carbs 17, protein 8

548. Chives Dip

Preparation time: ten mins
Cooking time: 0 minutes
Servings: 4

Ingredients:

- 2 tablespoons chives, chopped
- 1 shallot, minced
- 1 tablespoon freshly squeezed lemon juice
- A pinch of black pepper

- 2 ounces low-fat cheese, shredded
- 1 cup coconut cream

Directions:

1. 1.In a bowl, combine the chives with all the shallot, freshly squeezed lemon juice, black pepper, cheese and coconut cream, whisk well and serve as a celebration dip.
2. Enjoy!

Nutrition Value: calories 211, fat 3, fiber 5, carbs 15, protein 6

549. Dill Dip

Preparation time: ten mins
Cooking time: 0 minutes
Servings: 6

Ingredients:

- 8 ounces coconut cream
- ¼ cup horseradish
- 2 tablespoons dill
- A pinch of black pepper

Directions:

1. 1.In a bowl, combine the cream using the horseradish, dill and black pepper, stir very well and serve as a celebration dip.
2. Enjoy!

Nutrition Value: calories 181, fat 3, fiber 7, carbs 16, protein 7

550. Chickpeas Salsa

Preparation time: ten mins
Cooking time: 0 minutes
Servings: 6

Ingredients:

- 15 ounces canned chickpeas, no-salt-added, drained and rinsed
- 4 scallions, chopped
- 2 roasted red peppers, chopped
- 1 cup baby arugula leaves
- 2 tablespoons freshly squeezed lemon juice
- 2 tablespoons essential olive oil
- A pinch of black pepper

Directions:

1. 1.In a bowl, combine the chickpeas while using scallions, red peppers, arugula, fresh

fresh lemon juice, oil and black pepper, toss, divide into small bowls and serve.
2. Enjoy!

Nutrition Value: calories 189, fat 3, fiber 6, carbs 14, protein 6

551. Cilantro Dip

Preparation time: 10 mins
Cooking time: 0 minutes
Servings: 6

Ingredients:

- 2 bunches cilantro leaves
- ½ cup ginger, sliced
- 3 tablespoons balsamic vinegar
- ½ cup organic olive oil
- 2 tablespoons coconut aminos
- 2 teaspoons sesame oil

Directions:

1. 1.In your blender, combine the cilantro with the ginger, vinegar, oil, aminos and sesame oil, pulse well, divide into small cups and serve.
2. Enjoy!

Nutrition Value: calories 188, fat 4, fiber 6, carbs 7, protein 8

552. Yogurt and Dill Dip

Preparation time: ten mins
Cooking time: 0 minutes
Servings: 4

Ingredients:

- 2 cup non-fat yogurt
- 1 garlic cloves, minced
- ¼ cup walnuts, chopped
- ¼ cup dill, chopped

Directions:

1. 1.In a bowl, combine the yogurt while using garlic, walnuts and dill, stir well and serve cold.
2. Enjoy!

Nutrition Value: calories 181, fat 2, fiber 6, carbs 11, protein 7

553. Broccoli Dip

Preparation time: ten mins

Cooking time: 0 minutes

Servings: 4

Ingredients:

- 14 ounces broccoli florets
- 1 cup low-fat some kinds of cheese
- A pinch of black pepper

Directions:

1. 1.In the meat processor, combine the broccoli because of the cheese and black pepper, pulse well, divide into small cups and serve.
2. Enjoy!

Nutrition Value: calories 189, fat 4, fiber 6, carbs 15, protein 7

554. Easy Salmon Spread

Preparation time: ten mins

Cooking time: 0 minutes

Servings: 4

Ingredients:

- 2 tablespoons horseradish
- 8 ounces low-fat cream cheese
- 2 tablespoons dill, chopped
- ¼ pound smoked salmon, chopped
- A pinch of black pepper

Directions:

1. In a bowl, combine the horseradish while using the cream cheese, dill, salmon and black pepper, stir well and serve as a celebration spread.
2. Enjoy!

Nutrition Value: calories 212, fat 3, fiber 6, carbs 14, protein 7

555. Turkey Wraps

Preparation time: 10 minutes

Cooking time: 0 minutes

Servings: 2

Ingredients:

- 1 peach, cut into 8 wedges
- 3 ounces turkey breast, cooked and cut into 8 pieces

Directions:

1. Roll 2 peach wedges by 50 percent slices of turkey, wrap, secure which has a toothpick, repeat with all the rest inside the peach wedges and turkey and serve being a snack.
2. Enjoy!

Nutrition Value: calories 200, fat 2, fiber 5, carbs 13, protein 9

556. Plantain Chips

Preparation time: 10 mins

Cooking time: 10 mins

Servings: 4

Ingredients:

- 4 green plantains, peeled and thinly sliced
- 4 cups coconut oil, melted
- A pinch of red pepper flakes

Directions:

1. Heat up a pan because of the coconut oil over medium-high heat, add plantain chips, sprinkle pepper flakes, fry them for 5 minutes on both sides, transfer to paper towels, drain grease, divide into bowls and serve as a snack.
2. Enjoy!

Nutrition Value: calories 180, fat 3, fiber 3, carbs 8, protein 12

557. Green Beans Snack

Preparation time: ten mins

Cooking time: 16 minutes

Servings: 8

Ingredients:

- 1/3 cup coconut oil, melted
- 5 pounds green beans
- 1 teaspoon garlic powder
- 1 teaspoon onion powder

Directions:

1. In a bowl, mix green beans with coconut oil, garlic and onion powder, toss to coat adequately, spread for the lined baking sheet, introduce in the oven and bake at 425 degrees F for 16 minutes.
2. 2.Serve cold being a snack.
3. Enjoy!

Nutrition Value: calories 120, fat 3, fiber 4, carbs

7, protein 7

558. Dates Snack

Preparation time: ten mins
Cooking time: 0 minutes
Servings: 2

Ingredients:

- 4 medjool dates, cut around the one hand
- 6 pistachios, raw and chopped
- 1 teaspoon coconut, shredded

Directions:

1. In a bowl, mix chopped pistachios with coconut, stir, stuff the dates using this, divide into bowls and serve.
2. Enjoy!

Nutrition Value: calories 100, fat 1, fiber 2, carbs 2, protein 6

559. Baby Spinach Snack

Preparation time: ten mins
Cooking time: 10 minutes
Servings: 3

Ingredients:

- 2 cups baby spinach, washed
- A pinch of black pepper
- ½ tablespoon extra virgin organic olive oil
- ½ teaspoon garlic powder

Directions:

1. Spread the newborn spinach around the lined baking sheet, add oil, black pepper and garlic powder, toss a lttle bit, introduce inside oven, bake at 350 degrees F for ten mins, divide into bowls and serve being a snack.
2. Enjoy!

Nutrition Value: calories 125, fat 4, fiber 1, carbs 4, protein 2

560. Potato Bites

Preparation time: ten mins
Cooking time: 20 mins
Servings: 3

Ingredients:

- 1 potato, sliced

- 2 bacon slices, already cooked and crumbled
- 1 small avocado, pitted and cubed
- Cooking spray

Directions:

1. Spread potato slices on the lined baking sheet, spray with extra virgin olive oil, introduce in the oven at 350 degrees F, bake for 20 mins, arrange using a platter, top each slice with avocado and crumbled bacon and serve as a snack.
2. Enjoy!

Nutrition Value: calories 180, fat 4, fiber 1, carbs 8, protein 6

561. Sesame Dip

Preparation time: ten mins
Cooking time: 0 minutes
Servings: 6

Ingredients:

- 1 cup sesame seed paste, pure
- Black pepper around the taste
- 1 cup veggie stock
- ½ cup freshly squeezed lemon juice
- ½ teaspoon cumin, ground
- 3 garlic cloves, chopped

Directions:

1. In the meat processor, mix the sesame paste with black pepper, stock, fresh freshly squeezed lemon juice, cumin and garlic, pulse well, divide into bowls and serve as a celebration dip.
2. Enjoy!

Nutrition Value: calories 120, fat 12, fiber 2, carbs 7, protein 4

562. Rosemary Squash Dip

Preparation time: 10 mins
Cooking time: 40 minutes
Servings: 4

Ingredients:

- 1 cup butternut squash, peeled and cubed
- 1 tablespoon water
- Cooking spray

- 2 tablespoons coconut milk
- 2 teaspoons rosemary, dried
- Black pepper for the taste

Directions:

1. Spread squash cubes on the lined baking sheet, spray some oil, introduce inside oven, bake at 365 degrees F for 40 minutes, transfer on your blender, add water, milk, rosemary and black pepper, pulse well, divide into small bowls and serve
2. Enjoy!

Nutrition Value: calories 182, fat 5, fiber 7, carbs 12, protein 5

563. Bean Spread

Preparation time: ten mins
Cooking time: 7 hours
Servings: 4

Ingredients:

- 1 cup white beans, dried
- 1 teaspoon using apple cider vinegar
- 1 cup veggie stock
- 1 tablespoon water

Directions:

1. In your slow cooker, mix beans with stock, stir, cover, cook on Low for 6 hours, drain, transfer for the meat processor, add vinegar and water, pulse well, divide into bowls and serve.
2. Enjoy!

Nutrition Value: calories 181, fat 6, fiber 5, carbs 9, protein 7

564. Vanilla Whole30 Ice Cream

Preparation time: 3 hours 10 minutes
Servings: 6

Ingredients:

- 4 eggs; yolks and whites separated
- 1/2 cup swerve
- 1¼ cup heavy whipping cream
- 1 tablespoon vanilla extract
- 1/4 teaspoon cream of tartar

Directions:

1. In a bowl, mix egg whites with cream of tartar and swerve and stir using your mixer.
2. In another bowl, whisk cream with vanilla extract and blend very well.
3. Combine the 2 mixtures and stir gently.
4. In another bowl, whisk egg yolks very well and then add the two egg whites mix.
5. Stir gently, pour this into a container and keep in the freezer for 3 hours before serving your ice cream.

Nutrition Values: Calories: 243; Fat : 22; Fiber : 0; Carbs : 2; Protein : 4

565. Whole30 Coconut Ice Cream

Preparation time: 10 minutes
Servings: 4
Ingredients:

- 14 ounces coconut cream; frozen
- 1 mango; sliced

Directions:

1. In your food processor, mix mango with the cream and pulse well.
2. Divide into bowls and serve right away.

Nutrition Values: Calories: 150; Fat : 12; Fiber : 2; Carbs : 6; Protein : 1

566. Ricotta Mousse

Preparation time: 2 hours 10 minutes
Servings: 10

Ingredients:

- 1/2 cup hot coffee

- 2 cups ricotta cheese
- 2½ teaspoons gelatin
- 1 teaspoon espresso powder
- 1 teaspoon vanilla stevia
- 1 teaspoon vanilla extract
- 1 cup whipping cream
- A pinch of salt

Directions:

1. In a bowl, mix coffee with gelatin; stir well and leave aside until coffee is cold.
2. In a bowl, mix espresso, stevia, salt, vanilla extract and ricotta and stir using a mixer.
3. Add coffee mix and stir everything well.
4. Add whipping cream and blend mixture again.
5. Divide into dessert bowls and serve after you've kept it in the fridge for 2 hours

Nutrition Values: Calories: 160; Fat : 13; Fiber : 0; Carbs : 2; Protein : 7

567. amazing Granola

Preparation time: 45 minutes
Servings: 4

Ingredients:

- 1 cup coconut; unsweetened and shredded
- 1 cup almonds and pecans; chopped.
- 2 tablespoons coconut oil
- 1 teaspoon nutmeg; ground
- 2 tablespoons stevia
- 1/2 cup pumpkin seeds
- 1/2 cup sunflower seeds
- 1 teaspoon apple pie spice mix

Directions:

1. In a bowl, mix almonds and pecans with pumpkin seeds, sunflower seeds, coconut, nutmeg and apple pie spice mix and stir well.
2. Heat up a pan with the coconut oil over medium heat; add stevia and stir until they combine
3. Pour this over nuts and coconut mix and stir well.

4. Spread this on a lined baking sheet, introduce in the oven at 300 degrees F and bake for 30 minutes
5. Leave your granola to cool down, cut and serve it.

Nutrition Values: Calories: 120; Fat : 2; Fiber : 2; Carbs : 4; Protein : 7

568. Chocolate Cookies

Preparation time: 50 minutes
Servings: 12

Ingredients:

- 1 teaspoon vanilla extract
- 1/2 cup unsweetened chocolate chips
- 1/4 cup swerve
- 1/2 cup ghee
- 1 egg
- 2 tablespoons coconut sugar
- 2 cups almond flour
- A pinch of salt

Directions:

1. Heat up a pan with the ghee over medium heat; stir and cook until it browns
2. Take this off heat and leave aside for 5 minutes
3. In a bowl, mix egg with vanilla extract, coconut sugar and swerve and stir.
4. Add melted ghee, flour, salt and half of the chocolate chips and stir everything.
5. Transfer this to a pan, spread the rest of the chocolate chips on top, introduce in the oven at 350 degrees F and bake for 30 minutes
6. Slice when it's cold and serve

Nutrition Values: Calories: 230; Fat : 12; Fiber : 2; Carbs : 4; Protein : 5

569. Chocolate Cups

Preparation time: 35 minutes
Servings: 20

Ingredients:

- 1/2 cup coconut butter
- 1/4 teaspoon vanilla extract
- 1/2 cup coconut oil
- 1 ounces chocolate; unsweetened
- 1/4 cup cocoa powder
- 1/2 cup coconut; shredded
- 1/4 cup swerve
- 3 tablespoons swerve
- 5 ounce cocoa butter

Directions:

1. In a pan, mix coconut butter with coconut oil; stir and heat up over medium heat.
2. Add coconut and 3 tablespoons swerve; stir well, take off heat; scoop into a lined muffins pan and keep in the fridge for 30 minutes
3. Meanwhile; in a bowl, mix cocoa butter with chocolate, vanilla extract and 1/4 cup swerve and stir well.
4. Place this over a bowl filled with boiling water and stir until everything is smooth.
5. Spoon this over coconut cupcakes, keep in the fridge for 15 minutes more and then serve

Nutrition Values: Calories: 240; Fat : 23; Fiber : 4; Carbs : 5; Protein : 2

570. Special Whole30 Pudding

Preparation time: 4 hours 13 minutes
Servings: 2

Ingredients:

- 1 cup coconut milk
- 4 teaspoons gelatin
- 1/4 teaspoon ginger; ground
- 1/4 teaspoon liquid stevia
- A pinch of nutmeg; ground
- A pinch of cardamom; ground

Directions:

1. In a bowl, mix 1/4 cup milk with gelatin and stir well.
2. Put the rest of the coconut milk in a pot and heat up over medium heat.
3. Add gelatin mix; stir, take off heat; leave aside to cool down and then keep in the fridge for 4 hours
4. Transfer this to a food processor, add stevia, cardamom, nutmeg and ginger and blend for a couple of minutes
5. Divide into dessert cups and serve cold.

Nutrition Values: Calories: 150; Fat : 1; Fiber : 0;

Carbs : 2; Protein : 6

571. Whole30 Scones

Preparation time: 20 minutes
Servings: 10

Ingredients:

- 1 cup blueberries
- 1/2 cup coconut flour
- 2 eggs
- 5 tablespoons stevia
- 1/2 cup ghee
- 1/2 cup almond flour
- 2 teaspoons vanilla extract
- 2 teaspoons baking powder
- 1/2 cup heavy cream
- A pinch of salt

Directions:

1. In a bowl, mix almond flour with coconut flour, salt, baking powder and blueberries and stir well.
2. In another bowl, mix heavy cream with ghee, vanilla extract, stevia and eggs and stir well.
3. Combine the 2 mixtures and stir until you obtain your dough.
4. Shape 10 triangles from this mix, place them on a lined baking sheet, introduce in the oven at 350 degrees F and bake for 10 minutes Serve them cold.

Nutrition Values: Calories: 130; Fat : 2; Fiber : 2; Carbs : 4; Protein : 3

572. Dessert Smoothie

Preparation time: 5 minutes
Servings: 2

Ingredients:

- 1/2 cup coconut milk
- 1½ cup avocado; pitted and peeled
- 1 mango thinly sliced for serving
- 2 tablespoons green tea powder
- 1 tablespoon coconut sugar
- 2 teaspoons lime zest

Directions:

1. In your smoothie maker, combine milk

with avocado, green tea powder and lime zest and pulse well.
2. Add sugar, blend well, divide into 2 glasses and serve with mango slices on top.

Nutrition Values: Calories: 87; Fat : 5; Fiber : 3; Carbs : 6; Protein : 8

573. Avocado Pudding

Preparation time: 10 minutes
Servings: 4

Ingredients:

- 2 avocados; pitted, peeled and chopped.
- 1 tablespoon lime juice
- 2 teaspoons vanilla extract
- 14 ounces canned coconut milk
- 80 drops stevia

Directions:

1. In your blender, mix avocado with coconut milk, vanilla extract, stevia and lime juice, blend well, spoon into dessert bowls and keep in the fridge until you serve it.

Nutrition Values: Calories: 150; Fat : 3; Fiber : 3; Carbs : 5; Protein : 6

574. Lime Cheesecake

Preparation time: 12 minutes
Servings: 10

Ingredients:

- 4 ounces almond meal
- 2 tablespoons ghee; melted
- 2 teaspoons granulated stevia
- 1/4 cup coconut; unsweetened and shredded
- For the filling:
- 1 pound cream cheese
- 2 cup hot water
- 2 sachets sugar free lime jelly
- Zest from 1 lime
- Juice from 1 lime

Directions:

1. Heat up a small pan over medium heat; add ghee and stir until it melts
2. In a bowl, mix coconut with almond meal, ghee and stevia and stir well.

3. Press this on the bottom of a round pan and keep in the fridge for now.
4. Meanwhile; put hot water in a bowl, add jelly sachets and stir until it dissolves
5. Put cream cheese in a bowl, add jelly and stir very well.
6. Add lime juice and zest and blend using your mixer.
7. Pour this over base, spread and keep the cheesecake in the fridge until you serve it.

Nutrition Values: Calories: 300; Fat : 23; Fiber : 2; Carbs : 5; Protein : 7

575. Easy Lemon Custard

Preparation time: 40 minutes
Servings: 6

Ingredients:

- 1⅓ pint almond milk
- 5 tablespoons swerve
- 4 eggs
- 2 tablespoons lemon juice
- 4 tablespoons lemon zest

Directions:

1. In a bowl, mix eggs with milk and swerve and stir very well.
2. Add lemon zest and lemon juice, whisk well, pour into ramekins and place them into a baking dish with some water on the bottom.
3. Bake in the oven at 360 degrees F for 30 minutes
4. Leave custard to cool down before serving it.

Nutrition Values: Calories: 120; Fat : 6; Fiber : 2; Carbs : 5; Protein : 7

576. Seafood Stew

Ingredients:

- Smallish Fillets of Gilthead (Skinned)-8
- Fresh clams- 500g. About 1lb.
- One small finely sliced onion (2 or 3 Good shallots will do)
- Thinly sliced Garlic-2 cloves
- The Juice from one large lemon.
- Dry white wine- 1 pint-2 cups

- Chopped coriander-1 bunch (the quantity is up to you, but we will like a lot).
- Diced plum tomatoes - 2
- Cornflour.
- Chillis crumbled or 2 Cayenne peppers

Directions:

1. In a Non-Stick Frypan, poach your fish fillets in the white wine using a pinch of salt.
2. Drain and keep warm.
3. Place the shallots, garlic, chillis, lemon juice, a little of the finely sliced rind, and some coriander (remain a little to sprinkle at the end).
4. Drain the liquid till its half.
5. Pour the tomatoes and return to boil.
6. Put the clams and stir until they are all opened.
7. In some cold water, slake a spoonful of Cornflour (corn starch) and add it little by little until you achieve the desired consistency. Make it funny, but not watery.
8. Put the fish fillets in four bowls, dish over the saucy clams, and sprinkle over the remaining coriander
9. Serve straight away.

577. Stargazy Fish Pie Recipe

Ingredients:

- Skinned and pin-boned Salmon Fillet-1lb. 450g.
- Skinned Monkfish Fillet -1lb. 450g.
- Good quality Raw-Shell on Prawns Shrimps-Gambas-1lb. 450g.
- Extra Shells on Prawns Shrimp Gambas for the Star Gazing Garnish-6
- Large Tomatoes sliced in 3 4" 2cm. Cubes - 2
- Wilted Spinach leaves (chopped)-1 2lb. 220g.
- Large Onion Sliced-1
- Finely chopped Garlic-6 Cloves
- Thinly sliced Potato -1 Kilo 2.2lb.
- Grounded Chillis or Dried Cayenne Peppers - 4
- Chorizo chopped into 1 2" 1cm. Cubes - 4ozs 100g.

- Small Red pepper – 1 (1" 2.5cm)
- Small Green Pepper – 1 (1" 2.5cm)
- Lemon – 1 (only the Juice and Zest is needed)
- Extra Virgin Olive Oil - 1 2 liter.
- Sugar-1 Teaspoon
- Parmesan (freshly grated) -2ozs. 50g.
- Fresh Basil chopped (A good handful)
- Salt
- Black pepper to taste
- Deep earthenware Casserole dish sized 1 13" 33cm X 2-1 2" 6cm.

Directions:

1. Start by arranging your tomatoes and wilted spinach at the bottom of the earthenware casserole.
2. Next, arrange your fish - shelling the shrimps.
3. Put it away
4. Pour a good amount of Extra Virgin Olive Oil and fry the sliced onion with some sugar on medium heat. (The sugar helps the onion to caramelize).
5. Add your peppers
6. Sprinkle some salt and the crushed chillis.
7. Reduce heat
8. Put the garlic.
9. Ensure that everything is cooked
10. Add to your casserole.
11. Pour in your lemon juice and zest and the basil.
12. For the potato topping. Start by placing your Prawns at strategic places at the edge of the casserole, like they are gazing up to the stars.
13. Arrange those potatoes all around with a good drizzle of olive oil between each layer and a sprinkling of salt.
14. Grind large amounts of Black Pepper at the top.
15. Cover these with Aluminum foil
16. Allow to Cook in a hot oven - 200°c. 400°f. For an hour.
17. Remove the foil and sprinkle your grated Parmesan on top with some more extra virgin olive oil.
18. Take it back to the oven and bake for a further 20 minutes till the top turns crisp

and golden.

578. Whole30 Sole Meuniere

Ingredients:

- Dover Sole fillets or Lemon Sole- 4 good sized fillets.
- Plain Flour- 2ozs. 50g.
- Butter 2ozs. 50g.
- Extra virgin olive oil -2 Tablespoons
- The juice of a Large lemon
- Finely chopped garlic-2cloves
- A Handful of chopped flat leaf parsley.
- Salt to taste
- Freshly ground black pepper.

Directions:

1. Begin by seasoning the flour with lots of salt and black pepper. Coat the Sole fillets well and shake off any excess flour.
2. Heat the oil and butter together in a Large Non-Stick Fry Pan (the oil will stop the butter from burning) and add the fish fillets.
3. Cook gently on both sides for about ten minutes (depending on the thickness of the fillets), until cooked and golden.
4. Take the fish out of the pan
5. Keep it warm.
6. Add the garlic to the pan
7. Cook gently for about two minutes.
8. Pour the parsley then stir.
9. Lastly, whisk the lemon juice.
10. Check for seasoning
11. In four plates, arrange the fish fillets four and spoon over the sauce.
12. Conclude with a last sprinkling of parsley.

579. Swordfish Recipe

Ingredients:

- Four Swordfish Steaks -(6 - 8ozs. 150 200g. each)
- Extra virgin olive oil- 2 tablespoons
- Salt
- Freshly ground black pepper
- Either Salsa Verde or Tomato Salsa - you decide!

Directions:

1. Remove the skin and every dark bit from the steaks (these dark, bloody bits never look nice and don't taste very nice too!).
2. Season with salt and black pepper.
3. Turn them in the oil and ensure they are well covered.
4. Allow marinating for about an hour.
5. Make your sauce and keep it warm (for the salsa Verde) -If decided on the Tomato Salsa, warm it thoroughly before serving.
6. Dry fry or griddle the Swordfish steaks on every side till it's cooked through but leave some moist in the middle. Take about 2-3 minutes on every side
7. Serve on warm dinner plates and dish over the sauce.

580. Fishcake Recipe

Ingredients:

- Extra virgin Olive oil
- Peeled potato-250g 9oz
- Roasted red pepper (small diced)-1 med
- Finely chopped onion-1 medium
- Finely chopped cloves of garlic- 2 plumps
- Good solid white fish -350g. 12ozs.
- Lemon - 1 (juice and zest only)
- grounded Dried Chilies - 2
- Pimenton (smoked Spanish paprika)-1 teaspoon
- Chopped parsley and coriander- 1 handful each
- Dry white wine-1glass
- Dried dill-1 teaspoon
- Egg (whisked)- 1
- Fresh bread crumbs (dried out)-50g. 2ozs.

Directions:

1. Begin by cutting the potato into 1" cubes and Boil them in salted water until it gets tender.
2. Drain in a colander until it's quite dried and Mash with a fork.
3. Pour the roasted red pepper to the potato and Mash well in a bowl.
4. Fry the onion in the extra virgin olive oil until it's soft and adds the garlic at the end.
5. Put the fish, the wine, chilies, paprika, the lemon juice, and the zest and herbs. Leave

it to cook over low heat till the fish flakes and all the liquid has boiled away.
6. Allow it cool and Mix in with your potatoes and red peppers.
7. Form into patties - around 3" x 3 4". If you chose to make Tapas, shape the mixture into 1" balls.
8. Cover the patties with the egg and roll them in the crumbs.
9. In a large Non-stick fry pan, Place about 1 4" of olive oil and fry the fish cakes until it turns golden on every side.
10. Squeeze over the remaining lemon juice and serve with our tasty tomato salsa.

581. Dorado – Baked Fish

Ingredients:

- Olive oil
- Finely chopped medium onion – 1
- Finely chopped garlic cloves – 2
- Dorados in whole – 2 (it should be scored 3 to 4 times on each of its sides using a knife that is sharp)
- Finely sliced large potatoes – 2
- Diced large red pepper – 1 (1 inch 2.5cm)
- Roughly chopped large tomatoes – 2
- Fine slices of lemon – 1
- Dried chilies – 2 (bashed inside a mortar with a pestle)
- Pimento – 1 tsp (Spanish paprika smoked)
- Dry white wine – ½ bottle
- Sliced large mushrooms – 6
- Good quality olives – 12
- Fresh herbs in a handful – parsley and mint-coriander is used
- Salt
- Fresh black pepper

Directions:

1. Have the potatoes, garlic, onions, red pepper and the mushrooms fried inside a medium fry pan that is non-sticky. Use plenty of the olive oil, till you see it has gotten soft and brown
2. Have them arranged at a deep baking pan bottom
3. Have the fish set on top of it
4. After this, have your lemon slices placed

on the fish top

5. Have the chilies and the paprika mixed inside the wine and have it poured in
6. Add in your olives and herbs\
7. Have it seasoned with the black pepper and salt
8. Make use of the kitchen foil to seal and cover the baking tray
9. Have it baked in a medium-hot oven of 4000F or 2000C for about 45 minutes
10. Remove the cover and serve with crusty bread.

582. The Whole30 Tilapia

Ingredients:

- Tilapia Fillets - 4 (150g 6ozs per one)
- Good sized shrimp prawns – 12 (still raw in their shells)
- Ingredient for the sauce
- Finely chopped small onion – 1
- Chopped and bashed garlic clove – 1
- Diced red bell pepper – ½
- Small diced medium zucchini courgette – 1
- Flaked red chili – 1
- A glass of white wine – 125ml
- Extra virgin olive oil – 1tbs
- Dried Herbes de Provence – ½ Tsp
- Ground black pepper and salt

Directions:

1. Firstly have the prawns shelled and then set aside along with the fish fillets – have it seasoned lightly with black pepper and salt
2. Inside a non-stick fry pan that is big have the prawn heads sauté and have it shelled over a medium heat inside a little olive oil, and make use you have them crashed to squeeze out all the juices
3. Add in a little salt and the wine
4. Let the liquid go down a bit
5. Have the stock put inside a sieve for the prawn bits to be removed and keep it at a side
6. Now you can have the red pepper and onions fried inside the olive oil till you can see it nicely browned
7. Add in the zucchini courgette and cook for like 5 minutes

8. Have the heat lowered and add in the chili and garlic and cook further for like two minutes
9. Add in the herbs and the stock of the sieved prawn shell and get it reduced to a consistency that is sticky
10. Have the prawns and fillets cooked on a grill pan or hot griddle to give them several colors
11. After that, have the sticky sauce spooned into warm dinner plates, put the fish fillets on the top and for the crowning glory the prawns.

583. Scampi Provencale - Shrimp Prawn Recipe

Ingredients:

- Olive oil (for frying)
- Finely chopped, peeled medium onion- 1
- Crushed and peeled garlic cloves – 3
- Olive oil – 2 tbsp
- Tomato purée – 1tsp
- White wine – 50ml (a splash)
- Roughly chopped tomatoes – 10 or can of chopped tomatoes – 400g
- Fresh black pepper and salt
- Chopped parsley – a handful
- Cornstarch cornflour – ½ (if necessary slacked with water a little)

Directions:

1. Prepare the sauce firstly by having the garlic and onion fried inside a frying pan that is non-sticky with olive oil for some minutes without giving it color
2. Have the tomato purée stirred in, zest, lemon juice, and white wine. Allow it simmer for one minute
3. Add your tomatoes, have it seasoned and let it simmer for 5 to 6 minutes till the tomatoes are beginning to open up
4. Have the prawns shrimps added and allow it to simmer till it has turned to pink. This takes about 3 to 4 minutes. Be careful about having it overcooked
5. If many juices come out from the scampi shrimp while cooking, it might be necessary to have the sauce thickened by using the cornflour mixture. Just have it

stirred in and let it simmer

6. Have the chopped parsley stirred in and check your seasoning
7. Have it stirred immediately with vegetables or rice.

584. Lubina a la sal – Sea Bass

Ingredients:

- Cleaned whole sea bass – 2 (¼ lb or 550g)
- Coarse sea salt – 4 (½ lb or 2k)
- Crushed garlic clove – 1
- Extra virgin olive oil – 4tbls.
- Fresh lemon juice – 2tbls.
- Salt – 1 leveled tsp.
- Honey – 2tsps.
- Dried dill – 1 heaped tsp.
- Aromatic chili oil – 1 Tsp.

Directions:

1. Firstly, have a big earthenware dish laid (it should be big enough to have the fish in without it touching the sides) along with a ½ inch of salt
2. Take the dish and lay it on the salt
3. Put the remaining salt on top of it
4. Have it patted down and have little water sprinkled on top of it to keep it moist
5. Have the earthenware placed inside an oven that is preheated to 400oF or 200oC for about 30 minutes
6. Have your sauce prepared- have all the Ingredients: put inside a glass bowl except the oil
7. Have the oil whisked in a tablespoon one at a time using a hand whisk
8. Have the fish eaten out of the oven, turn it down to low and put in the dinner plates to make it warm
9. The salt would have turned into a crust that is hard, so have it broken with a mallet gently and remove it from the fish
10. The skin would come off easily, and you can be able to have the fillets removed and have them arranged on the dinner plates
11. You can have the sauce sprinkled and begin to eat
12. If it's the traditional method you prefer- make use of a pinch of salt and have the lemon juice squeezed.

585. Grilled Shrimp

Ingredients:

- Uncooked shell large prawns – 800g
- Crushed garlic cloves – 2
- Crumbled dried chili – 2 to 3
- Lime zest and juice
- Chopped fresh coriander – a handful
- Extra virgin olive oil – 4 tablespoons
- Fresh black pepper and salt

Directions:

1. Have the prawns shelled and leave 2- it will be used for garnishing the dish
2. Have the marinade made by having all the other Ingredients: combined in a big bowl evenly? Have little of the chopped coriander kept for garnishing
3. Have the shelled prawns added and have them mixed into the marinade well
4. Cover it and leave it for about an hour
5. Have the prawns threaded onto the skewers neatly-like 5 on the stick each
6. Have the marinade remains poured inside a baking tin that has sides and has it placed inside a warm oven to slightly heat it
7. Have the griddle on high heat and firstly have the 2 shell prawns grilled for like 2 to 3 minutes on each of its sides. And put it at a side. Then have the skewered prawns cooked on one side for about 2 minutes on both sides only
8. Have the heat taken off and have the skewered prawns placed into the marinade tin. Have them turned over for a few times to have the juices picked up.
9. Have it served immediately on a shredded lettuce bed, and have the warm marinade poured on it.
10. Have it garnished with the shell prawn, coriander, lime wedges, and tomato.

586. Marinated Chicken

Ingredients:

- Scored and skinned chicken legs with separated wings – 2
- Greek yogurt – 1 x 4oz or 125g
- Finely chopped garlic cloves – 2
- Lemon juice – 1

- Finely chopped medium red pepper – ½
- Paprika – 2 teaspoons
- Comino (cumin) – 2 teaspoons
- Spanish Colorante – ½ teaspoons or yellow food coloring or Turmeric – 2 drops
- Fresh black pepper and salt

Directions:

1. This is quite easy! Inside a mixing bowl have the garlic, yogurt, red pepper spices. Lemon juice and the food coloring combined.
2. Have it seasoned with black pepper and salt
3. Add in your chicken wings and legs and have them mixed inside the marinade well
4. Have it covered and leave it for 2 hours or if possible longer
5. Now have the chicken arranged on a rack that is over a roasting tray with water
6. Have it roasted at 180oC or 350oF. after 20 minutes have the chicken turned over and then roast again for 20 minutes
7. While it's cooking, you can have the water topped up as its evaporating
8. To prepare the sauce: have the remaining marinade poured into a small saucepan and let it boil on a medium heat
9. If you want it to be a little creamier add an extra spoon of the Greek yogurt before you have it served with chicken.

587. Poached Salmon

Ingredients:

- Boned and skinned salmon fillets – 2 (about 225g each)
- A glass of white wine – 125ml
- Fresh black pepper and salt
- Water – 50ml
- Roughly chopped fresh dill – 1 teaspoon
- Dijon mustard – 1 teaspoon leveled
- Honey – 1 teaspoon leveled
- Cornstarch cornflour – 1 teaspoon flat with a little water to thicken it

Directions:

1. This is quite easy and quick! Take out a frying pan that is non-sticky and have the water and wine poured in, add the pepper,

salt, and dill. Have the salmon fillets placed inside the pan.
2. Let it boil over medium heat and allow it to simmer for 3 minutes and have the fillets turned over and simmer again for 3 minutes
3. Have the fillets removed from the pan and keep it warm
4. To prepare the sauce: have the pan placed
5. To prepare the sauce: have the pan placed back on the medium-heat, have the crème Fraiche or cream whisked, the honey and mustard and let it boil
6. Have the heat turned down and add in little slacked cornflour mixture for the sauce to get thickened and smooth pouring consistency
7. Have the fish arranged on plates and have the sauce poured on it
8. Serve it immediately with vegetables and potatoes
9. You can try it also with our crunchy baked potato or our pesto mash dish

588. Fish Fillet

Ingredients:

- Large thick fillets without bones – 4 (boning is very easy by these pliers---you can make use of cod, Rosada, etc. any white fish, a firm would be ok)
- Extra virgin oil
- Fresh black pepper and salt
- Finely chopped garlic cloves – 2
- Chopped parsley or dill or dried mixed herbs – a teaspoon
- Wholemeal breadcrumbs – 4oz 110g
- Small lemon juice

Directions:

1. Firstly, have the baking tray oiled and it should be big enough to have all the fish fillets cooked
2. Have the fillets arranged on the tray putting small gaps in between each of them
3. Have each of them sprinkled with a little salt and pepper
4. Have it followed with sprinkling the garlic and then the dried or chopped herbs
5. Finish it off with evenly spreading of the

breadcrumbs and drizzle olive oil on it

6. Have the tray put on the top shelf and have the oven pre-heated to 425oF or 220oC then let it cook for 10 to 15 minutes depending on the thickness of the fillets

7. When the flakes easily separate with a knife, then the fish is cooked

8. Have it taken out and arrange it on the plates, squeezing lemon juice a little on each of the fillets

9. Have it served immediately with vegetable of your choice, and you can as well try it out the crispy fried potatoes or the crunchy baked potatoes

589. Whole Fish

Ingredients:

- Large snapper or a fish that is similar – 1 (about 3 ½ to 4lb or 1 ½ to 2 kilos) descale and clean the fishmonger
- Fresh black pepper and salt
- Finely sliced garlic cloves – 4
- Finely grated fresh ginger – 2 inch
- Zest and lemon juices finely grated- 2
- Fresh coriander roughly chopped – a handful
- Pine nuts – a handful
- Small extra virgin oil

Directions:

1. Have the fish washed inside and out well underneath the tap and dry it off with a kitchen paper

2. Have a large oven tray which can hold it with cooking oil and use olive oil to have it greased well, or make use of a fish baker that goes from the oven to the table

3. Have the fish laid on the tray and have it opened up and have it seasoned with salt and black pepper

4. Have the inside stuffed with ginger, chili, garlic, lime juice and zest, ½ of the pine nuts and ¾ of coriander evenly

5. Have the fish closed up and have the remaining coriander, and the pine nuts sprinkled on top of it

6. Finish it up with the drizzling of olive oil all over the fish and do some extra seasoning

7. Haven the fish put into the oven uncovered at 190ēc 375ēc for about 45 minutes. Have the oven turned off and let the fish be there for like 15 minutes

8. When serving, have the fish removed from the tray, have it slide off the foil into a serving platter pouring the cooking juice all over, or have it brought out in its baker and have the cooking juices spooned over before you serve. Have it garnished with fresh coriander leaves and lime wedges

590. Sole Recipe

Ingredients:

- Roughly chopped ripe tomatoes – 1lb ½ kilo or can of whole plum tomatoes – 16oz
- Olive oil – 1 teaspoon
- Finely chopped medium onion – 1
- Bashed garlic cloves – 2
- Zest and juice of a lemon – ½
- Strong vegetable stock – 1 pint 450ml
- Tomato purée – 1 tablespoon
- Bay leaf – 1
- Black pepper and salt
- Roughly chopped fresh basil – 1 bunch or dried – 1 teaspoon heaped
- Capers – 1 tablespoon
- Halved and pitted black olives – about 10
- Ingredient for the sole:
- Sole fillet – 6oz 175g per person
- Fresh black pepper and salt
- Extra virgin oil to grease the foil and grill the fish

Directions:

1. Have the fish fillets washed underneath a tap and have it dried using a kitchen paper

2. Put it at a side till you have prepared the sauce

3. Inside the olive oil have the onion fried on medium heat till it has softened then turn the heat down and add your garlic

4. Cook it for like 3 to 4 minutes while stirring it

5. Add in the fresh tomatoes or have the can opened and pour the juice, have the tomatoes inside the can chop roughly using a sharp knife and have it poured inside the

pan

6. Add all the other Ingredients: except for the capers, olives, and basil

7. Let it simmer for like 20 minutes while occasionally stirring it

8. Have the bay leaf removed and discard it. Add in your basil

9. Have the tomato sauce blended using a stick blender or any other food processor type until it isn't entirely smooth. Its best for the sauce to have some texture retained

10. Add in your capers and olives and set it aside

11. Have a foil that is well greased placed on the grill pan for it to have the fish fillets accommodated

12. Have the fillets arranged evenly inside the foil, have it seasoned with black pepper and salt

13. Have little bit drizzled on it

14. Have it placed underneath a preheated hot grill for 5 minutes – depending on the fish fillet thickness

15. Per inch of the thickness is 10 minutes cooking time for the rule of thumb

16. Have a cocktail stick inserted at the center of the fillet that is very thick. If there isn't a resistance, then the fish is cooked- if not, have it cooked for a while and retest

17. Have the sauce reheated gently and bring it under a boil

18. Have the fillets arranged evenly between the warm dinner plates

19. Top it up with the sauce and have it served immediately

591. Seafood and Chicken Paella Recipe

Ingredients:

- Traditional Paella pan (Paellera) - 13 inches
- Paella rice - 2 cups
- Monkfish fillet (minute pieces)- 12 ozs
- Prawns (medium-sized)- 11lb.
- Plump chicken breast (boned and skinned)- 1
- Fish and shellfish stock- 1 Quart
- Fresh mussels - 12
- Chopped Chorizo- 4 ozs

- Peas- 1 2 a cup
- Parsley- 1bunch
- Finely chopped garlic - 3 cloves
- Small squid calamari- 2
- Roughly chopped onions-1
- Red pepper- 1 piece chopped into 1" dices
- Chopped mushrooms- 1 4 lbs.
- Lemons- chopped in quarters lengthwise
- Black pepper
- Salt
- Extra virgin olive oil
- 12 threads of saffron

Directions:

1. Slice squid into bite-sized pieces.

2. Slice chicken into 1" dices.

3. In a little portion of water, cook mussels until they open up and discard any that do not open.

4. Remove the half shell and put away the mussels and add the liquid to your stock.

5. Shell some of the prawns and leave 8 prawns with their shells.

6. Pour 2-3 tablespoons of olive oil into your Paellera.

7. Fry red pepper, onions, mushrooms, with the calamari and chicken pieces on high heat. Stir frequently for up to five minutes to avoid burning; you want them to color.

8. Lower the heat and add the chorizo and garlic then stir for 2 minutes.

9. Add the rice and stir for some minutes till it becomes opaque.

10. If it looks too dry add more oil.

11. Take away the paellera from the heat.

12. Boil the stock with the saffron for about 10 minutes.

13. Put back the Paellera on high heat and add half the stock giving it a final stir.

14. Layout the fish and prawns in the liquid and put the shell-on prawns on top.

15. Let the liquid lessen- do not stir again and put the remaining stock.

16. Keep the paellera on heat until there's almost no liquid left, then remove from heat.

17. Line up mussels around the perimeter of the paellera.

18. Cover the paellera with a clean cloth and

leave for about 10 minutes to allow the rice to absorb all the liquid.

19. Arrange the already cut lemons around the perimeter.

20. Chop some parsley and liberally sprinkle it over the Paella.

592. Mackerel Recipe

Ingredients:

- Filleted fresh Mackerel - 2 (medium sized)
- Clams - 1 2lb. 250g bag
- Spring onions- 4 (sliced)
- Dried dill
- Wholemeal breadcrumbs- 2 heaped tbsp
- Garlic- 2 cloves
- Dry white wine - 1 2 a bottle
- Flake chills
- Cornflour- 1heaped tbsp (cornstarch)
- Salt
- Pepper
- Lemon juice
- Olive oil

Directions:

1. Get an oven tray large enough for the four fillets
2. Pour a little oil and add half the breadcrumbs (already seasoned with freshly ground black pepper and salt)
3. Put the fish fillets on top of the bread crumbs; skin side up and cover it up with the other half of the breadcrumbs
4. Heat oven up to about 400°F
5. At the same time, get a pan large enough for the clams and reduce the wine by at least half.
6. Add the clams, spring onions and garlic and stir until the clams open.
7. Then add half the lemon juice.
8. Put in the dill and thicken the liquid with cornstarch.
9. Cook the fish fillets for about 10 minutes.
10. Into two bowls, put in the clams and arrange the mackerel fillets on top.
11. Add the remaining lemon juice and serve the meal.

593. Seafood Salad Recipe

(Salpicon De Mariscos)

Ingredients:

- Crab sticks- (1 2" cube) 4ozs. 100g
- Shrimp prawns- (1 2" pieces) 4ozs. 100g
- Tomatoes- 2 pieces (roughly chopped)
- Salaf leaves
- Roasted Red Bell Pepper- (1 2" squares) 2ozs. 50g
- Cucumber- small, peeled, roughly chopped
- A handful of chopped parsley
- Dressing:
- One lemon (juice)
- Vegetable oil(twice as much)
- Dijon mustard (1tsp)
- Liquid honey (2tsps)
- Salt (1 level tsp)
- Crushed chili (optional)
- Dried dill (1 level tsp)

Directions:

1. Mix the fish and the other salad Ingredients: in a glass bowl (save some parsley for sprinkling)
2. Take enough dressing to coat the salad and toss.
3. Set salad leaves in your plates and serve your seafood salad
4. Sprinkle the remaining parsley and enjoy your Salpicon de Mariscos.

594. Grilled Monkfish Recipe

Ingredients:

- Monkfish fillets (9ozs. 250g)- slice into 1" 2.5 cms. cubes
- Shrimp large prawns- 8 pieces; raw, skinned and deveined
- Mushrooms- 8 pieces cut into 1" cubes
- Green bell pepper(medium sized)- slice into 1" 2.5cms. slices
- Red bell pepper(medium sized)- slice 1" 2.5cms. slices
- Salt
- Wooden skewers- 4-10" 25cms
- Ingredients: for the Marinade:
- Garlic- 2 cloves (finely chopped)

- Fresh coriander - a handful; chopped
- Small crushed dried chilis
- Large lime(juice)
- Extra virgin olive oil (2 tbsps)

Directions:

1. Get a shallow dish large enough to hold the kebab and mix the Ingredients: for the marinade together (save half the coriander for later).
2. Starting with a mushroom string the other Ingredients: onto the skewers; a piece of fish, a square of pepper, prawn and finish with another mushroom. (There should be about 3 pieces of fish and two prawns on each skewer)
3. Set up the kebabs in the marinade and whirl around until it is fully coated.
4. Allow to marinate for about an hour and turn once or twice.
5. Set your grill in motion
6. Add the remaining marinade and the remaining coriander.
7. Enjoy your meal immediately with any vegetables of your choice.

595. Fish Pie Recipe

Ingredients:

- Firm white fish- 8ozs. 200g
- Mashed potatoes- 1lb. 450g
- Large shrimps prawns- 8ozs. 200g (raw, shelled and deveined)
- Garlic- 2 cloves (chopped)
- Zucchini Courgette (medium sized)- slice in 1 2" cubes.
- Fish stock- 250ml
- Wholemeal breadcrumbs-25g 1oz.
- Dry white wine- 125ml
- Cornflour cornstarch- 1tsp. (Slaked in water)
- Roasted red bell pepper- 50g 2ozs. (Chopped)
- Finely grated Parmesan cheese- 50g 2ozs.
- Single cream-125ml
- Dried dill- 1 heaped tsp
- Salt
- Black pepper(freshly grounded)

- Olive oil to fry

Directions:

1. Mash potatoes and keep it warm in the oven on low heat.
2. At the same time, mix all liquid and add the garlic
3. Cook liquid gently for 10 minutes
4. Also, quickly fry the courgette zucchini in olive oil(little) and allow to turn brown.
5. Add prawns, fish, dill and red pepper to the liquid and bring to boil.
6. Keep cooking until prawns fish turn pink, and fish becomes firm.
7. Please take out the fish and prawn and allow them to stay warm.
8. Set the fish, prawns and courgettes zucchini on top of the mashed potatoes.
9. Add cornflour cornstarch to thicken the sauce and put it on the top.
10. Sprinkle cheese and bread crumbs on the fish pie and put in a hot grill or broiler to give it a perfect taste.

596. Cod Recipe

Ingredients:

- Cod fillets- 2; weighing about 8oz 220g; skinned and boned
- Baby clams- 8ozs. 220g (that have sat in a bowl of cold water and expelled sand)
- Garlic- 2 cloves
- Cornflour cornstarch
- Coriander- 2 tbsp
- Red pepper- finely sliced
- Dry white wine- 1 glass
- Fish stock - 1 glass
- Dried chili (finely sliced)
- Lemon juice
- Salt
- Black pepper

Directions:

1. In a medium sized fry pan, add wine and stock and allow to boil.
2. Put in chili and garlic and leave to simmer for 2-3minutes.
3. Put in the clams and allow to simmer until they are opened; take out clams with a

designated spoon so that the cooking liquor seeps back into the pan.

4. Remove the shells from the clams and cover it to keep it warm.

5. Add red pepper to the pan and leave to simmer for 5 minutes.

6. Add the cod fillets into the pan and allow to boil. Reduce heat and leave to simmer for 2 minutes, turn over and allow to simmer for another 2 minutes.

7. Remove the cods and prawns from the pan and keep warm.

8. Put the lemon juice and coriander, check if seasoning is adequate.

9. Reheat the liquor and allow to boil then thicken with cornflour cornstarch till required consistency is achieved.

10. Add the cods and clams back into the pan and reheat immediately.

11. In two bowls, put the cod in the center and put the clams around it; then your sauce.

12. Serve immediately.

13. Serving options include brown rice, potatoes or brown bread.

597. Baked Salmon in Pastry Crust (Salmon en Croute) Recipe

Ingredients:

- Salmon fillets; boned, skinned, weighing about 60 ozs 150gmvj9a
- Extra virgin olive oil
- Lemon juice
- Lemon slice
- Nutmeg - a pinch
- Melted butter
- Coriander- freshly chopped
- Fresh spinach leaves - 150g
- Filo pastry- 2 sheets 480x255mm
- Dried dill- 1 Tsp
- Salt
- Black pepper (freshly ground)
- Sauce Ingredients:
- Honey- 1 2 Tsp
- White win3- 3tbsp
- Dijon mustard - 1 2 Tsp
- Dried or fresh dill- 1 2tsp

Directions:

1. Put a little olive oil in a frying pan and add the spinach, chili, lemon juice, dill, nutmeg, coriander, and seasoning; cook all together until the spinach shrivels.

2. Drain the mixture in a sieve and compress with a wooden spoon over a mixing bowl until all of the excess liquid is drained, and it is as dry as possible. Set the liquid and spinach aside.

3. Lay a sheet of filo pastry lengthwise on a clean work surface and smear the melted butter over it with a brush.

4. Fold filo pastry in half from right to left and smear evenly with more melted butter.

5. Place half of the already cooled spinach in the center of the pastry and top it with a salmon fillet and half the slice of lemon.

6. Fold pastry over the salmon and squeeze ends together until it is sealed package.

7. Place on an oiled baking sheet

8. With the remaining Ingredients:, make another package.

9. Smear packages evenly with melted butter and put it in a preheated oven 400°F on quite a high shelf

10. As the packages are baking, make the sauce

11. Pour the spinach liquid into a small sized pan and allow to boil, add the dried wine and allow to reduce to half.

12. Put in the extra dill and then add the mustard and honey. Mix well and take away from heat.

13. Let the salmon en croute stay in the oven for 15 minutes (an extra 5 minutes if you prefer it very well done)

14. Immediately serve with sauce on the side.

15. Serving options include baked potatoes and some rocket salad.

598. Anchovy Recipe

Ingredients:

- Fresh anchovies boquerones- 1-1 2 lb. 600g
- Olive oil
- Kitchen paper
- Plain White flour (already seasoned with salt and black pepper)
- Lemon wedges (to be squeezed over

cooked fish)

Directions:

1. Wash anchovies boquerones in cold running water and drain well.
2. To fillet: With a sharp knife, cut around the head of the fish just below the gill.
3. Then with the fish in one hand use the other hand to ease the head away from the body and ensure that the backbone comes away as well. Continue pulling until you remove the tail; the guts will come out as well. (You'll get better with practice)
4. Do this again and lay the fillets flat on a large tray.
5. After doing this, wash well with cold water, drain and dry with kitchen paper.
6. Now, coat each anchovy boquerone evenly with the already seasoned plain white flour.
7. Place them on a large floured tray without touching each other.
8. Using a deep fat fryer or a deep pan with enough olive oil; oil should be approximately 360°F.
9. Drop each fish singly into the hot oil in batches. Fry each batch for 1- 1-1 2 minutes until it turns golden brown.
10. Remove from oil and place on a kitchen paper to drain; keep warm in a low heat oven.
11. Keep doing this until all fish is cooked
12. Place in your serving plates.
13. Serving options include lemon wedges and crisp salad. You may also serve with sauce tartare and garlic mayonnaise.

599. Sardine Recipe

Ingredients:

- Fresh sardines- 1-1 2lb. 600g
- Extra virgin olive oil
- Fresh white breadcrumbs- 2ozs. 50g
- Garlic- 2 cloves (finely chopped)
- Whole lemon (cut in half)
- Salt
- Black pepper

Directions:

1. Descale sardines in a sink of cold running water; also done by working the back of a

knife from the tail to the head; do this underwater to prevent scales from flying around.
2. Gut the fish and wash the cavities
3. To fillet the fish; using a sharp knife cut into the backbone just behind the head and slide knife towards the tail. Turn the fish over and repeat the same process.
4. Oil an oven tray with the extra virgin olive oil and place half of the breadcrumbs across the bottom.
5. Sprinkle some salt and pepper and half the garlic on top of the fillet.
6. Place the sardine fillets with the skin side up. Then cover with the remaining garlic and sprinkle more salt and pepper.
7. Spread the remaining breadcrumbs on top and spritz more olive oil on it.
8. Bake in a preheated oven at 400°F for 8-10minutes.
9. Serve; with half a lemon in each plate and a crisp salad.

600. Crab Cake Recipe

Ingredients:

- Spice mix:
- Dried chili-1
- Comino seeds- 1 tsp
- Black peppercorns- 1 2tsp
- Fennel seeds- 1tsp
- Crab Cake:
- White crab meat(fresh or frozen)-8ozs. 250g
- Cooked potatoes (mashed)-8ozs. 250g
- Juice and grated zest of 1 2lime
- Medium sized onion (finely chopped)
- Chopped coriander- a handful
- Garlic- 1 clove(finely chopped)
- Salt
- Coating:
- Plain flour- 4 tbsps mixed with salt
- Olive oil
- Egg- 1 (beaten)
- Fresh white breadcrumbs- 4ozs 125g

Directions:

1. Using an electric coffee grinder or a pestle

and mortar, blend all the spices until it becomes a fine powder.

2. Put all the Ingredients: in a mixing bowl and mix well until it becomes uniform.

3. Make the mixture into cakes of your choice.

4. Spread the flour in a plate, the beaten egg in a bowl and the breadcrumbs in another bowl.

5. Coat each cake with flour and then dip into the egg and coat evenly then coat with breadcrumbs.

6. Pour some olive oil in a nonstick fry pan and heat up, then gently cook the crab cakes on one side until it turns golden brown and turns over until the other side also turns golden brown.

7. Serve immediately.

8. Serving options: garnish with salad leaves, tomato salad on the side; you can also sprinkle some chopped coriander.

601. Salmon Escabeche

Ingredients:

- Salmon fillets- 2lbs. 900g
- Dry white wine- 10fl.ozs 1 2 a pint
- White wine vinegar- 10fl.ozs 1 2 a pint
- Soft brown sugar- 3tsps
- Garlic- 3 cloves(sliced)
- Carrot-1 (French cut- like match sticks)
- Olive oil-4ybsps
- Salt-2 Tsp
- Red bell pepper (small-sized)- 1 (French cut)
- Black peppercorns- 12
- Star anise- 2
- Onion(medium sized)- 1 (sliced)
- Coriander seeds-12
- Salt
- Pepper

Directions:

1. Season salmon fillets with salt and freshly ground black pepper, brown in olive oil and set aside.

2. Then add the remaining Ingredients: except for the wine, vinegar, and salt to frypan and fry until golden.

3. Add the wine, vinegar, sugar, and salt then boil till it is reduced by half.

4. Set the salmon fillets in a shallow dish and pour the marinade over and ensure that the fillets are completely covered.

5. Cover with a plastic wrap and leave to cool.

6. Keep in the refrigerator overnight.

7. Enjoy your meal.

602. Seafood Risotto

Ingredients:

- Raw mussels-8 (debearded and raw)
- Small clams- 4ozs. 125g
- Whitefish (Hake, cod or similar)- 4ozs. (Cut into 5cm 2" pieces)
- Raw jumbo shrimps king prawns- 1 2kilo 1lb (shelled and deveined keep 4 aside for garnishing, save the heads for the stock)
- Stock (fish or vegetable stock)- 700mls
- Onion(medium-sized)- 1 (finely chopped)
- Round grain tice- 200g 7ozs
- Celery- 2 sticks(finely sliced)
- Extra virgin olive oil- 2-3 tbsp's
- Garlic- 2 cloves (bashed)
- Fresh dill- 1 tbsp (chopped)
- Dry white wine or vermouth- 1 glass (add to stock after cooking the fish, allow to stay warm but do not boil)
- Salt
- Freshly ground black pepper
- Parsley- handful (chopped)

Directions:

1. Pour stock into a medium-sized saucepan and allow to boil over on high heat.

2. Put all the fish into the pan and cook for 2 minutes only.

3. Remove the fish from the pan and keep in a covered bowl to keep warm.

4. Then add the prawn heads and allow to simmer for 5 minutes.

5. Remove prawn heads from stock and dispose of.

6. Add the dill then reduce the heat.

7. Then add the wine or vermouth; keep the stock under the boil but ensure it stays hot.

8. In a medium-sized heavy based pan, fry the onion and celery in the olive oil over

medium heat until they become translucent.

9. Add the garlic and cook for another minute.
10. Add the rice and seasoning and cook for 2-3minutes stirring continuously until it becomes opaque.
11. Increase the heat to medium level.
12. Start adding the stock wine mixture little by little, a small portion at a time stirring continuously.
13. As the rice simmers down; it will reduce in size, then add another portion of the stock wine mixture.
14. Continue doing this and ensure that the risotto is well reduced before adding more liquid.
15. At this point, the rice mixture will start to look creamy as the rice cooks until all the liquid has been added. This takes about 15-20minutes.
16. Put in all the fish except the prawns with their shells and the mussels and mix gently.
17. Remove pan from the heather and cover it with its lid; then allow to cool for 3-4minures- this allows the flavors to seep into the rice and produces a creamier risotto.
18. Make sure the seasoning is adequate.
19. Serve immediately and garnish with the whole prawns and the mussels on the half shell.
20. Sprinkle parsley on top.
21. Serve immediately.

603. Fish Casserole Recipe

Ingredients:

- Raw hake fillets - 750g 1 1 2lb(cut into about 2" 5cm square pieces)
- Raw jumbo shrimp king prawns - 750g 1 1 2lb(deveined and shelled)
- Juice and zest of a big lemon
- Extra Virgin olive oil- 3 tbsps
- Garlic- 3 cloves (bashed)
- Small dried chili- 2 (grounded in a pestle and mortar)
- Fresh parsley- handful (chopped)
- Salt

- Freshly ground black pepper

Directions:

1. Place the hake fillets in the base of an ovenproof casserole dish.
2. Place the prawns shrimps evenly on top of the hake fillets.
3. Mix garlic with the lemon juice and zest and pour equally over the fish.
4. Sprinkle the parsley and chili over the fish.
5. Spritz the olive oil over it.
6. Then add salt and black pepper to taste.
7. Cover the casserole with aluminum foil(double sheet) and ensure that it is properly sealed.
8. This prevents the loss of steam during cooking.
9. Place in a hot oven 450°F for 20-25minutes.
10. Remove from oven and leave to rest (still covered) for about 5 minutes.
11. Serve immediately.
12. Add extra lemons if desired.

604. Tiramisu Pudding

Preparation time: 2 hours 10 minutes
Servings: 1)

Ingredients:

- 8 ounces cream cheese
- 16 ounces cottage cheese
- 4 tablespoons almond milk
- 1½ cup splenda
- 1 teaspoon instant coffee
- 2 tablespoons cocoa powder

Directions:

1. In your food processor, mix cottage cheese with cream cheese, cocoa powder and coffee and blend very well.
2. Add splenda and almond milk, blend again and divide into dessert cups
3. Keep in the fridge until you serve

Nutrition Values: Calories: 200; Fat : 2; Fiber : 2; Carbs : 5; Protein : 5

605. Whole30 Nutella

Preparation time: 10 minutes
Servings: 6)

Ingredients:

- 2 ounces coconut oil
- 4 tablespoons cocoa powder
- 1 cup walnuts; halved
- 4 tablespoons stevia
- 1 teaspoon vanilla extract

Directions:

1. In your food processor, mix cocoa powder with oil, vanilla, walnuts and stevia and blend very well.
2. Keep in the fridge for a couple of hours and then serve

Nutrition Values: Calories: 100; Fat : 10; Fiber : 1; Carbs : 3; Protein : 2

606. Pumpkin Custard

Preparation time: 15 minutes
Servings: 6)

Ingredients:

- 14 ounces canned coconut milk
- 14 ounces canned pumpkin puree
- 2 teaspoons vanilla extract
- 8 scoops stevia
- 3 tablespoons erythritol
- 1 tablespoon gelatin
- 1/4 cup warm water
- A pinch of salt
- 1 teaspoon cinnamon powder
- 1 teaspoon pumpkin pie spice

Directions:

1. In a pot, mix pumpkin puree with coconut milk, a pinch of salt, vanilla extract, cinnamon powder, stevia, erythritol and pumpkin pie spice; stir well and heat up for a couple of minutes
2. In a bowl, mix gelatin and water and stir.
3. Combine the 2 mixtures; stir well, divide custard into ramekins and leave aside to cool down.
4. Keep in the fridge until you serve it.

Nutrition Values: Calories: 200; Fat : 2; Fiber : 1; Carbs : 3; Protein : 5

607. Mix Berries Dessert

Preparation time: 10 minutes

Servings: 4

Ingredients:

- 14 ounces heavy cream
- 2 tablespoons stevia
- 3 tablespoons cocoa powder
- 1 cup raspberries
- Some coconut chips
- 1 cup blackberries

Directions:

1. In a bowl, whisk cocoa powder with stevia and heavy cream.
2. Divide some of this mix into dessert bowls, add blackberries, raspberries and coconut chips, then spread another layer of cream and top with berries and chips Serve these cold.

Nutrition Values: Calories: 245; Fat : 34; Fiber : 2; Carbs : 6; Protein : 2

608. Cookie Dough Balls

Preparation time: 10 minutes
Servings: 10

Ingredients:

- 1/2 cup almond butter
- 1/2 teaspoon vanilla extract
- 3 tablespoons coconut sugar
- 1 teaspoon cinnamon; powder
- 3 tablespoons coconut flour
- 3 tablespoons coconut milk
- 15 drops vanilla stevia
- A pinch of salt

For the topping:

- 3 tablespoons granulated swerve
- 1½ teaspoon cinnamon powder

Directions:

1. In a bowl, mix almond butter with 1 teaspoon cinnamon, coconut flour, coconut milk, coconut sugar, vanilla extract, vanilla stevia and a pinch of salt and stir well.
2. Shape balls out of this mix.
3. In another bowl mix 1½ teaspoon cinnamon powder with swerve and stir well.